Demos is an independent think-tank focused on power and politics. We develop and spread ideas to give people more power over their own lives. Our vision is of a democracy of powerful citizens, with an equal stake in society.

Demos has several core research programmes in 2010: Capabilities, Citizenship, Security, Economic Life, Progressive Austerity and Extremism. We also have two political research programmes: the Progressive Conservatism Project and Open Left, investigating the future of the centre-Right and centre-Left.

In all our work we bring together people from a wide range of backgrounds to develop ideas that will shape debate in the UK and beyond, and engage a broad and diverse audience worldwide.

Find out more about our work at www.demos.co.uk.

D1586068

First published in 2010
© Demos. Some rights reserved
Magdalen House, 136 Tooley Street,
London, SE1 2TU, UK

ISBN 978 1 906693 46 6
Series design by modernactivity
Typeset by Chat Noir Design, Charente
Printed by Lecturis, Eindhoven

Set in Gotham Rounded
and Baskerville 10
Cover paper: Flora Gardenia
Text paper: Munken Premium White

IN LOCO PARENTIS

Celia Hannon
Louise Bazalgette
Claudia Wood

DEMOS

Contents

Contents

Acknowledgements

We are very grateful to all those at Barnardo's who made this project possible, in particular Enver Solomon, Julian Walker, Pam Hibbert and Martin Narey.

The care journey costings contained in this report would not have been possible without the important work of researchers at the Centre for Child and Family Research at Loughborough University. We are especially grateful to Jean Soper, Lisa Holmes and Harriet Ward for collaborating with us on this element of the project.

To build a rounded picture of the care system it is vital to listen closely to the views of looked after children and care leavers, so our thanks go to those who took the time to share their thoughts and personal stories with us. Foster carer and residential staff were similarly generous with their time, and we benefited greatly from their first hand knowledge. Our thanks also go to all the professionals, practitioners and the staff in local authorities who helped us to arrange case study visits and interviews; including those in Northern Ireland and Scotland.

Throughout this report we draw heavily on the extensive research that has been conducted by academics and experts who have studied the care system over many years. Without this rigorous body of evidence we would know far less about what works for looked after children than we do today. We have endeavoured to represent this research as accurately as possible but apologise for any omissions. We are similarly grateful for the input of the many experts, policymakers and academics who gave us feedback and advice, in particular; Caroline Abrahams, Liz Cooke, Nina Biehal, Mike Stein, John Simmonds, Julie Selwyn and Madeleine Tearse.

At Demos, Howard Reed worked closely with us on developing the quantitative dimension of the research. During the writing process we also received invaluable support and feedback from Julia Margo, Sonia Sodha, Kitty Ussher, Richard Reeves and Jen Lexmond. We were also able to draw on organisational and research support from Ivan Yiga, Sarah Kennedy, Tom Bousfield and Maria Holly. Finally, Claire Coulier and Beatrice Karol Burks expertly steered the publication through the production process and the launch.

The text was expertly copy edited by Susannah Wright. As ever, all errors and omissions are our own.

Celia Hannon
Claudia Wood
Louise Bazalgette
2010

Executive summary

In media debate and policy discussions the care system is frequently described as failing. This negative view of care in England is closely related to how it is evaluated and the way that data on young people's outcomes is misinterpreted – both of which tell a misleading story about its impact. In reality, there is a dissonance between the evidence on the impact of care, and the public perception of the system. Currently, this stigmatisation of the care system, combined with concern about the upfront costs to the state, means that some children who might benefit from the care system do not do so.

Children enter care for a variety of reasons and go on to have very different journeys while they are there. If the care system is to be successful, it needs to be flexible and responsive enough to address the needs of individual children, their carers and their birth families. When the care system is used effectively in this way it can be a powerful tool for improving the lives of vulnerable children and young people.

A strong body of evidence and our own primary research shows the most positive experiences of care, and the best outcomes for looked-after children, to be associated with the following three factors:

· early intervention and minimum delay
· stability during care
· supported transitions to independence

In this report we will consider what the care system would look like if it were reconfigured to avoid the delay, instability and abrupt transitions that many young people still experience. We go on to show that this type of system could also be less costly to the state in both the short term and over the long term.

Section 1 The purpose and the impact of care

Broadly speaking, there has been a 'pendulum' movement in the history of the care system between two approaches. The first approach sees the purpose of care as supporting families and enabling children to remain with or return to their birth parents (a 'preventative' approach). According to the second approach, the purpose of care should to be to safeguard children and provide them with permanency beyond the birth family (a 'permanency' approach). Both of these philosophies are rooted in the idea that children's exposure to public care should be minimised.

In practice there will always be a group of children for whom prevention from entering care or permanent solutions such as adoption are not realistic outcomes. Instead of oscillating between these positions of 'prevention' and 'permanency' we should aim to use public care far more proactively to:

· provide support to families as soon as they need it rather than waiting until they reach crisis point
· achieve early permanency for those children who cannot return to their families
· provide stability for those children and young people for whom a permanent solution is not desirable or feasible

The care population

Children enter care for a variety of reasons and have very different needs and characteristics when they arrive. If we are to understand the many purposes served by the care system, we must be aware of the heterogeneous nature of the care population:

· Over the past 30 years, the numbers of children in care in absolute terms has gradually fallen. Between 1994 and 2004 there was a slight rise in the number of children in care; this was due to fewer children entering care but those that did tending to stay for longer.
· A number of factors indicate there is a high concentration of disadvantage in today's care population.

- The care careers and placements of children vary considerably according to the age of the child and their age at entry, their reasons for entry, and their behaviour and needs.
- Many children entering care are over the age of 10, and many will only have a short stay in care. Consequently, a child's pre-care experience is one of the most important influences on their care journey. Evidence suggests that many of the children and young people who eventually become looked after already have a high level of mental and physical health problems at their point of entry to care.

The complex makeup of the care population reaffirms the range of purposes the system serves and the limitations inherent in pursuing a 'one size fits all' approach.

Does care 'fail'?

Society's view of whether care is, at the most simplistic level, 'good' or 'bad' exerts considerable influence over the use of care in practice. The mistaken belief that care consigns all looked-after children to a lifetime of underachievement and poor outcomes creates a culture of uncertainty, increasing delay and leading to instability later on. To challenge these misconceptions we need to recognise the following:

- The way that we measure and present looked-after children's 'outcomes' is flawed.
- There is now a substantial body of academic evidence that provides a longer-term and more nuanced perspective on looked-after children's lives, taking into account the nature of their pre-care experiences and comparing them with more appropriate control groups.
- This evidence shows that care can be a positive intervention for many groups of children.

However, care clearly serves some groups of children better than others. Rather than focusing on 'preventing' entry into care in cases where that might not be in the best interests of the child, we should differentiate between types of care journey and identify the factors that do impact on children's wellbeing.

Section 2 What works for children in care?

Child development literature tells us that if children are to develop in a psychologically healthy way and develop the important character traits and skills they need to succeed in life (such as application, self-regulation, empathy and resilience), they need to experience:

· a secure attachment
· 'authoritative' parenting that provides a combination of 'responsiveness' and 'demandingness' (or warmth and consistent boundaries)
· stability

A care system that promotes stability, resilience and healthy psychological development for looked-after children, should be based around an early or decisive entry to care (where appropriate), stable and high-quality placements that provide good parenting and are responsive to the child's needs, and a supported transition to independent adulthood.

Early or decisive entry to care

Academic evidence shows that there is a strong association between children's age of entry to care, the likelihood that they will experience emotional and behavioural difficulties and their chance of achieving stability in care. Some groups of children whose entry to care is delayed by indecision or drift are at risk of experiencing:

· a longer exposure to pre-care adversity
· higher emotional and behavioural problems
· placement disruption and instability

These findings emphasise the need to avoid delay in intervening and to initiate permanency plans for children as early as possible if it is unlikely they will be able to return to their family, although it should be noted that entry to care at a younger age is clearly not appropriate in many circumstances.

High quality and stable placements

Stability can promote resilience for looked-after children in two respects: by providing the young person with a secure attachment (which can also reduce the likelihood of placement breakdown), and by providing continuity in other areas of the child's life, such as their school and their friendship group.

Placement stability and attachment

Attachment and placement stability are strongly linked. Evidence suggests that adoption provides children who are to be looked after in the long-term with the best opportunities to develop attachment. However, adoption is only suitable for a small proportion of looked-after children and most are placed with foster carers (73 per cent in 2009). Factors that contribute to children developing secure attachments with their carers and feeling stable and secure in their placements are:

· 'sensitive parenting'
· a combination of warmth and consistent boundaries being set

If residential care is to promote resilience and stability for children, it must promote opportunities for children to develop secure attachments. Influential research suggests that high ratios of staff to children and high turnovers of staff and young people are counterproductive. Other important relationships that can contribute to children's sense of stability and continuity include their relationships with social workers and with their birth families.

Stability and educational attainment

Being able to stay at the same school and avoid disruption to their education has a strong association with educational attainment for looked-after children. Care leavers who go on to higher education are more likely to have had stable care experiences, continuity in their schooling, to have been encouraged by their birth parents, and to have been assisted by their foster carers in their schooling.

Stability and mental health

Emotional and behavioural problems have a strong association with placement breakdown. Placements may disrupt if children's carers feel unable to cope with their challenging behaviour. Placement instability can then exacerbate children and young people's mental health problems, increasing their vulnerability to further placement breakdown. Children need to receive high quality emotional and professional support and stable placements from the start of their care journeys to address these problems and build their resilience.

Supporting stable placements

To reduce the risk of placement breakdown it is essential that adequate support is provided to looked-after children and their carers. Some adoptive parents may require a level of support that is comparable to foster carers. Forms of support valued by foster carers in our primary research included specialist training, social work support, and access to short breaks from caring.

Placement stability and quality

Stability is of vital importance but should not always be prioritised as an end in itself; in some cases a young person will feel that the benefits of moving to a more suitable placement outweigh the negative impact of instability and change. Children's wellbeing should be a higher priority than stability.

Listening to looked-after children

Ensuring that looked-after children's views are listened to and that they are able to influence care planning will make it more likely that children's placements meet their emotional needs and is also likely to reduce placement disruption.

Smooth exit and supported transitions

There are four factors that can significantly improve a young person's experience of leaving care and give young people a chance of better adult outcomes: the age at which young people leave care; the speed of their transition; their access to preparation before leaving care and support after leaving care; and maintaining stability and secure attachments after leaving care.

The age at which a young person leaves care

Looked-after children who leave care early, for example at 16, tend to do less well than those who leave care later. Evidence suggests they have a higher instance of substance abuse, homelessness, unemployment and poor educational outcomes. Young people doing well with their careers tended to have left care later.

The speed of transition

If we are to promote resilience in looked-after children and young people, there needs to be more recognition of the nature and *timing* of young people's transitions from care, including the psychological space needed to cope with the significant changes taking place in their lives.

Preparation before and support after leaving care

A number of studies have associated positive outcomes for care leavers with:

· receiving adequate planning and preparation before leaving care, so they had developed strong life and social skills
· being engaged in education, employment or training

- having a positive sense of their own wellbeing
- having a network of informal support, including family and friends
- having access to 'good' housing on leaving care: those who failed to secure good housing arrangements early on tended to fare worse over the follow-up period
- having good-quality support in accommodation after leaving care

To support positive outcomes for care leavers and build their resilience, the care system must provide emotional preparation before they leave care and continued emotional support throughout young people's transition to independence. The stress and depression reported by many care leavers may be linked to the rapid series of changes and the withdrawal of support that many experience at this time. Stable housing in particular has been identified as a critical element for a successful transition from care. Supported accommodation could provide care leavers with an important 'middle way' between care and complete independence.

Research suggests that some care leavers suffer from a 'cluster' of negative outcomes that are mutually reinforcing, for example substance misuse, emotional and behavioural difficulties and offending. Those with such difficulties will often face further problems in areas such as housing, career, occupation and general wellbeing. This suggests that support for care leavers once they have left care needs to be carried out holistically. Care leavers have identified holistic services, multi-agency leaving care teams and third sector 'one-stop shops' as a helpful and accessible type of support.

Stability and attachments

Stability and the maintenance of attachments with adults are vital factors in a positive care experience. Leaving care can represent an abrupt ending of a stable placement and break in attachments, which can impact negatively on care leavers' resilience, self-esteem and sense of security. Maintaining links with care leaving teams, foster carers and family members can provide care leavers with an important source of ongoing support.

Section 3 Areas in need of reform

As we outline in section 1, there is no 'typical' care journey; looked-after children's experiences before and during care are diverse and not *all* children will have experience of the issues outlined below. However, evidence from academic sources and our primary research shows that some poor care experiences are all too common and need to be addressed.

Delay in entering care
Pre-care experiences

Evidence suggests that provision of early family support remains patchy and dependent on the culture of individual local authorities, which have very different interpretations regarding the 'right' amount of support a family should receive before their child is placed in care, and indeed the 'right' moment at which a child should be taken into care. This means that in some cases children go into care because they have too little family support, when this might have been easily avoided, while in others *too much* emphasis on keeping the family together can lead to a delay of the inevitable.

The point of entering care – delays in the process

Taking a child into care is a complex administrative and legal process, which means delay can occur at a number of stages. Resource pressures exacerbate this problem. For those children coming from situations of abuse or neglect, such delays may result in an increased risk of mental health or emotional and behavioural problems. Children entering care at an older age are also less likely to be adopted or to secure a stable placement.

The role of our philosophical approach to care

The British cultural attitude to children and the family sees children as 'private goods' – the responsibility of the family and the individual unit – while in some other European countries, children are seen as 'social goods' – part of society and its wider responsibility. This means taking children from the family normally only occurs when all other options have been deemed to fail. This philosophy of so-called 'last resortism' can create administrative delay in care proceedings as social work teams must prove beyond all reasonable doubt that a child had to be removed from their birth family. In some cases this may lead to children being taken into care too late, when significant problems have developed, and when their chances of a stable placement are greatly reduced.

Instability in the care journey
Multiple placements

In 2009 10.7 per cent of children had three or more placement moves in a year, while 67 per cent were in a long-term placement (defined at more than 2.5 years). There was significant local variation, with nine local authorities having 15–19 per cent of their children experiencing three or more placements in a year. In our interviews with children in care and care leavers, many young people reported having experienced up to ten placement moves, short term, emergency placements, and sudden unexpected moves. The frequency with which social workers changed was also felt to be destabilising. One study found that 43 per cent of placement moves were initiated and planned by the local authority, and were often resource or practice-led, as a result of a shortage of suitable placements or lack of planning.

Failed attempts at family reunification

Evidence suggests that a large proportion of children in care experience at least one failed return to their family, and a recent study found that 16 per cent of the children in their sample experienced two failed family reunifications. These reunifications may fail because they lack assessment and post-reunification support. Children who return to care following a failed reunification will rarely if ever be able to return to their former foster family, which creates further instability.

A lack of placement support

Many placements end in an unplanned way; this breakdown may result from lack of support, particularly mental health support. The support given by child and adolescent mental health services (CAMHS) to children in care – foster and residential care – and to adopted children is patchy, with many local authorities having no teams in place dedicated to helping children in care or those who had been adopted. This lack of coherent mental health support is particularly concerning when we consider that several studies have established poor mental health as both a cause and a result of children having unstable care journeys.

A lack of choice

The national shortage of foster carers and foster care placements means that some children do not have an adequate choice of placement. This can increase the risk of instability because placements that are not properly matched are more likely to break down, or because social workers may need to place children in short-term placements before an appropriate long-term placement can be identified.

Instability in residential care

The high instance of mental health problems in residential care may be due to the fact that in the UK residential care tends to be viewed as an 'end of the line' option for children and young people whose previous placements have failed. This can mean that the poor outcomes associated with residential care become a self-fulfilling prophecy as only most troubled children are ultimately placed there. However, it may be that for children for whom foster care is not suitable, residential care placements could be a valuable source of stability and opportunity to develop peer relationships. To improve the quality of residential care we need to address staff retention and shift patterns to provide young people with greater stability and continuity. Currently, the lack of availability of care homes also reduces choice, increasing the chances of a mismatch between the child's needs and the home selected, which may lead to placement breakdown or a series of temporary placements.

An abrupt exit from care

The transition from care to independence is a critical period for young people, and needs to be handled carefully to prevent a traumatic break from the stability and attachments formed during care. The following areas are in need of reform:

An abrupt and compressed transition from care

Every year, around 6,000 looked-after children leave care for good; 21 per cent are 16, 17 per cent are 17 and 61 per cent are 18. This ought to be compared with the average age when young people leave home in the general population: 24. This means a significant proportion of young people are still leaving care prematurely to live alone in private accommodation, ill prepared for the realities of adult life. In addition to the departure from care being premature for many young people, the process itself is compressed. The speed with which a young care leaver finds themselves 'independent' has been reported to be traumatic for many, as they are ill prepared practically and emotionally for what this transition entails.

A lack of transition support

The 'cliff edge' style of transition from care is all the more concerning because care leavers are not given adequate practical, emotional and financial care and support once they leave care. A number of surveys carried out with care leavers found that many are in unstable and poor quality housing.

The importance of mental health support

There is a growing concern that care leavers living on their own display a range of emotional and psychological problems. Research suggests that local authorities tend to overlook the need for emotional and psychological preparation for those on the verge of leaving care and living independently, focusing instead on practical issues.

Section 4 The cost of care journeys and later life outcomes

The failure to provide looked-after children with a stable, high quality experience of care will not only result in a less positive care journey for them, but can also lead to escalating costs to children's services. To illustrate this problem we have modelled and costed two exemplar care journeys, which typify the best and the worst of the current system. They do not attempt to prove that certain care journeys *cause* certain outcomes, so it is important to note that we have not attempted to prove causality at any stage. These exemplar journeys are therefore only designed to illustrate the costs associated with two experiences at each end of the spectrum.

One journey is designed to reflect the experience of the very top range of 5–10 per cent of children in care who are fortunate enough to have long-term, stable placements and supported transitions; the other reflects the 5–10 per cent of children who have a journey characterised by instability, disruption and abrupt exits. We drew on DCSF data from the Department for Children, Schools and Families (DCSF; now the Department for Education) about looked-after children to build these journeys, and used a number of small scale academic studies to identify the associations (but not causality) between the factors of late entry, poor mental health, instability and late exit.

In comparing the costs to children's services for two exemplar care journeys ('child A' and 'child B') we found the following:

· The variation in costs is significant: the stable care journey cost £352,053 over a 14-year period, while the unstable care journey cost £393,579 over a 7-year period (a difference of £41,526).
· This translates to a much larger difference in annual costs per year (£23,470.20 for child A and £56,225.57 for child B) once their length of stay in care is taken into account (15 versus 7 years).
· There is a cost of £32,755.37 more per year for childB's care journey than for child A's

Some of this variation can be attributed to the additional social worker time needed to make a larger number of placement moves, but more importantly, we identify a cyclical escalation of poor care experience and costs: a child with a delayed entry into care is less likely to maintain a stable placement, which is associated with poorer mental health and potentially behavioural problems, which in turn may undermine placement stability. This cycle leads to a need for increasingly costly support. Of course, it is also important to note that children will enter care for a range of different reasons and have widely differing personal characteristics – child A's journey would not be applicable in many instances.

We also went on to consider the adult outcomes that might be associated with each scenario (again causality was not proven) to estimate their possible costs to the state up to age 30:

· Child A leaves care at 18, following a stable placement, with good qualifications.
· Child B leaves care at 16½, has no qualifications, and has mental health problems.

Rather than starting their adult costs at different points, the analysis begins at age 16. This is because although both children are still technically in care at this point, their costs to the state (as distinct from the costs of their care to children's services) begin at 16, as this is the end of their compulsory schooling. Assumptions about adult outcomes for child A and child B:

· We assume child A lives outside London, where she stays at school to 18, then attends a university to age 21, living away from home. On graduating, she finds a job and is employed at an average starting salary.
· We assume child B also lives outside London. She leaves school at 16 with no qualifications, and moves out of her care placement at 16½. We know from her care journey (above) that she is likely to have mental health problems. Based on a range of national data, we are able to estimate the risks of child B being unemployed during her life, and a range of costs associated with this.

By collating the costs of these very different adult outcomes, we have calculated the estimated costs to the state of each young person from age 16 to age 30.

- 'Child A', may cost the state £20,119.10 by age 30 if she goes on to university and secures a graduate job.
- 'Child B' may cost the state £111,923.99 if she experiences unemployment, underemployment and mental health problems.
- Between age 16 and age 30 there is a difference between Child A's and Child B's costs to the state of £91,804.89.

The difference here can be attributed in large part to the very different mental health and educational attainment out-comes associated with the two care journeys. The main costs of child A are associated with a young person attending university after care, which only happens in the minority of cases.

In reality, most children in care will experience something between these two extreme examples of care journeys. However, in demonstrating the significant range of care journeys and types of outcomes that the current care system is capable of producing, we hope to show not only that there is considerable room for improvement, but more importantly that this improvement is eminently attainable.

With this in mind, we should consider the range of adult outcomes than can be achieved by today's care system, from those children who have a positive, nurturing care experience and go on to university and a successful life, through to those who end up more or less dependent on the state and health services. In total the difference could be £133,330.89 per child to age 30 if we take both the costs of the care journey and outcomes into account. As there are currently nearly 61,000 children in care, the contrast between the two creates a powerful argument for investing in good care experiences to avoid greater costs now and in the future.

At whatever age a child enters care, greater stability and improved mental health can reduce *immediate* costs to the local authority by reducing social workers' time, use of expensive agency and residential placements, and therapeutic support. These are not distant cost savings beyond the budgetary cycle, but in this case amount to an average of £32,755.37 saved per child each year while that child is in care. This difference in cost between a stable and unstable care journey should be borne in mind in section 5, where we present our recommendations.

Section 5 What next for care?

While recent reforms have done much to improve the framework and legislation surrounding the care system they have not gone far enough in tackling the parenting deficit in the lives of many looked-after children.

What must care achieve?

Although children come into care for different reasons, at different ages, and for different periods of time, there is no reason why all children, when living away from their families, should not benefit from warm relationships and a sense of stability. It is for this reason that we differentiate between *permanence* (which would imply a permanent care solution or adoption) and *stability*. While the latter may be delivered effectively through the former, we should also bear in mind that when a permanent care solution is not viable, stability can and should still be sought.

Drawing on best practice and case studies, the following recommendations, therefore, all seek to create permanency (where appropriate), stability of good quality placements and continuity of support. These can be achieved in very different ways at each phase of a care journey – from entry, during and at exit. Given the current fiscal climate, we have not included a number of recommendations that would have been more costly, and we have instead focused on changes that we believe would provide a high impact for the costs involved. In some cases recommendations are close to cost-neutral. Given the escalating spending associated with poor care journeys we believe that the relatively modest investment we propose in particular areas makes economic sense, and will help to make the care system more sustainable in the future.

Systemic reform

The poor usage of public care can be linked, in part, to society's belief that the care system is destined only ever to be a poor second to the quality of care provided by any birth family. This points towards a self-fulfilling prophecy: a lack of confidence in the care system to generate positive outcomes leads to its poor use, and its poor use is associated with poor outcomes. Poor outcomes reinforce the underlying lack of confidence in the system. However, in spite of popular misconceptions, the care system as it currently stands can and does create stable, nurturing environments. To promote positive outcomes more consistently for young people Demos believes that the following shift in our approach to care is necessary:

1 A more pro-active, positive use of care
Demos urges the government to adopt a more confident stance on the capacity of the care system to achieve positive outcomes. We should create a new virtuous circle – one where care is used earlier and more effectively and in turn becomes more effective.

2 Care as family support and early intervention projects
Corporate parenting and birth parenting should not always be seen as mutually exclusive. The state should be recognised as capable of acting as a 'parallel parent' for children and families who need such ongoing support. The government must embark on a concerted effort to destigmatise care as a form of family support. We set out in our specific recommendations below how parallel parenting could work in practice for some families with packages of 'support care'.

3 Improved data on children in care
We currently compare children from backgrounds of deprivation, neglect and abuse with children from stable family backgrounds, and attribute the difference in outcomes to the care system (in which children may only have stayed for a matter of months.) By failing to take into account or controlling for background characteristics, we generate a fundamentally flawed picture of the care system. Demos recommends that outcomes data relating to children in care must adopt a 'value added' approach that is able to take children's backgrounds into account. Rather than publishing annual data 'snapshots', the Department for Education (DfE) should publish analysis of

longitudinal data that links looked-after children's pre-care and in-care experiences to their later life outcomes.

4 A better understanding of placement and care journey costs

Value-added and longitudinal measures of children's outcomes may help change perceptions of the care system, but will not drive real reform unless spending decisions at local level change. To achieve this, local authorities need a better understanding of the outcomes of different types of care placement, *and* of the costs associated with these placements. We suggest local authorities look to the cost calculator for children's services (CCFCS)[1] developed at Loughborough University to break down their costs more accurately.

However, annual budgeting may make it difficult to take into account longer term outcomes or attribute cost savings to them, and may also make it difficult for authorities to understand how placement delays generate costs over time. There are reports that some children's services departments have already shifted to multi-year spending plans (in line with the comprehensive spending review) allowing annual budgets to be carried over from year to year. Multi-year spending plans are an important step in the right direction, and where appropriate other Local Authorities should use these to manage annual budgets more flexibly for looked-after children. Some children's services departments have already shifted their annual budgets to multi-year cycles, in line with multi-year children and young people's plans and the comprehensive spending review, which is an important step in the right direction.

Demos is also making a number of targeted recommendations, set out below.

Recommendations for early intervention and less delay

1 Demos recommends there should be a government audit of local authority policies on managing their care populations and research into associated child outcomes.
2 Demos recommends the 'tapering' of the care system for families in need of occasional support, for example by local authorities

making 'support care' arrangements matching foster carers and families more widely available.

3 Demos recommends there should be a statutory duty on local authorities to offer family group conferencing.

4 Demos calls for the government to provide seed funding for concurrent planning in local authorities wishing to pilot the service.

5 Demos calls for a renewed government focus on adoption timeliness and a DfE review of the 12-month target.

6 Demos recommends that all local authorities consider establishing permanency planning tracking panels.

Recommendations for stability

7 Demos recommends that the DfE makes mental health assessments of children entering care mandatory, using a standardised multi-disciplinary measure.

8 Demos calls for the Children's Workforce Development Council (CWDC) to include mental health training in training standards for foster and residential care workers.

9 Demos recommends that primary care trusts commission on-site CAMHS support for children in residential care and residential staff.

10 Demos recommends that local authorities make short breaks and placement support workers available to foster carers on request.

11 Demos proposes introducing social pedagogy training in CWDC standards in order to spread existing good practice in residential care work.

12 Demos calls on the DfE to amend care planning guidance to ensure there are fewer failed reunifications, and to introduce better resourced and time limited reunification plans.

Recommendations for supported transition to independence

13 Demos recommends that looked-after children teams and 16 plus teams shadow one another before and after transition.

14 Demos calls for local authorities to use personal advisers at an earlier age and for CWDC to outline specific training requirements.

15 Demos urges the government to raise the care leaving age to 18 and asks the DfE to support flexible approaches to allow young people to stay on in placements to 21.

16 Demos recommends that DfE amends transition support guidance to prioritise emotional and mental health support.

17 Demos recommends that DfE guidance explicitly applies the resilience model to transition planning, and independent reviewing officers are trained accordingly.

18 Demos calls for the wider availability of supported accommodation through commissioning and active promotion by government and local authorities.

19 Demos recommends floating support services are made more readily available by local authorities, and calls for the government to create a statutory 'right to return' for all care leavers.

Conclusion

Every child is different and will need something different from the care system; from a short break away from home to a lifelong adoptive placement. By no means do we underestimate the difficulty of meeting the needs of each individual child, and of making the right decisions at key moments in that child's life. Nevertheless, a shift of resources and investment to the beginning of a child's care journey could have real long-term benefits for that child, and minimise the costs associated with unstable placements.

In the context of the immediate resource constraints confronting central and local government, the interventions and recommendations outlined in this publication should be seen as part of a long-term, ongoing project to raise standards in the care system. But we also believe that the escalating costs associated with poor care journeys and placement disruption have short-term resource implications for local authorities, meaning there are cost savings attached to better care journeys in the here and now.

Of course, intervening earlier through focused family support or placements away from home is not always possible or appropriate, and so we must also focus on the key ingredients proven to make a difference at any stage of a care journey, namely a high quality stable placement and a supported, smoother transition to independence. The edges of the system also need to be 'tapered'; entering care should not be seen as an all-or-nothing intervention to be used only when all else fails. Recognising that care can, and often does, succeed enables us to be more ambitious for the system as a whole, and by extension for the children and young people who pass through it.

Introduction

By presenting young people in and leaving care solely as 'victims' of systems that fail them, we risk ignoring and undermining the role they themselves play in their own futures, and the resilience that many possess.
Sonia Jackson[2]

The British care system is mired in the language of failure. Social workers and directors of children's services are regularly described as 'incompetent',[3] while the care system itself is promoting an underclass and 'blighting' the life chances of care leavers.[4] In the public consciousness this idea is reinforced by the reporting of poor outcomes for children who pass through the care system. But how correct is this view, and what are the consequences of regarding care as a damaging intervention to be avoided?

In Loco Parentis shows the care system can be an effective tool and should be used earlier and more proactively. The negative perception of care in England is closely related to how it is evaluated and the way that data on young people's outcomes is misinterpreted – both of which tell a misleading story about its impact. Acknowledging that some elements of public care do have a positive impact is far from arguing that that the care system is good enough. Of course it is right to demand better for one of the most disadvantaged and vulnerable groups in society. There are groups of children who are still let down by the parenting they receive from the state, and many problems in our care system persist. But one of the unintended consequences of labelling care 'a failure' is that in so doing we compound those problems in our system.

Concerns about the damaging impact of care can lead to delays in taking decisive action, whether that means providing intensive family support or finding children stable placements away from home. In some cases this exposes children to abusive or neglectful situations for longer. As a result some groups of children enter the system at an older age with more entrenched emotional and behavioural difficulties, and they are less likely to find a stable placement or permanent alternatives such as adoption. Further oscillations in and out of care contribute to this instability and poorer outcomes in academic attainment and wellbeing. These outcomes confirm the assumption that care is damaging, undermining our confidence in the system still further and establishing a vicious cycle.

In England this cycle is also fuelled by our unease about the idea of the state taking on the 'parenting' role. This can be traced back to a strong belief in the primacy of the birth family, a view which is stronger in the UK than in, for example, some Scandinavian countries. The oxymoronic term 'corporate parenting,' now commonly used to describe public care, perfectly expresses this unease. Understandably, we struggle with the idea that the 'corporate' state should be drawn into the intimate arena of family relationships. This historical reluctance to intervene in the private sphere of family life has manifested itself in confusion about the purpose of public care in England.

Over recent decades we have moved between two policy-making positions: supporting children to remain in the family home or taking more children into care with the aim of finding them permanent solutions such as adoption as quickly as possible.

This 'pendulum effect' has afflicted children's social services for decades, leading to fluctuations in the size of the care population, usually in reaction to a child's death from abuse or neglect, a damning review or the exposure of failing services. Whether the state prioritises a preventative 'birth family is best' approach or safeguarding at any given moment in time is often related to where we are in this unstable cycle. Considering this, it is perhaps unsurprising that huge variation persists in the cultures of different local authorities and the type of services they provide.

The reactive nature of the care system in England is proof that we are in need of greater clarity about the use and purpose of public care for children. It is vital that we turn this vicious circle into a virtuous circle – re-casting the care system as a proactive tool which *can* deliver for children – to identify where and how it succeeds and replicate that success elsewhere. The first step towards doing so is differentiating between the many types of journey looked-after children experience. Care is not a homogenous intervention and the care population is characterised by huge diversity. Consequently, we should not regard care as 'all or nothing intervention'. The system should be used to achieve early permanency for those children for whom it is appropriate, stability for when a permanent solution is not possible, and to deliver early family support before a child's development is affected.

An important moment for care

Over the past decade the government has done much to improve legislative frameworks and the quality of placements so that children in and leaving care are supported with better planning, educational facilities and accommodation. The true impact of this activity may not be apparent for several years to come. In this respect the 'corporate' dimension to the parenting role has been heavily invested in, with a particular focus on new guidelines, structures and safeguarding processes. The larger challenge of addressing the parenting dimension of the 'corporate parent' role has still to be met. Far less attention has been paid to parenting deficit in children's lives and enabling them to form enduring attachments while in care, although it is this resilience which will underpin other positive outcomes throughout their life.

Nevertheless, the investment in the care system over recent years has undoubtedly been key in delivering real change throughout the care system and incremental improvements in outcomes. But the associated increase in the costs to the state (for example, there was a 100 per cent real terms increase in total expenditure on children looked after between 1994 and 2005/6[5]) means that the squeeze on public spending is likely to have big implications for the future of services for looked-after children.

The fiscal pressure on the system will also be stepped up by the influx of children into care following the death of Baby Peter, and the renewed emphasis on safeguarding. The case led to an immediate 40 per cent surge in referrals to the courts to take children into care. Latest quarterly figures from Cafcass, the Children and Family Court Advisory and Support Service, suggest that although the initial increase in referrals has levelled off, it has still settled at historically higher levels. The courts received 2,185 section 31 care applications from October to December 2009, up 21 per cent on the same quarter in 2008.[6] As safeguarding, family support and looked-after children services are funded from the same children's services budget, the shift to child protection could lead to a diversion of resources away from families in need of support services and children who are *already* in care. In meeting these new demands, the care system will find itself needing to do more with less.

However, the temptation to intervene later and cut frontline spending for vulnerable children and families would be a counter-productive cost cutting exercise. In this report we look at the evidence on children that come into care later with higher levels of need, and go on to have unstable care journeys which are more expensive. For care leavers in later life we show the wide disparity between the low costs to the state for those who exit care with qualifications and good mental health, versus the considerable cost to the state when a young person leaves with neither of those things. If we do not meet the needs of vulnerable children today through focused family support or high quality placements, we will foot the bill in the future.

This report

Social services always say that our lives were not good with our parents and that's why we ended up in care so, therefore, they should be giving us the same opportunities like every other kid. They should be giving us at least what they think our parents couldn't give us.
Care leaver interview

Guiding the next phase of reform should be the principle that when the state acts *in loco parentis* it should be providing the same quality of care that birth parents would hope to give their own children. This ideal should continue to be a driver of innovation and higher standards. With this report we aimed to raise the status of care as a positive option for children and a less stigmatised source of support to their families.

However, there are some policy areas that we do not interrogate in depth with this report, such as safeguarding, the questions confronting the future of the social work profession and court processes. All of these issues also shape a child's care journey, but are undergoing considerable reform at present and demand detailed assessment in their own right. It should also be noted that we deal only with the care system in England and Wales, and that the system of local authority care, although sharing many common features, operates differently in Scotland and Northern Ireland. We do draw comparisons with Scotland and Northern Ireland but do not seek to address those nations as separate systems.

We will look at the interventions, strategies and innovations which could deliver a good care journey to a greater proportion of the care population. We also look to existing academic research, which tells us a great deal about the ingredients of a good care experience and the impact on children. We ground our recommendations in our own primary research with experts, looked-after children, carers and care leavers. We find that the following three factors are key ingredients of a positive (and often less costly) care journey:

- early intervention or less delay
- stability
- supported transitions to independence

We consider what the care system would look like if it were reconfigured to avoid delay, instability and abrupt exit, in order to support the lifelong relationships that looked-after children need to sustain them as they move into adulthood.

Box 1 describes our methodology.

Box 1 **Methodology**

1 Literature reviews of domestic and international evidence
*The first phase of the project was to carry out a literature review
of the more recent body of research (academic literature, policy
documents and research by third sector organisations and
others) on looked-after children, identifying the most prominent
themes for the domestic (English and Welsh) care system.
Our desk-based research also included:*

- *a review of international practice in care in Northern Ireland,
  Scotland, Denmark, Germany, France, Finland, Spain,
  Sweden, Hungary and Australia*
- *a review of children in care legislation*
- *a review of consultations with children in care and care leavers
  over the past decade*
- *a review of academic studies (both domestic and international)
  that sought to identify the outcomes that are associated with
  different types of care journey*

2 Expert interviews
*We discussed our emerging thinking, informed by our desk-
based research, and sought feedback and ideas for further areas
of investigation from a number of policy and academic experts.
These included:*

- *Mary Sainsbury, Centre for Excellence and Outcomes in
  Children and Young People's Services (C4EO) and Social Care
  Institute for Excellence (SCIE)*
- *Sonia Jackson, Institute of Education*
- *David Holmes, British Association for Adoption and Fostering
  (BAAF)*
- *Lucy Sweetman, Sharn Bowley and Linda Briheim-Crookall,
  Catch 22 and National Care Advisory Service (NCAS)*
- *Robert Tapsfield, fostering network*
- *Hugh Thornberry, Action for Children*

- *Harvey Gallagher and Matthew Huggins, Care Matters Partnership*
- *Dionne Baptiste, Centrepoint*
- *Mike Stein, Social Policy Research Unit (SPRU), York University*
- *Nina Biehal, SPRU, York University*
- *Ian Sinclair, SPRU, York University*
- *Yvette Stanley, Director of the Merton Council Children, Schools and Families Department*
- *Deirdre Coyle, Health and Social Care Northern Ireland*

3 Domestic case studies

Based on our scoping work and discussions with experts, we visited or spoke to people in a number of projects and services to identify areas of good practice and innovation. These included:

- *Essex County Council Social Pedagogy Project*
- *Whistler Walk residential children's home, Kensington & Chelsea*
- *concurrent planning projects – Brighton & Hove and Devon local authorities and Coram in London*
- *Hackney local authority social pedagogy pilots and reclaiming social work scheme*
- *Horizon's Centre care leaver support, Ealing*
- *Placement Support Service, East Sussex*
- *Merton local authority, family support activities*

4 International scoping

To supplement the literature review of international practice, we also visited Northern Ireland to learn more about their leaving care services, and Scotland to speak to a number of policy makers, providers and academics to better understand the use of kinship care, Children's Hearings, and other aspects of the Scottish system that differ from the English and Welsh system.

5 Focus groups and interviews

The Demos team conducted primary research with care leavers, looked-after children and foster carers in nine local authority areas (Kensington and Chelsea, Tower Hamlets, Tunbridge Wells, Derby, Haringey, Richmond, Ealing, Barking and Dagenham, and East Sussex).

We conducted four focus groups with foster carers, in four different local authority areas, involving 26 carers in total. We asked them about their motivation for becoming foster carers; their role and professional status; how they work with other agencies; what causes placements to break down; which types of support they receive or would like to receive; and for their feedback on a number of our policy proposals.

We carried out semi-structured interviews in groups with 37 young people (23 care leavers and 14 looked-after children) ranging from age 7 to age 21, in five different local authorities. We asked about their experiences of care and opinions from the perspective of stability, continuity, attachments and transitions to independence.

6 Quantitative analysis

Demos carried out a substantial body of work to design two exemplar care journeys which represented the two extremes of experiences within the system. We constructed these care journeys on the basis of evidence about how particular experiences of care (eg age of entry, stability and age of exit) are associated with certain pathways through the care system. We then worked in partnership with Harriet Ward, Jean Soper and Lisa Holmes from the Centre for Child and Family Research (CCFR) at Loughborough University to cost these care journeys using their cost calculator for children's services. This tool was developed by Ward and colleagues in consultation with staff from social service departments in six local authorities. Through this consultation the team identified eight case management processes (eg finding a placement, care planning, maintaining a placement) that are involved in planning and supporting looked-after children's placements, and developed average unit costs associated with each of these activities, which vary according to placement type, frequency and duration of placements, and characteristics of the child.

To calculate an estimated cost for each of our exemplar care journeys, we put data on the children's characteristics (eg whether they have additional support needs such as emotional and behavioural difficulties or a disability), the number and type of placements they received and any other services they received into the cost calculator. This tool was then able to attribute an average unit cost to each of the case management processes that took place, and to any additional services provided by other agencies (eg CAMHS). The costs associated with each placement were then aggregated to calculate an estimated total cost for each of the care journeys.

Demos then went on to cost potential adult outcomes to age 30, based on the possible academic achievements and mental health of the children who had experienced these two exemplar journeys. We did this by using a number of national data sources including the Annual Survey of Hours and Earnings and Labour Force Survey to establish a relationship between qualifications and earning and risk of unemployment, and combining this data with current levels of employment support allowance, national insurance, income tax and so on to estimate costs of different levels of labour market activity. We limited our analysis to employment, earnings and mental health, and did not include possible offending behaviour, teen pregnancy or softer outcomes that might be associated with academic attainment and mental health.

In all cases, however, it is important that we did not establish causality between being in care and adult outcomes.

7 Policy seminar

To test the findings from our research, Demos hosted a policy seminar with a number of policy experts and practitioners in the field, including representatives from local government, academia, and community and voluntary sector organisations that represent the views of looked-after children, care leavers and foster carers.

Section 1
The purpose and impact
of care

However, the historical legacy of confusion about the purpose of care has had a lasting impact. Considerable local variation continues to be a stubborn characteristic of today's care system. On the basis of the findings presented to them, the Care Matters working group on the future of the care population concluded that 'the care system might more realistically be viewed as being not one but 150 different systems'. They expressed concern that

this high level of inter-authority variation is as likely to mean children who should be in care are being left at home in potentially dangerous situations for far too long, as it is to mean that many children made the subject of Care Orders should have been left at home with more intensive support programmes.[21]

This variation can be seen most clearly by looking at how many children are in care in each area – which cannot be entirely explained by local socio-economic disadvantage: there are 13 children per 10,000 of population in care in Rutland, compared with 221 per 10,000 in the City of London. The national average number of children in care per 10,000 of population is 55.[22] The variations in the use of care extends to the type of placements that local authorities opt to provide; the proportion of the care population in residential care varies significantly between local authorities (from 4 per cent to 28 per cent). Deloitte also found significant variation in the number of children in residential care by region. London and the North West place 24 per cent and 17 per cent respectively of the total number of children in residential care, while five regions place 10 percent or less of the total number of children in residential care.[23]

It is hardly surprising that outcomes for looked-after children also vary by local area – with the number of children in care getting one or more GCSEs ranging from 26 per cent to 89 per cent depending on the authority, and performance in 20 per cent of local authorities falling below an acceptable level.[24] In 2009 DCSF reported that 15 local authorities had over 80 per cent of their care leavers in education, employment and training, but 13 local authorities had less than 50 per cent.[25]

Looked at from a historical perspective the existence of different local cultures and approaches to the purpose of care is entirely unsurprising. That some emphasise prevention and 'birth family is best', and others stress safeguarding can be traced back to the swinging of the 'pendulum' over recent decades. The perceived cost disincentive associated with intervening earlier has also influenced the local authority use of care, although as we show in section 4, this is something of a false economy.

Box 2 **Landmarks in the last decade of policy**

The Children Act 1989 and 2004

The Children Act 1989 established the general duty of local authorities in England and Wales to safeguard and promote the welfare of children within their area who are in need. There was a clear promotion of parental responsibility in this act, with local authorities specifically tasked with promoting 'the upbringing of children by their own families if safe to do so' and working in partnership with parents. While the local authority can seek a court order when compulsory action is in the best interest of the child, the first option must be to work with the parents by voluntary arrangement unless to do so would clearly be placing the child at risk of significant harm.

The act also focused on court proceedings – a court can make an order to remove a child from his family only if it is better for the child than making no order, and the child's welfare must be the paramount consideration. The act also introduced the principle that delay in court proceedings is harmful to the child.

The Children Act 2004 did not change the functions of the 1989 act, but made a lot of changes to the delivery to promote far more cross-departmental working. It required local authorities to lead on integrated delivery through multi-agency children's trusts and local safeguarding boards; to draw up a single children and young people's plan; to appoint a children's commissioner and director of children's services; and to set up a shared database of children, containing information relevant to their welfare.

This act underpinned the 2004 Every Child Matters strategy, which presented a much wider cross-agency programme aimed at promoting the five outcomes for children – being healthy; staying safe; enjoying and achieving; making a positive contribution; and achieving economic wellbeing.[26]

The Children (Leaving Care) Act 2000

The Children (Leaving Care) Act 2000 introduced the personal adviser role to support care leavers. Personal advisers develop Pathways plans with care leavers to meet their support needs and help them prepare for independent living. They plan for personal support, accommodation, education and training, employment, family and social relationships, practical and other skills, financial support, health needs and contingency planning. Leaving care teams may also have specialist workers in areas such as mental health, accommodation or employment.

The act took a more prescriptive approach to the local authority's responsibilities for care leavers, in that it required local authorities to provide services in many cases where before they had only discretion but not a duty to provide them. Also, the types of services and the upper age limits for which they were responsible were also extended. pathway plans are for all over 16s until they are 21, or longer if they are in education. The main aims of the act were:

· *to delay young people's discharge from care until they are prepared and ready to leave*
· *to improve the assessment, preparation and planning for leaving care*
· *to provide better personal support for young people after leaving care*
· *to improve the financial arrangements for care leavers*

New local authority duties included that they should:

· *assess and meet needs*
· *provide pathway plans for all children in care 16 or over*

- *provide personal advisers for all over 16s*
- *give assistance to achieve goals agreed in pathway plans*
- *give support and accommodation*
- *provide financial support*
- *keep in touch with care leavers until they are at least 21*

Children and Young Persons Act 2008

In November 2006, the government published the green paper Care Matters: Transforming the lives of children and young people in care, *alongside papers from four working groups established to investigate best practice in making provision for looked-after children.*

Following a period of consultation, these papers fed into the June 2007 white paper, Care Matters: Time for change. *This set out the government's plans to improve outcomes for looked-after children and care leavers. The white paper was fairly comprehensive and radical in some ways (see below for a full summary of proposals).*

The Children and Young Persons Act 2008 reformed the statutory framework for the care system in England and Wales by implementing the proposals in the white paper that required primary legislation. The act also included provisions on the wellbeing of children and young people, private fostering, child death notification to local safeguarding children boards and appropriate national authorities, the powers of the secretary of state to conduct research and applications for the discharge of emergency protection orders.

The act:

- *makes provision to enable local authorities to delegate local authority functions in relation to looked-after children to providers of social work services and (following the pilot stage) places a general duty on the secretary of state to promote the wellbeing of children in England*
- *requires local authorities to take steps to secure sufficient accommodation in their area that is appropriate for the needs of children they look after*

- *amends the duties of local authorities in relation to the appointment of independent reviewing officers (IROs); adds to the functions of IROs; and provides powers for the appropriate national authority to establish a new national IRO service independent of local authorities in England and Wales*
- *places a new duty on local authorities to appoint a representative to visit all looked-after children, wherever they are living, and provides a power to extend the duty to other groups of children who were looked after but have ceased to be so*
- *extends the duty on local authorities to appoint an independent person to visit, befriend and advise any looked-after child if doing so is in the child's interests*
- *places a duty on governing bodies of maintained schools to designate a member of staff as having responsibility for promoting the educational achievement of registered pupils at the school who are looked after*
- *extends the duty on local authorities to appoint a personal adviser and keep the pathway plan under regular review to care leavers who are over 18 and who start or resume a programme of education or training after the age of 21 but under the age of 25 years*
- *requires local authorities to pay a bursary to a former care leaver who goes on to higher education*
- *extends the powers of local authorities to make cash payments to children in need and their families*
- *makes provision to enable registration authorities to issue compliance notices to children's home providers who are failing to meet required standards and to serve a notice preventing new admissions*
- *extends the period within which a registration scheme may be established for private fostering by three years*
- *extends the rights of relatives who are entitled to apply for a residence order or special guardianship order without leave of the court to those with whom the child has lived for a continuous period of one year; and ensures that where a court makes a residence order the order will normally continue until the child reaches the age of 18*[27]

It is worth noting that during the passage of the Children and Young Persons Bill, several amendments failed to be incorporated.[28] The most significant were:

· the right for all children to remain in foster care until 21, as opposed to 18 (the white paper announced pilots for extending the leaving age for foster care to 21, but campaigners wanted this to be put straight into legislation)
· for foster carers to be registered with a professional body, to increase their status giving councils responsibility for all children in care who enter custody (currently children who enter custody lose their looked-after status and the services and protection that go with it – see below)
· introducing compulsory registration of private fostering arrangements (ie children living with people who are not parents or relatives under a private arrangement). The Children Act 2004 set a deadline for 2008 for government to decide whether registration ought to be compulsory, but the Children and Young Persons Act extends that to 2011.

2   The care population

Children enter care for a variety of reasons and go on to have very different journeys while they are there. Understanding the heterogeneous nature of the care population is key to understanding the different purposes served by the care system. It also allows us to pinpoint the type of journeys that represent positive care careers, and focus on the groups that are less well served. The range in terms of the time children spend in the care system also points to the fact that the experience of being 'looked after' will affect them to differing degrees. Some may enter as young children and remain until they are 18, others may only spend several weeks in care. Consequently, for many young people their experience before entering care will exert more influence over their later outcomes than the time they spend in care.

A historical perspective

In general terms, the numbers of children in care in absolute terms has gradually fallen over the past 30 years. The lowest levels occurred in the mid-1990s; since then numbers began to rise. Figure 1 shows the trends in the size of the care population as a proportion of the overall under-18 population.

Future of the care population working group 2007[29]

It is clear from figure 1 that children in the late 1970s and early 1980s had a significantly higher chance of being in public care than at any time since. The rising care population during the 1970s was also driven by the idea that 'attending to the welfare needs of children would diminish their propensity for crime, with the result that "delinquent" children were drawn into the child welfare system'.[30] The 1969 Children and Young Person's Act

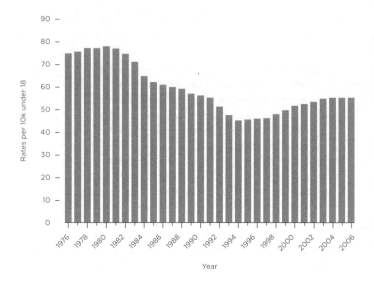

Figure 1 **Trends in size of care population as a proportion of overall under–18 population**

Rates per 10k under 18 / Year

introduced an ethos of treating youth offending and sometimes non-attendance at school as a child welfare issue and the courts made many care orders under section 7(7) of that act.

The decreasing rate of children in care during the late 1980s and early 1990s was quite pronounced and there is little sign that the 1989 act made an impact on this trend. There was a slight rise in the number of children in care from 1994 to 2004, but this had tailed off by 2004 and was much lower than the peak reached in 1980. Interestingly, this rise between 1994 and 2004 was the result of fewer children entering care but those that did staying longer.[31] An increasing proportion of these children were looked after under care orders rather than by voluntary agreement with parents.[32] Longer periods in care may be partly explained by the impact of policy and legislative initiatives such as the Children (Leaving Care) Act 2000, which attempted to ensure that young people left care later. And, according to analysis of the care population undertaken by Rowlands and Statham longer periods in care might also imply the emergence of:

a higher threshold for becoming looked after or a stronger discrimination in determining whether children should come into care or not. The implication is that a significant proportion of children entering care have more serious and enduring family problems that militate against an early return home.[33]

They suggest that over time these higher thresholds, policies and practices might have led to a 'care system with a high concentration of disadvantage, and this leads to poor outcomes overall'.[34]

While it is extremely difficult to draw meaningful international comparisons (because of the very different cultural approaches to the use of care in each country), the future of the care population working group's report notes that England now has a comparatively small per capita rate of care. They include analysis which shows that, at 55 children per 10,000, England's rate of care is lower than that of most European countries and approximately half that of Denmark and France.[35] So while direct comparisons are of limited use, this does seem to suggest that compared with some European countries there is likely to be a high concentration of disadvantage in the English care population of today.

The care population today

Compared with historic highs in the numbers in care, today's care population is comparatively small. There were 60,900 looked-after children at 31 March 2009, 2 per cent more than the figure for 2007/8 of 59,400.[36] There is evidence of a slight increase in the number of children who *started* to be looked after during 2008/9, when 25,400 children became looked after (an increase of 9 per cent from the previous year).[37]

The majority of the children entering care today can expect to be placed in a foster placement: 73 per cent of looked-after children were in foster care in 2009 while only 13 per cent were in residential settings.[38] This is in stark contrast to the use of residential care in the past. In the early 1980s the majority of looked-after children would have been in a residential placement; in the past these were 'used more extensively and [at] an earlier stage of intervention'.[39] It is also important to note that today only a minority of looked-after children achieve the type of permanency represented by adoption in any given year: 3,300 looked-after children were adopted during 2009.[40] Although overall young people are leaving care later today, DCSF statistics on care leavers in 2009 show that 38 per cent of young people still leave care before their 18th birthday, when they are 16 or 17.[41]

Of the 60,900 looked-after children in England, 36,200 were looked after under a care order. The percentage of children looked after under a voluntary agreement increased from 29 per cent to 32 per cent since 2007/8.[42] The majority of looked-after children in England are of white British origin (73 per cent). In 2009 there were 3,700 unaccompanied asylum seeking children in the system, which is an increase of around 200 children compared with 2008.

The age that children come into care often shapes the type of journey they go on to experience afterwards, something we will look at in more detail in section 2. The following statistics from 2009 show the range in ages for entrants to the care system (although it is important to note that this period in care may not be the first – young people in the older age groups may have spent a period in care when they were younger):

· 19 per cent are under 1 when they enter care
· 19 per cent are aged 1 to 4
· 16 per cent are aged 5 to 9
· 36 per cent are aged 10 to 15
· 11 per cent are 16 and over

It is striking that just under half of the entrants to the care system in 2009 were over the age of 10, and suggests that many are likely to have complex needs by the time they arrive.

To arrive at a more nuanced understanding of the dynamics of the care system, it is important to look at the duration of children's stay there. In reality, some groups of children move in

Table 1   **All children looked after at 31 March 2009**

Category of need	Percentage
Abuse or neglect	61%
Child's disability	4%
Parent's illness or disability	4%
Family in acute stress	9%
Family dysfunction	11%
Socially unacceptable behaviour	2%
Low income	0%
Absent parenting	9%

Source: DCSF, www.dcsf.gov.uk/rsgateway/DB/SFR/
s000878/index.shtml

and out of care rapidly and often do not stay for long periods. As of September 2009, only 43,200 of the care population had actually been looked after continuously for over a year.[43] Among the group of children and young people who ceased to be looked after in 2009, the average length of their last period in care was just under two and half years (874 days).[44] In 2009 48 per cent of children who ceased to be looked after had only spent less than a year in care,[45] and 25 per cent of children that year returned home within 8 weeks.[46] For those children who stay for very short periods in the care system, it seems clear that their home environment is likely to be more influential than their time in care.

Why do children enter care in the first place? Although government data does not allow us to look at this issue in depth, table 1 shows that the majority still become looked after because of abuse or neglect, but that the care system is also performing important functions in supporting families in difficulty or those with disabled children.

'Groups' of looked-after children

The care careers and placements of children vary with their age and age at entry, reasons for entry, behaviour and family characteristics. This was clearly reflected in the primary research conducted with looked-after children for this project, when we interviewed young people who had entered at a young age and enjoyed stable placement for over a decade and others who had entered later and moved in and out of care numerous times without ever finding stability.

In *The Pursuit of Permanence* (2007) Sinclair et al undertook a major study of the movements of children in and out of the care system in 13 councils. On the basis of their findings they managed to identify several distinct 'groups':

- *Young entrants (43 per cent of the sample)*. These children were under the age of 11, and were looked after primarily for reasons of abuse and neglect; 29 per cent of them had returned home at least once (which means they were counted as a 'repeat admission').[47]
- *Adolescent graduates (26 per cent of the sample)*. These young people were first admitted under the age of 11 but were now older than this and still looked after – they had generally entered for reasons of abuse or neglect; 56 per cent of this group had returned home at least once.
- *Abused adolescents (9 per cent)*. This group was first admitted over the age of 11 for reasons of neglect or abuse; they often exhibited challenging behaviour; 44 per cent of this group had returned home at least once.
- *Adolescent entrants (14 per cent)*. These young people were first admitted when aged 11 or over when their relationships at home had broken down; they also showed more challenging behaviour; 50 per cent had returned home at least once.

· *Children seeking asylum (5 per cent)*. These children were almost always over the age of 11 and were doing comparatively well at school, displaying less challenging behaviour. 21 per cent of this group had had at least one repeat admission.
· *Disabled children (3 per cent)*. These children had comparatively high levels of challenging behaviour but their families were not said to have many problems in their own right; 46 per cent had returned home at least once.[48]

According to Sinclair, these groups of children differed in their chances of achieving a permanent 'family placement' and in the way they were likely to find it. The young entrants were divided between those who were adopted, those who went home and those who stayed on in the care system. Adolescent graduates and the small group of severely disabled children were largely dependent on the care system for whatever stability they were going to achieve. Abused adolescents and adolescent entrants could go home or remain in the care system but in either case their chances of achieving a long-term stable family placement were less good than those of others.[49]

Alongside their age and reason for entering, one of the most important influences on the shape of a child's care journey is what happens to them *before* they enter the system. The majority have a history of abuse and neglect, and the impact of this pre-care adversity will often contribute to the emergence of emotional and behavioural difficulties later on. The evidence suggests that the group of children and young people who eventually become looked after already have a high level of mental and physical health problems, along with challenging behaviour at the outset of their care journey.

Sempik at al. looked at the emotional and behavioural difficulties of children at *entry* to care. Although problems were less common for younger age groups, they found that 72.3 per cent of looked-after children aged 5–15 in the study showed indications of behavioural or emotional problems.[50] In 2003 Meltzer et al found that once in care, about two-thirds of children living in residential care were assessed as having a mental disorder, compared with a half of those living independently, and about four in ten of those placed with foster carers or with their natural parents.[51]

The complex makeup of the care population and the range in pre-care experiences defeats any 'one size fits all' approach to care. It reaffirms the range of purposes the system serves and the difficulty in pursuing only 'permanence' or 'prevention' for such a diverse group. In any assessment of the performance of the care system, it is also essential to acknowledge the comparatively short periods that many actually spend in care and the frequency with which they return home.

3 Does care 'fail'?

In this chapter we investigate perceptions of the *impact* of care, to explore how well this is grounded in existing evidence. In this report we argue that society's view of whether care is at the most simplistic level 'good' or 'bad' has exerted considerable influence over the use of care in practice. Consequently it is essential that our collective understanding of care is grounded in the evidence wherever possible. Of course, challenging the view that care 'fails' on a catastrophic scale is far from arguing that the English care system is perfect. It is possible to acknowledge that there are many shortfalls in the system, and that care leavers are disadvantaged relative to the rest of the population, without accepting the care system is solely responsible for that disadvantage. This is an important distinction, but it is one that is frequently missing from the media or political debates on this issue.

The public discourse about care is undoubtedly shaped by the fact that many of the families and young people in contact with the care system experience multiple disadvantages and have problematic, sometimes chaotic, lives. As we will show later in this chapter, this gives rise to some confusion between cause and effect. The idea that the (very real) difficulties experienced by many care leavers are created by the care system has been in the ascendant in political and media circles for some time. In 2006 a Centre for Policy Studies report maintained that:

care is failing on a scale that is catastrophic. It is not just a tragedy for the individual. A successful system of care would transform this country. At a stroke, it would empty a third of our prisons and shift half of all prisoners under the age of 25 out of the criminal justice system. It would halve the number of prostitutes, reduce by between a third and a half the number of homeless and remove 80 per cent of Big Issue sellers from our street corners. Not only is our system failing the young people in care, it is failing society and perpetuating an underclass.[52]

The Centre for Social Justice has been similarly influential in promoting the view that the care system is in crisis, and in *Couldn't Care Less* set out its overall position on the effectiveness of the care system: 'Despite over a decade of reforming legislation and initiatives, the treatment of many children in care and those leaving the care system deserves to be a source of national shame.'[53]

This attitude towards the care system is by no means universal, but in the past two years it has been given added credibility by failures in safeguarding, interpreted as proof that the system lets children down across the board. The tragic death of Baby Peter in August 2007 sparked numerous articles about a care system that made a real impact on the public consciousness. One article, 'Children in care: how Britain is failing its most vulnerable', discussed the shortcomings of the care system and went on to draw a link between the perception that care fails and the consequent unwillingness of professionals to intervene:

Social workers are so familiar with the dismal outcomes from care that they see taking children into the system as something to be avoided at all costs. It is this conviction, combined with a sense that struggling families can be mended, that is understood at some unspoken level to have motivated child protection workers in Haringey to defer removing Baby P from his family, with disastrous consequences. No one can feel positive about taking a child into care when the official outcomes at the other end are so bleak.[54]

As we will argue in this report, the view that care consigns children to a lifetime of underachievement and poor outcomes plays a part in shaping the way we use public care, creating delay and instability later down the line. Given that this belief about a failing care system is so widely held it seems unlikely that it is entirely unfounded, so what fuels the idea that care impacts negatively on children? For an explanation we must look to the way we interpret outcome data for looked-after children.

'Outcomes' and the problem of interpretation

Statistics on the numbers of children and young people in care in England have been collected and published by the Department of Health at least since the Children and Young Persons Act 1969, and similarly in Scotland, Wales and Northern Ireland. Since 2004, statistical returns for 'outcomes' for children and young people have been collected and cover academic performance, employment and training, youth offending and some health-related outcomes. Since 2009 data on the emotional and behavioural health of looked-after children has also been collected, although only partial data was returned.[55] The SSDA903 collected from all local authorities is an important source of potential longitudinal data, as it is collected for individual children each year. However, the information on children from one year to the next has not yet been analysed and presented longitudinally, it has only been presented as a yearly snapshot.

This data has played an important part in the drive to improve standards and outcomes for looked-after children and care leavers, with a particular focus on improving academic attainment. Over recent years a number of targets for improvement have been set. For example, as part of the Comprehensive Spending Review (2008–11) the government set public service agreement (PSA) targets for local authorities on educational attainment. The current PSA target 11 aims to narrow the gap in educational achievement between children from lower income and disadvantaged backgrounds and their peers. This is underpinned by two indicators. Indicator 4 aims to increase the proportion of looked-after children achieving Level 4 in English to 60 per cent by 2011 and to increase the proportion achieving Level 4 in mathematics at Key Stage 2 to 55 per cent by 2011. Indicator 5 aims to increase the proportion of looked-after children achieving five grade A*–C GCSE results to 20 per cent by 2011. The reason these targets were introduced – the poor academic performance of looked-after children compared with the rest of the population – is clearly apparent from figure 2.

Despite incremental improvements on most measures over recent years, this type of outcome data certainly confirms the existence of a large gap between looked-after children and the

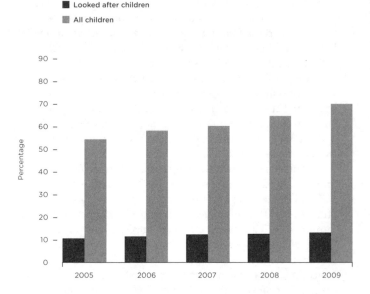

Figure 2 **Percentage of children continuously looked after for at least 12 months at 30 September 2005 to 2009 obtaining five grade A*–C GCSE results or GNVQ equivalents compared with all children**

■ Looked after children

■ All children

Source: Outcome Indicators for Children Looked After: Twelve months to 30 September 2009, England 21 April 2010, DCSF

rest of the population. For children looked after continuously for 12 months to September 2009, 9 per cent of those aged 10 or over were cautioned or convicted for an offence during the year, just over twice the rate for all children of this age.[56] The DCSF statistical release from 2009 showed that only 7 per cent of care leavers at 19 were in higher education (studies beyond A level).[57] On the basis of this type of outcome data, and other small scale academic studies,[58] it seems clear that looked-after children do perform worse academically, and have poorer mental and physical health and other outcomes compared with the rest of the population. But does this tell us anything about the impact of the care system?

Assuming that this type of data can tell us about the effect of care on children's outcomes is mistaken for several reasons. First, this information is only presented publicly as 'snapshot' data of those children who were in the care system at that moment in time; as we saw in chapter 2 children regularly move in and out of the care system and many do not remain looked after for more than two or three years. Consequently, the group of children in the snapshot are not the same from year to year. Second, to make comparisons between looked-after children and the rest of the child population is not to compare like with like. As we saw earlier, many children enter care for reasons of abuse or neglect, and have pre-existing emotional or behavioural difficulties. This level of pre-care adversity (combined with background socio-economic factors) means that entrants to the care system are already unlikely to perform as well as those children who have not been exposed to such experiences – so the rest of the population is not a meaningful control group to use. Furthermore, when entering care some children will be a very long way from achieving qualifications, and so any improvements they make will not be captured by academic measures.

Third, published government data does not follow young people beyond their 19th birthday into early adulthood so it is impossible to gather any meaningful information about later life outcomes on a large enough scale. Finally, and most importantly, published data is rarely longitudinal and so it is not possible to track children's progress *over time* spent in the care system. On the few occasions that a longitudinal element is included, it tells a slightly different story about the outcomes of children when they are looked after by the state. In 2006 DCSF published a highly detailed statistical release on outcomes for looked-after children in 2005, which would seem to indicate that children's educational outcomes improve the longer that they remain looked after (figure 3).[59]

This piece of data would appear to contradict the assumption that the longer a child remains in care the worse they are likely to perform academically. Additional longitudinal

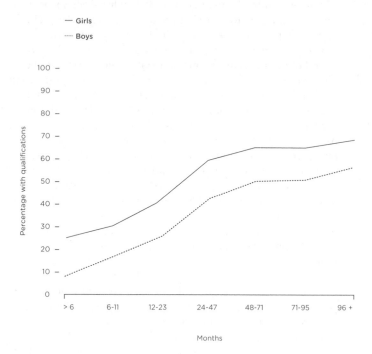

Figure 3 **Percentage of care leavers in 2005 with at least one GCSE or GNVQ by duration of last period of care (England)**

— Girls

···· Boys

Percentage with qualifications

Months

evidence on the care population is needed to explore this more thoroughly. Publishing an analysis of data which charted this group's progress through care (including number and type of placements, health information and educational attainment) from the point of entering care to leaving would be an important step towards untangling the impact of care from pre-care experiences.

Next, we turn to overviews of smaller-scale academic research that attempt to introduce this longitudinal element into assessments of the impact of care and to compare 'like with like'.

Alternative perspectives on the 'impact' of care

The simplistic view of care as failing 60,000 young people should be confined to the dustbin.
        Professor Mike Stein[60]

        At the outset of section 1 we emphasised the range of interventions and experiences covered by the concept of 'public care'. Generalisations about the impact of the whole care system are therefore almost impossible to make with any certainty. The care population is far from homogenous and the care system has also changed considerably over the past decade making long-term comparisons difficult. Nevertheless, there is a credible body of academic evidence that destabilises the view that care is somehow responsible for *creating* poor outcomes.
        In 2007 a significant overview of that evidence was commissioned by the Welsh Assembly, entitled *What is the Impact of Care on Children's Welfare?* Undertaken by Dr Donald Forrester and colleagues, the main focus of this review was British studies published between 1991 and 2006 that provided information on the welfare of children in care over time, though some international studies and important earlier research were also considered.[61] Given the comprehensive nature of this review we will quote from the findings in some detail. Forrester and his team divided British studies between 1991 and 2006 into the following categories:

(a) Studies that compared outcomes for children who entered care with those for comparable children who did not
        Only two studies provided data on this (with a third published in 2007 that was included). Two of the studies suggested significant improvements for children who entered care compared to those who did not. One indicated little difference.
(b) Studies that looked at the progress of children in care over time
        Eleven studies were included within this section. The focus of most of these studies was the progress of children in permanent placements (such as adoption or long-term fostering), though a smaller number considered the impact of foster care and a few covered a cross-section of children in care.

Key findings were:
· *Children's welfare improved over time in every study – whatever type of placement was the focus of research;*
· *There was strong evidence that children traditionally considered difficult to place in permanent placements (i.e. older children, sibling groups and children from ethnic minorities) could nonetheless benefit from such placements;*
· *Nonetheless, the older the child and the more serious their problems the more likely there were to be problems in the placement;*
· *Children in foster care generally made good progress, even when this was a temporary or uncertain option;*

(c) Studies that compared adults who had been in care with other adults who had experienced adversity or difficulty
Such approaches tended to use existing datasets. There are significant difficulties in such approaches – with the most important being that the adversities that care was compared with (such as coming from a one parent family or being working class) did not take account of issues such as abuse or neglect that might be expected to have a negative impact on children. The studies cannot therefore unpick the contribution of care to later difficulties.
Overall adults who had been in care had somewhat higher problems than those who had not, but this was not a very strong relationship. If children in care were compared with others who might have experienced some level of disadvantage, their outcomes were broadly similar.[62]

While acknowledging important gaps in the research, on the basis of this evidence the authors came to this conclusion:

There was little evidence of the care system having a negative impact on children's welfare. Indeed, the picture suggested the opposite – in the vast majority of studies children's welfare improved. This picture was fairly consistent. This overall pattern leads us to conclude that on the whole care is a positive experience for most children and that it appears to either improve or at the least not harm their welfare.[63]

The review also stresses the impact of pre-care adversity; so, given the difficulties many entrants to the care system have experienced it would be unreasonable to expect all their problems to have been resolved after being placed. As a result, the outcomes of the general population will always be an inappropriate point of comparison.

As well as Forrester's study, there has been another review carried out by C4EO, the Centre for Excellence and Outcomes in Children and Young People's Services, which was funded by DCSF to identify effective practice in improving educational outcomes. It found that 'for most young people entry to care was considered to have been beneficial for their welfare, including their education'.[64] High quality placements are, of course, essential to achieving this type of positive impact on educational outcomes.

When we look at other studies which attempt to compare care leavers' outcomes with a group of similarly disadvantaged young people, a similar picture of the impact of care emerges to that painted by these reviews.

Cameron et al's 2007 study sought to compare outcomes among care leavers with a *comparable* peer group.[65] This non-care in 'difficulty' group, aged 16–29, was defined as those who were homeless and/or had two or more of the following difficulties in their lives: living apart from family; pregnancy or parenthood; addiction problems for example with alcohol or illicit drugs; a criminal record or offending behaviour; unemployment; learning or physical disabilities; belonging to a minority ethnic group; and leaving school with no qualifications. Both care leavers and young people 'in difficulty' were more likely than young people in the general population to have had mental health problems, to be disabled in some way, to have had a pregnancy and to have substance misuse problems. However, the team concluded that, overall, care leavers seemed to be doing rather better than young people who had not been in care. Care leavers were doing better than young people 'in difficulty 'when measuring access to housing, educational participation, being in employment, and self-assessment of their health and wellbeing.

In 2009 Pritchard and Williams used Home Office records to compare 438 formerly looked-after children (LAC) aged 16–23 (who had spent some time in care) with 215 males who were permanently excluded from school (PEF).[66] The PEFs were, almost by definition, likely to be educational under-achievers, which is linked to unemployment, poor skills, low income, poor housing, high crime, ill-health and family breakdown. This study found that the subsequent offending rate by LAC was 44 per cent, which was significantly lower than the subsequent offending rate of former PEFs (64 per cent). Although LAC and PEFs had higher rates of being victims of crime than the general population, LAC men were significantly more often victims of sex and violent crimes. However, there were no suicides among LAC but the suicide rate of PEFs was 133 times that of their peers in the general population. Overall, the researchers argue that 'despite starting from a more disadvantaged situation, former LAC did significantly better than the PEF young men'.[67]

This dissonance between the perception of care as damaging and the academic evidence is striking. This is not to say that the care system is necessarily *good enough*, rather that when care is compared to the alternative, it does not necessarily have a negative impact and can often improve things for some children. The fact that care could be improved for many children is not incompatible with the idea that, overall, care does not seem to be solely responsible for the bad outcomes which are often attributed to the system.

The evidence outlined above also raises important questions about the consequences of seeing care as a 'last resort'. The stigmatisation of care, and the upfront costs to the state, mean that children who might benefit from early intervention or family services do not do so. As we will see later in this report, delays in taking decisive action means children can enter care later and develop more emotional and behavioural difficulties as a result of their pre-care experiences. Consequently, they may go on to experience unstable care journeys, which are ultimately more costly to the state. This vicious cycle is one of the underlying problems of the care system, and can be traced back to the historical debates about the purpose of care outlined in the beginning of this section.

However, given the variety in children's needs and care experiences it is important to acknowledge that there is a vast range in how positive an experience of care can be. In *Costs and Consequences of Placing Children in Care* Ward et al demonstrate the costs associated with different care journeys for children with a range of support needs. They find that although those with the least extensive needs often seemed to benefit the most from placements, the group with the highest level of need were actually served least well by the care system:

By and large children with the least extensive needs appeared to cost least and benefit most from care or accommodation. The group who appeared least likely to benefit were those with the most extensive needs, particularly young people with no evidence of physical or learning disability, but who displayed emotional or behavioural difficulties and also committed offences. Many of these young people had extensive and entrenched needs; they would have been likely to require intensive expert services wherever they were placed.[68]

This points us towards differentiating between types of care journey and developing a more sophisticated understanding of the 'impact of care' for different groups of children. What is it that defines a *good* journey through care and how can this become the experience of the majority? It is to this question that we turn in section 2 of this report.

Section 2
What works for children in care?

In this section we review the evidence on key factors that contribute to all children and young people's healthy psychological development, before considering how these theories can best be applied to different aspects of the care system.

Proximal processes

Child development research has consistently shown that a child's home environment and the parenting they receive have the most significant impact on their psychological development and later life outcomes.[69] Bronfenbrenner's ecological model of human development distinguishes between 'proximal' factors, which describe the influence of the child's social relationships within their family and wider social network, and 'distal' or background factors, which describe the influence of the socio-economic, geographical and demographic environment surrounding the child.[70]

Within this framework, 'proximal' interactions that take place daily between the child and their family have been shown to have the most *direct* influence on children's development.[71] Important examples of proximal processes are demonstrated by the relationship between child and parent, which may involve warmth and affection, use of discipline, attitudes towards learning and shared aspirations towards the child's future. Distal factors such as income and family background interact with and influence family relationships (for example, low income can cause stress and poor mental health, which can impact on a parent's ability to parent well) but unlike proximal influences they are not the primary determinants of children's outcomes.[72]

Attachment, warmth, and setting of boundaries

Research on attachment has also shown how important it is for young children's development that they experience a warm bond with their primary caregiver.[73] The caregiver's show of affection and responsiveness towards the child gives the child the sense of security they need to develop an attachment with their carer.[74] Through this process of *attunement* with their caregiver, children are able to develop empathy, which provides the basis for other social skills and the ability to form relationships.[75] Children who do not experience attunement with a caregiver may fail to develop empathy altogether.[76]

Secure attachment is therefore fundamental to children's socialisation and wellbeing. However, as Diana Baumrind has highlighted, responsiveness is only one-half of the picture; the parenting that contributes best to children's development must combine attachment with 'demandingness', which refers to a parent's ability to impose consistent rules.[77] Using these two dimensions, Baumrind has constructed a typology that divides parenting behaviour into the following four categories:[78]

· *Authoritative parents* are both demanding and responsive. They are warm and nurturing towards their children, set clear boundaries for their children's behaviour and provide discipline in a way that is supportive.
· *Authoritarian parents* are demanding towards their children but not warm and responsive. They provide an ordered environment and monitor their children's behaviour carefully.
· *Permissive parents* are responsive and affectionate towards their children but not demanding. Rather than imposing consistent boundaries, they are lenient with their children's behaviour and avoid confrontation.
· *Rejecting–neglecting or 'disengaged' parents* are neither demanding nor responsive. They do not structure or monitor their child's behaviour and environment and do not provide affection or support. Disengaged parents 'may be actively rejecting or else neglect their childrearing responsibilities altogether'.[79]

Empirical studies show that children who were raised by *authoritative* parents consistently had better social skills, a stronger sense of agency, and were more cognitively advanced.[80] A recent study by Demos analysed data from the Millennium Cohort Study (MCS) to identify how these different varieties of parenting were associated with children's development of key character traits that are important to children's social and emotional development and later life outcomes. This study found that the authoritative parenting style, which combines strong attachment between carer and child and consistent rule enforcement, was best able to help children develop important character traits. Demos's analysis of the MCS found that permissive parenting was slightly more effective than authoritarian parenting, and disengaged parenting had the most negative outcomes for children. The analysis concluded that 'overall, warmth registers as more important than discipline in impacting on child behavioural outcomes'.[81]

In our own research with children in care and care leavers, a number of their comments showed their appreciation for the rules and boundaries that had been enforced by their foster carers, as signs that their carers were concerned about them and wanted to prepare them for independence:

Even if we've been through a lot, I think we need that toughness.

Stability and consistency

The research carried out for this project, including interviewing a number of children in care and care leavers, identified negative experiences of unwelcome change as a consistent theme. Changing home, school and local area through placement moves were seen as practically and emotionally disruptive. Most significant were disruptions to relationships –with both social workers and carers. One care leaver told us that even though she disliked her school, she was glad she was able to remain there despite several placement moves:

It was a good thing in a way because I was moving a lot. It was probably the most consistent period in my life.

Another care leaver told us how much she had disliked being moved to a placement in another borough; this had led to the breakdown of her placement:

I wanted to come back and I actually ran away.

Other studies have emphasised the important role that stability and consistency in children's and young people's relationships and immediate environment plays in contributing towards their sense of security and wellbeing. Recent research by the Children's Society investigated the association between children's wellbeing and recent changes in their lives related to family structure, home, school and local area. The study found that change had a markedly negative effect on young people's wellbeing. In particular, young people who had experienced a recent change in the adults with whom they lived had significantly lower wellbeing than young people who had not. Other changes in home, school or local area were also associated with lower wellbeing for young people, but not to the same extent as changes in their family structure.[82] This reflects the significant negative impact that disruption to children's attachments has on their wellbeing.

In order to cope well with change and negative life events, young people need to build their resilience, defined as:

The quality that enables some young people to find fulfilment in their lives despite their disadvantaged backgrounds, the problems or adversity they may have undergone, or the pressures they may experience.[83]

One study found that young people's resilience at age 10 (measured according to their locus of control, application, self-esteem and other indicators) has a significant relationship with their mental health outcomes at age 16.[84] Michael Rutter argues that a young person's level of resilience is determined by the presence of 'multiple risk and protective factors', including genetic and environmental factors, and that 'the reduction of negative, and increase of positive, chain reactions influences the extent to which the effects of adversity persist over time'.[85]

Resilience in young people from disadvantaged families has been found to be associated with a secure attachment with a family member or other caregiver; a positive experience of school; feeling that you have control over decisions in your life; 'being given the chance of a "turning point", such as a new opportunity or break from a high-risk area'; having a high IQ; and having positive relationships with friends.[86] While a child may have experienced adversity in their early life, the introduction of protective factors at a later stage in their life can help build their resilience and compensate for previous disadvantage.

The remainder of this section will outline how the care system can best provide looked-after children and young people with the factors outlined above: warm and secure relationships, consistency and stability, which are known to support children's wellbeing, educational attainment and resiliency. Chapters 4 to 6 will show that looked-after children's opportunities for positive psychological development and good later life outcomes can be influenced by three critical factors: the point at which they enter care or whether they experience delay, the stability they experience while in care, and the support they receive in making the transition to independent adulthood.

4   Early or decisive entry to care

There is now a compelling body of evidence showing that children who are exposed to abuse or neglect and whose entry to care is delayed by indecision or 'drift' in case management are more at risk of experiencing emotional and behavioural difficulties and are less likely to experience the positive outcomes of being adopted or having a stable placement while in care.

Many children entering care have already experienced a high degree of uncertainty and instability in their lives and some will be severely traumatised by their exposure to abuse or neglect. Of the children and young people who entered care in 2009, 61 per cent did so as a result of abuse or neglect and a further 29 per cent became looked after as a result of 'absent parenting' or because their family was dysfunctional or experiencing acute stress. Monck's review of attachment theory in relation to adoption highlights the impact that troubled and broken attachment relationships can have on the psychological development of children who have been exposed to abuse or neglect and have subsequently entered care. A child who has experienced 'persistent inconsistency or rejection by the primary carers... is more likely to develop disturbed behaviour patterns, including counter rejection of the caregiver and others'.[87]

A number of studies have found a strong association between children's age at entry to care and their level of emotional and behavioural problems. A study by Sempik et al found that the incidence of emotional and behavioural difficulties demonstrated by children at entry to care increased sharply between the 0–4 age group (18.4 per cent) and the 5–10 age group (67.8 per cent).[88] They commented:

It is often assumed that such high levels of need are the result of children's adverse experiences in care, however, the children in this study had no previous experience of care and were assessed at entry to the care system and their difficulties, therefore, will reflect adverse experiences in the home environment.[89]

Administrative or legal delays in taking a child into care can therefore lead to a child spending longer in an abusive or neglectful situation and being more psychologically damaged as a result. The impact of unnecessary delay and the associated increase in emotional and behavioural difficulties this can cause is far-reaching; Sempik et al observed that the emotional and behavioural problems experienced by young children at entry to care can become more serious as the child grows older and in some cases can be a cause of placement disruption.

This link between the timeliness with which children enter care, their level of emotional and behavioural difficulties and their chance of experiencing a stable long-term placement while in care has been explored in more detail in other research. Selwyn et al's study of the effect of delay on the placement outcomes of 130 children over a period of seven years found that 26 per cent of the original group had not been adopted but went on to have a long-term foster care placement or another type of permanent placement, and 12 per cent of the original group did not achieve a stable placement. Factors that predicted whether children would be in this latter 'unstable group' included being older at the time that permanency planning began, having been exposed to more forms of abuse, and having more serious emotional and behavioural problems.[90] These children were also more likely than those who had stable adoptive or long-term foster care placements to have experienced a failed attempt to reunify them with their family (44 per cent of the group) and to have had more placements since they entered care. Selwyn et al estimated that for these children the odds of not being adopted increased 1.5 for every year of age at entry to care.[91] They comment:

Practice decisions and legal uncertainties clearly had a profound influence on a child's age at entry to care... The extent of children's recovery from abuse and neglect is known to be inversely related to the depth and length of their experience of adversity... In this sample, delay affected not only the length of children's adverse experiences but also their range and depth.[92]

Biehal et al's study comparing the characteristics of children placed for adoption or long-term foster care who went on to experience stable and unstable placements over a seven-year period also found a strong association between the age at which children entering care and their placement outcome. The mean ages at which the different groups of children had last entered care, according to their placement outcome, were: adopted by strangers (1.5 years); adopted by carers (3.1 years); in stable foster care (3.9 years); and in 'unstable care' (5.3 years).[93] The study found that children who went on to experience placement disruptions had already had a higher level of emotional and behavioural difficulties eight years earlier, compared with those who were adopted or settled in long-term foster care placements. Less serious emotional and behavioural difficulties were associated with the children having entering their current placement at the age of 3 or younger.[94]

These studies show a strong association between age of entry to care, the likelihood that a child will experience emotional and behavioural difficulties, and their chance of achieving stability in care. The close relationship between these three factors emphasises the damage that can be caused by allowing children to be exposed to situations of abuse and neglect for too long before they enter care. Of course it is not always possible or appropriate to take children into care at a younger age, and this step should only ever be taken if the circumstances demand it. However, delay and drift in the system can be avoided at any age. To give children a better chance of achieving stability and associated outcomes of better mental health, wellbeing and educational attainment (explored in more detail below), it is important that decisions on taking children into care are made as early and decisively as possible and that poorly planned or unsupported reunification attempts are minimised.

5 High quality and stable placements

To compensate for many children's pre-care exposure to abuse and neglect, and to reduce the psychological impact of these experiences, the care system must seek to build looked-after children's and young people's resilience by maximising the number of protective factors in children's lives, such as a stable base, a secure attachment to a carer and positive school experiences and peer relationships. Mike Stein comments:

Resilient young people have, in the main, had stability in their lives… it seems likely that the link between stability and improved life chances for care leavers is associated with some care leavers having experienced compensatory secure attachments, especially through long-term fostering, and, for others, the stability, although not necessarily resulting in secure attachment, has provided them with security and continuity in their lives. [95]

Stein argues that stability can promote resilience for looked-after children in two respects: by providing the young person with a secure attachment, which can help to make placement disruption less likely; and by providing continuity in other areas of the child's life, such as their school and friendship group. [96]

Placement stability and attachment

A significant body of research has found adoption offers looked-after children who cannot return home to their families the best chance of achieving stability and developing a secure attachment. As mentioned above, it is likely that adoption is associated with lower disruption rates than long-term foster care because adopted children tend to have entered care at a younger age, have experienced a shorter period of exposure to pre-care adversity, have experienced fewer placements and have had fewer failed reunifications with their birth parents.[97] However, Biehal et al's study also emphasises the additional sense of stability and belonging that can be felt by later-placed looked-after children who are adopted by their carers: 'Two children who had been placed with their adoptive families at the age of five expressed great relief at having achieved the legal security of adoption.'[98] This leads Biehal et al to recommend that, where appropriate, local authorities should support carers to adopt. Our own primary research with foster carers found that a number of foster carers had adopted, or had tried to adopt children they cared for, sometimes despite a significant level of resistance from their social worker:

Yes, I went in for it [adoption]. But foster carers are strongly discouraged. They say that you can't deal with attachment issues.

This discouragement of foster carers from adopting is likely to reflect the great pressure that social workers are under to maintain an adequate stock of foster care placements as a result of the endemic shortages of foster carers. However, it is clear that discouraging adoption in these circumstances is unlikely to be in the best interests of the child concerned.

Only a very small proportion of looked-after children are adopted each year. In 2009 just over 5 per cent of looked-after children were adopted, while 73 per cent of looked-after children were placed with foster carers, including family and friends carers.

A significant factor in the success and stability of these placements is whether the child or young person feels integrated in their foster carer's family and is able to develop a secure attachment with their carers. Some of the looked-after children and young people we spoke to during our primary research had developed very strong relationships with their foster families:

I refer to them as family and my foster carer as my mum. They are basically my family.

They're like real brothers and sisters.

However, others had found it difficult to develop a close and trusting relationship:

I lived with mine for seven years and there was never really a family bond.

It's a lot harder when you're living with someone who's got their own children because they tend to keep you in the dark about certain things. You are there just to live with the family and not to be part of the family.

A number of studies have associated carers' personal qualities with success in achieving stable placements.[99] Schofield and Beek's study of a cohort of children placed in foster care, who were a 'high risk' group according to the age at which they were placed and the abuse and neglect they had been exposed to, found that the degree of 'sensitive parenting' demonstrated by one or both carers was associated with whether children settled stably in their placement and made good progress. 'Sensitive parenting' was defined as:

The carer's capacity to put themselves 'in the shoes of the child', to reflect on the child's thoughts, feelings and behaviour and their own thoughts, feelings and parenting style – all features of reflective function that link to resilience in the carers themselves as well as to resilience-promoting parenting.[100]

Another important dimension of 'sensitive parenting' mentioned by Schofield and Beek was sensitivity to the child's need to feel accepted as a 'full family member'.[101] One dimension of being a 'full family member' in their foster family that was appreciated by the young people we spoke to was having chores to do like other family members and being expected to obey the house rules. Their comments reflected Baumrind's parenting typology, which identifies effective parenting with a combination of displaying warmth and setting consistent boundaries. One of the young people we spoke to compared her experience of foster care favourably with the time she had spent in residential care, which she had found impersonal:

You didn't really learn life skills because meals were cooked for you… but in foster care, it was like a family with different allocated chores.

Another young person had found that his placement in residential care had provided too much freedom and lacked structure and security:

In a foster home they treat you like proper kids with proper rules.

Several of the young people we spoke to who had experienced placements in residential care explained that they found the changes in staff destabilising and that it was more difficult to form attachments than in foster families. The young people who described positive experiences of residential care attributed this to the close relationships they had been able to form with staff: 'some of them treated me like their own' or with other children:

My children's home was good and me and the kids there got really attached together and none of us wanted to separate any more because we were all we knew and that's what we thought was family.

These young people's experiences of residential care – both negative and positive – reflect Bowlby's critique of residential care, which he argued could have a damaging impact on young people if care was provided in an impersonal way and young people had little opportunity to form 'selective attachments' with their carers.[102] Petrie et al's analysis of attachment theory in relation to residential care identifies two potential solutions to this: first, that effective residential care must promote opportunities for young people to develop secure attachments and, second, that residential care workers must show 'sensitivity to the child as an individual with a mind, rather than as a collection of needs, behaviours or risk factors'.[103]

Petrie et al's recent and very influential study *Working with Children in Care: European Perspectives*, which compared residential care in England with care homes in Denmark and Germany, found significantly higher turnovers of both staff and young people in residential homes in England compared with the other two countries, and a higher ratio of staff to young people, factors that make it more difficult for young people to develop personal relationships with carers.[104] They suggest that the social pedagogic training that residential workers in Denmark and Germany receive is responsible for some of the differences in culture that promote better outcomes for young people in residential care in these countries. Pedagogic training, which most residential staff in Denmark complete to degree level, and in Germany to a medium or high level, promotes a child-centred approach to care, an emphasis on building a relationship between staff and children and on the importance of listening to and communicating with children, and reflective and mutually supportive professional practice. In 2007 the *Care Matters* white paper announced a national pilot to test the effectiveness of the European social pedagogic approach in residential care homes in England. This pilot is running between 2008-2011 in children's homes in ten Local Authority areas and the Universities of Bristol and York are conducting an independent evaluation.

Foster carers and residential carers were not the only important attachment figures in the lives of the looked-after children and young people we spoke to; the social workers of some young people had provided an important source of continuity throughout the placement changes they had experienced. One young person referred to a very positive relationship she had with one of her previous social workers, whom she had stayed in contact with and still visited frequently: 'even when I had a problem with a new social worker, I would call her and she would sort it out'. Another young person had had the same social worker for 13 years, until her retirement. However, as we will discuss in more detail in section 3, the majority of the young people we spoke to had experienced very frequent changes of social workers, which had prevented them from developing a close and supportive relationship with them.

Staying in contact with members of their birth family had also provided many of the young people we spoke to with continuous relationships throughout their experience of care:

I am pretty close to my family and have always been in contact with them. It's only because my mum couldn't deal with me that I was put into care.

However, some of the young people described a feeling of loss as a result of having lost contact with their siblings and other family members. One young person speculated that 'maybe if I had more contact with my family I would have settled down'. As chapter 6 will consider in more detail, the birth families of some young people can provide an important source of emotional and practical support when they leave care and are making the transition to independence. However, it is important to note that frequent contact with birth families will not always be appropriate and can sometimes undermine children's sense of stability; studies by Biehal and Schofield and Beek showed that complex and troubled relationships with birth family members can be a cause of anxiety for children[105] and can sometimes contribute to 'conflicts of loyalty' with their foster families.[106]

Stability and educational attainment

For looked-after children, placement stability (which usually enables children to stay at the same school and avoid disrupting their education) has a strong association with educational attainment. This relationship was highlighted by one of the care leavers we spoke to when he told us that leaving care early and moving between different accommodation had impacted badly on his GCSEs. A number of studies have shown that moving children into 'independent living' when they are 16, soon before their GCSEs, has a particularly negative impact on their achievement.[107] A study by Biehal et al found that the children in their sample who had had an unstable experience of care were doing worse than children in stable placements on all measures of educational participation, including truanting behaviour and exclusions, and they were making less educational progress.[108] Jackson and Simon's study investigating the characteristics and experiences of care leavers who go on to higher education also demonstrates this link between stability and educational attainment. The study found that care leavers who went to university had experienced relatively stable care careers with only one or two placements, had had continuity in their schooling, had been encouraged by their birth parents, and had received significant support from foster carers with their education.[109]

In addition to supporting better educational attainment, continuity in schooling can also make an important contribution to looked-after children's broader wellbeing, as Dixon et al have commented:

[School] may also provide a source of structure and stability in an otherwise troubled life and can provide a forum for developing positive self-esteem and confidence either through formal or less formal non-academic achievements, such as sport, music or getting a part in the school play. It is important therefore that young people are able to continue to participate in their education with as little interruption as possible.[110]

Some of the care leavers we spoke to emphasised the importance to their feelings of stability and continuity of being able to continue attending the same school throughout times when they experienced many changes of placement. Children consulted by the Children's Rights Director also reflected this view when asked which rules should be included in new planning, placement and review regulations. The rule that 'If possible, you should not have to move to a new school or college when you move to a new placement' was the third most popular statement out of a possible seven, with the first being that children should have a choice of placement and the second that children should have a back up placement if they did not settle in their first placement. Being able to stay at the same school was given a higher priority than being placed with siblings or being placed near your home.[111]

However, while consistent attendance at the same school is likely to benefit the majority of looked-after children, it is important to note that a change of school can also sometimes be a positive experience for young people; in another survey by the Children's Rights Director in 2009, just over half of the children who had changed schools when they moved to a new placement felt that the change of school had been in their best interests.[112]

This evidence of the positive influence that change can also have reflects Rutter et al's finding that giving children an opportunity for a 'turning point' can contribute to their resiliency.

Stability and mental health

A strong body of research has shown children and young people's mental health and their emotional wellbeing to have a very strong association with the stability of their placements. As discussed above, the age at which children enter care – and the length of exposure they have had to neglectful or abusive home environments – is a key indicator of their level of emotional and behavioural difficulties. Poor mental health is associated with a higher risk of placement breakdown, as carers may struggle to cope with children and young people's emotional problems and challenging behaviours.[113] One study found that a group of children who experienced a high number of disrupted placements had *all* shown aggressive and defiant behaviour before they entered care; whereas only 30 per cent of the control group who had few placement moves had exhibited these behaviours before they entered care.[114]

Another study found that children whose long-term foster placements disrupted after three or more years had particularly serious emotional and behavioural difficulties and that these problems both contributed to placement instability and predicted a higher risk of doing badly at school.[115]

While there is a clear link between emotional and behavioural problems and placement instability, the subsequent impact that placement stability *itself* can have on children's mental health is more difficult to judge. A recent study by Rubin et al in the USA took on the challenge to:

Disentangle the cascading relationship between a child's problems and his or her subsequent placement stability, and thereby establish the innate contribution of a child's placement stability toward his or her risk for behavioural problems 18 months after entering foster care.[116]

This study assessed 729 children's behavioural wellbeing at entry to care and established controls for their baseline attributes and pre-care experiences. It then measured the impact of instability in foster care over a period of 18 months on the children's behavioural outcomes. The study found that regardless of their characteristics and pre-care experiences, instability significantly increased the probability that the children would have behavioural problems. Those children who did not achieve placement stability in foster care were estimated to have a 36–63 per cent increased risk of behavioural problems compared to those who did achieve a stable placement. This study suggests that the experience of placement breakdown and instability can exacerbate or even be a cause of emotional and behavioural problems for looked-after children. As Ward et al have observed, this can lead to a downward spiral in which children's worsening emotional and behavioural problems increase their risk of experiencing further placement breakdown and add to the difficulty of finding them a suitable placement, leading to escalating costs for the local authority.[117]

This research emphasises the great importance of ensuring that children who enter care with emotional and behavioural problems have these problems identified at an early point and receive a high quality of emotional and professional support from the very start to resolve these problems and build their resilience.[118] Many young people will need to receive specialist therapeutic support to resolve their feelings of anger and complex emotional issues that are legacies of their pre-care experiences. One of the care leavers we spoke to in the course of our primary research told us:

I still feel those emotions from when I was little and the more the pressure I get from moving out, the more my emotions come out and the more I get upset.

She explained that she had often released her emotions through anger, and that this had earned her a reputation among social workers and foster carers as being difficult to manage. She acknowledged that several of her placement breakdowns had been initiated by her own behaviour when she felt trapped in placements where she was unhappy:

I used to smash up the place and go out drinking so that they could move me.

Reflecting on her time in care, she thought that she could have benefited from 'emotional support plus being settled', as she had never had a carer who was a consistent presence in her life and could help her manage her emotions. Section 3 will examine the quality of emotional and therapeutic support that is currently available to looked-after children in more detail.

Supporting stable placements

To reduce the risk of placement disruption for children with challenging behaviour or significant needs, it is essential that their carers are well trained and supported to help them understand and respond to the children's emotional and behavioural needs. The types of support they need may range from specialist training in understanding autism or managing hyperactivity, to simple emotional support to affirm their efforts and encourage them to persist under difficult circumstances.

Children who are adopted from care may have equivalent mental health needs to children who are in long-term foster care, in which case adoptive parents will need the same level of support that is given to foster carers.[119] In Rushton's 2007 review of adoption outcomes he compares the adoption breakdown rates for non-infant adoption reported in two studies: in one study 23 per cent of the adoptive placements disrupted and in another 17 per cent of the adoptions. He observes that both studies indicated adoption can provide stability for most children, but that many of these children's problems were not resolved soon after the placement was made: in the second study only two-fifths of the children were free from behavioural problems seven years later. This suggests that some adoptive parents may need support over a period of many years if breakdown is to be avoided.[120]

Beek and Schofield's study of children with challenging emotional and behavioural needs who were placed in long-term foster care found that the level of social work support that the foster carers received was associated with the success of the placement. All of the children in the 'good progress' group had received regular social work support from their child care social workers, who had helped their carers to understand their needs and ensure that these were met. In the 'uncertain progress' and 'downward spiral' groups of children, Beek and Schofield observed that 'some carers were becoming overwhelmed and exhausted by the high levels of neediness of their foster children'. In these cases, a lack of professional support was a particular risk factor for the placement, with carers often feeling 'a sense of isolation and helplessness'.[121]

The focus groups with foster carers that we conducted in our primary research highlighted the challenges of caring for children with very complex needs and the difficulty they often experienced in trying to access the resources these children needed. For example, one foster carer said:

Our child comes from horrendous abuse and she's got very severe learning difficulties, behavioural problems, and severe autism, so we need a lot of resources. And that is really hard to get hold of, speech therapy, psychologist, community nurses, appointments at hospitals, you have to fight and fight. I've had to go to MPs before.

They spoke of the great importance of having access to specialist training to help them understand the children's needs, strong social work support and short breaks to prevent them from reaching crisis-point:

When I was at the end of my tether, they offered me respite – I had to go in and ask for it, mind you. I now take it every two weeks. It makes a real difference.

In many cases it was felt that social workers did not understand or appreciate the extent of the strain that the foster carers were under. Foster carers also felt that social workers concealed information about the extent of a child's emotional or behavioural problems that might dissuade them from accepting a placement. This added to the stress of caring for children as problems would quickly emerge that the foster carers felt ill-equipped to cope with.

Caring for adolescent young people was mentioned as being particularly problematic by many of the foster carers. One foster carer described the difficulty of getting adolescent children to accept her house rules:

What stresses me out is when children don't obey the boundaries: they go out, and switch their phone off, come home late. They sometimes make you want to stop fostering, so many times at the police station, you know... You're so worried about their safety.

A large body of evidence shows young people who enter care in adolescence to be most at risk of instability. A study by Sinclair et al that looked at a sample of 7,399 children in care found that children who had experienced three or more placements in one year were more likely to be aged 11 or over and to have entered care for the first time over the age of 11.[122] This study concluded that 'really long-term placements were effectively only available to children who entered care under the age of 11'.[123] Other studies have found that about 40 per cent of placements for 11–15-year-olds break down within the first year.[124] These studies highlight the importance of ensuring that placements for these older children, who are at higher risk of instability, are matched with the same care as for younger children, and that their placements are well supported to reduce the risk of breakdown.

To build evidence of how specialist therapeutic care can mitigate the risk of instability associated with entering care in adolescence, DCSF commissioned a national pilot to test the effectiveness of the evidence-based Multidimensional Treatment Foster Care (MTFC) programme with this age group. The young people admitted to the programme have complex and challenging needs which put them at high risk of placement breakdown and two-thirds of those admitted so far had already experienced three or more placements. Two important features of the programme are the robust assessment that young people receive on entry to the programme to identify their educational and emotional and behavioural support needs, and the level of support that is provided to the foster carers to reduce the risk of placement breakdown.

All young people who enter the MTFC programme in England receive a full assessment of their mental health needs, family history and significant harm, high risk behaviours, placement moves and educational needs. This assessment is used to create a personal support plan around the child drawing on the expertise of a multi-agency team including their foster carer, a skills coach, an individual therapist, an education worker, a birth family therapist and a foster carer recruiter who provides the foster carer with access to 24 hour support. The model also recommends a minimum provision of one respite carer to seven foster care placements, to provide the foster carers with frequent access to short breaks. The foster carer is at the centre of the treatment programme, supported by the work of the other team members, and is trained in a behaviour management technique that is designed to 'teach pro-social skills, reinforce positive behaviour and attitudes through tangible rewards and offer sanctions for problem behaviour'.[125] The most recent evaluation of the programme commented that:

Learning from the MTFC-A programme has influenced local authorities to consider the needs of children in residential establishments for assessments and clear behaviour management strategies and of the need for greater provision of support for mainstream fostering.[126]

The positive results already achieved by this programme in increased stability and the reduction of risk behaviours for over half of those young people who have left the programme so far,[127] indicate the importance of ensuring that young people's holistic support needs, and in particular their emotional and behavioural needs, are properly assessed at entry to care, that they receive tailored professional support to help them address any emotional or behavioural difficulties they may have, and that the foster carers who care for young people with particularly challenging needs have access to the support they need to perform this role effectively.

Placement stability and quality

However, although it is important to support stable placements where possible, it is important to note that stability will not always be a good thing in its own right. As Ward et al have observed, a young person's challenging behaviour can be an indication of poor wellbeing, suggesting that their current placement may not be meeting their needs.[128] One of the care leavers we spoke to recalled his change of placement as being a positive experience: 'my first placement was one I didn't really enjoy... but when I moved into my second placement it worked really well'. In a recent consultation conducted by the Children's Rights Director with over a thousand looked-after children, just over two-thirds (68 per cent) of the children surveyed said that their last placement move had been in their best interests. For the majority of these children, the benefits of moving to a more suitable placement were felt to outweigh the negative impact of instability and change.

The government's national indicators 62 and 63, which measure the number and length of looked-after children's placements, rightly emphasise the importance that children's placements are not changed frequently and without good reason, as a result of poor planning or lack of resources. However, as Sinclair et al have argued, it is important that these performance indicators do not lead to placement stability being prioritised over children's wellbeing.[129] Draft guidance recently issued by NICE commented:

Length of placement on its own is a poor quality indicator as a child or young person may be placed in an unhappy and uncaring environment that does little to reinforce their healthy emotional development and resilience.[130]

To address this problem, the programme development group responsible for this draft guidance suggest that 'government and regulators should take a wider view of placement stability and develop indicators that reflect a more holistic understanding of stability'.[131]

Sinclair et al's study found that the quality of a child's placement was only associated with the likelihood of placement disruption if the child was over 11. With children who were under the age of 11, placements that were not high quality often lasted as long as those that were. This suggests that younger children may be less able to articulate their feelings and influence placement decisions, and may be more likely to remain in placements where they are unhappy than older children.[132]

Listening to looked-after children

If we are to prioritise looked-after children's and young people's emotional wellbeing, it is essential that they are able to influence decisions that affect them. All of the young people we spoke to mentioned the importance of feeling that their views and feelings were being listened to and acted on:

They should have looked more into things you want and ask for rather than just saying no.

[Social workers] should be able to listen to you. If I was to talk to my mum, she would listen to me.

Many of the young people also described how powerless they had felt when key decisions about changing placement or leaving care were being made:

I just sort of sat there and saw them boss my life around.

I asked why [my placement had to change], what [had] happened, but the answer was not clear.

Social services have their discussions and because you are a child in care, they will tell you nothing.

Judy Cashmore has identified four key reasons why it is essential to involve looked-after children and young people in making decisions that affect them:

- Although children who live at home tend to have decisions made for them by one or two familiar adults, care decisions are often made on behalf of looked-after children by a range of adults, some of whom may be unknown to the child.
- It is important to children's self-esteem and confidence to have their opinions respected, particularly if they have previously suffered abuse or neglect, as it can help them to feel like 'active agents' as opposed to being 'the powerless victims of the whims of adults'.[133]
- There is an association between children having a choice about their placement and placement stability, as decisions that have taken the child's point of view into account are likely to be 'more appropriate and more acceptable to the child'.[134]
- Being helped to participate in decisions can build children's resilience and sense of agency, preparing them to take control of their lives when they reach independence.

This final point encapsulates a critical and often unsuccessfully executed role of the care system: preparing looked-after children for independence. The fact remains that children in care are in a temporary and somewhat conditional relationship with the state as corporate parent, and that at some point – whether that be at 16, 17 or 18 – they will eventually face a situation where that temporary relationship ends. This poses a significant risk to secure attachments and other protective factors that may have contributed to a child's resilience while in care. Moreover, care leavers face significant change – moving home, starting a new college or job – just as this support is withdrawn. It is a key moment of transition, which needs to be handled carefully and will be discussed in detail in the following chapter.

6 Supported transitions from care

There are a number of factors which can significantly improve a young person's experience of leaving care and give that young person a greater chance of better adult outcomes.

The age at which a young person leaves care

As one might expect, looked-after children who leave care early, say at 16, tend to do less well than those who leave care later. Those who leave earlier have a higher instance of substance abuse, homelessness, unemployment and poor educational outcomes.[135] Dixon et al[136] also found that young people who were doing well with their careers tended to have left care at an older age.

Poorer outcomes could be a result of these young people leaving care early (and therefore unprepared for independence), or could be a result of their poor experiences in care. Evidence suggests that those young people who leave care earlier tend also to have had the least stable and most negative experiences in care,[137] and, as we will see in the following section, this is associated with poorer educational outcomes and mental health. This in turn could be driving poorer later life outcomes for care leavers who leave care early. Nonetheless, it is likely to be a combination of these two factors – the emotional problems and poor education generated by a poor care career, *combined* with becoming independent at a very early age, which generates poor outcomes. Indeed, it could be argued that those who leave care the earliest are probably those least able to cope with the responsibility this new found independence brings.

Of course, it is unlikely any young person (let alone one leaving care potentially with existing emotional problems and very little in the way of a family support network) would be emotionally and practically prepared for living independently at 16.

Stein et al point to findings from the research programme of the Joseph Rowntree Foundation called Young People in Transition, which illustrated that the major decline in the youth labour market, increase in house prices, and extension of further and higher education means that young people are more dependent on their families for emotional, financial and practical support, often into their early 20s.[138] They argue that it is ironic that the very people who are the most likely to lack the range and depth of help given by families (children in care) are expected to cope on their own at a far younger age than young people living with their families.

Based on outcomes research and qualitative studies with care leavers, a large number of academic experts and charities working in this field are extremely critical of the practice of allowing children to leave care at 16. Indeed, they have called for children in care to be expected to stay until they are 18 and to be given the option to leave at 21.

The speed of transition

In addition to leaving care later, young people also need a more gradual, transitional care-leaving process. As one care leaver told us:

It comes on quite fast though, doesn't it? They say, ok you've got to this point, and they move you out.

Stein explains that psychological research suggests that most young people cope with the major changes in their lives consecutively during their journey to adulthood – dealing with one issue, then moving onto another, over a period of time.[139] But young people who have to cope with the greatest number of life changes in a shorter time have far poorer outcomes, including fewer educational qualifications and lower self-esteem.[140] The ESRC found that young people are less effective at managing change (such as changing home, moving from school to college, getting a job) if they have to cope with these events simultaneously.[141]

Anthropological research also suggests that young people tend to deal with change by using a transition phase – known as the 'liminal state' or opportunity to 'space out'. This liminal state provides a time for freedom, exploration, reflection, risk taking and identity search,[142] which is critical to the promotion of resilience in adulthood. This time exposes young people to challenging situations that provide opportunities to develop problem-solving abilities and emotional coping skills. For a majority of young people today, this is gained through the experience of further and higher education, but could also be achieved through graduated responsibilities being taken on in line with graduated independence.

Stein et al conclude that in promoting resilience, there needs to be more recognition of the nature and timing of young people's transitions from care, including the psychological space needed to cope with changes over time, and the significance of the middle-stage 'liminal stage' of transition.

Charities such as Barnardo's and Rainer[143] carrying out research into the experiences and outcomes of children leaving care have suggested that care leavers – in line with the experience of children leaving their birth families – should be able to return to a supported environment after they have left care if they feel they cannot cope.[144] Rainer's support for this proposal stems from a survey it carried out with care leavers in 2006 as part of their project What Makes The Difference?, which found that 88 per cent of leavers felt they should have had the option to return to supported accommodation if a move to independent living was not successful.[145]

Preparation before and support after leaving care:

Several studies interviewing and assessing groups of care leavers at leaving and then at follow up a few months to years later associate positive after-care outcomes with:

- receiving adequate planning and preparation before leaving care, so they had developed strong life and social skills
- being engaged in education, employment or training
- having a positive sense of their own wellbeing
- having a network of informal support, including family and friends
- having access to 'good' housing on leaving care; those who failed to secure good housing arrangements early on tended to fair worse over the follow-up period
- having good-quality support in accommodation after leaving care[146]

Emotional preparation and support

Leaving care is not simply a practical challenge for young people – it is also an emotional and psychological one. One care leaver told us:

I've never felt so lonely in my life. I've always felt kind of lonely growing up in care but that night, I just wished I was back home in my bed.

Research suggests that in addition to practical life skills training (such as cooking, cleaning, and budgeting), children in care also need preparation to help them cope emotionally with the independence and potential isolating experience of living alone. In particular, Stein et al's work showed that encouraging self-esteem, opportunities to contribute and facilitating social networks and relationships are all important elements in helping care leavers cope with change and stressful situations.[147] Education and extracurricular activities, such as hobbies and leisure pursuits, are also important vehicles for this, and so also need to be encouraged for children in preparation for leaving care.

Centrepoint's study found that a major reported problem was loneliness, with many care leavers finding it hard to adapt to coming home from college or work and having no one there. It found that loneliness could turn into depression, which had a negative effect on education and work.[148] Based on interviews,

Centrepoint generated a list of areas leavers would have wanted to be prepared for. These included:

· self-awareness, self-esteem and identity
· exploring and managing feelings
· developing personal values
· understanding others
· communication skills and interpersonal skills
· negotiation skills
· problem solving skills
· skills in taking action
· skills in planning and reviewing action[149]

Given the prevalence of mental health problems among children in care, it would seem obvious that in addition to emotional preparation before leaving, targeted emotional and mental health support for young people after leaving would also be a priority. A rapid break with carers, change of home and living alone may well trigger or exacerbate underlying mental health problems.

Dixon et al's study seems to support this reasoning.[150] At baseline interview, 38 per cent of care leavers in the study reported having a physical or mental health problem or a disability which affected their daily life, while 61 per cent reported problems at follow-up nine months later. Most notably, more young people reported mental health problems (24 per cent at follow-up compared with 12 per cent at baseline). This was largely reported in terms of stress and depression, although at least four young people had made suicide attempts over the previous nine months.

Dixon et al suggest that the type of problems reported (stress, depression, weight loss, flu, asthma) could be linked to the process of transition from care to independent living and changes in lifestyle, including periods of homelessness, insecure housing or unemployment and low income.

Accommodation

Housing in particular has been identified as a critical element for a successful transition from care. Where a care leaver first lives clearly has a huge impact on their subsequent outcomes (for example, their ability to attend college, hold down a job, and so on), and research by the University of York found that good housing was the factor most closely associated with good mental health among care leavers.[151]

This may be because accommodation is a vehicle for stability, which (being at the same college or job, with the same group of friends) can often be best assured if a care leaver stays in one place. Therefore any post-care accommodation which can ensure care leavers *remain there*, and thus have a stable post-care placement, is vital. For some care leavers, however, maintaining stable accommodation can be difficult without support, as they do not have either the practical or emotional skills to cope in a private tenancy, for example.

In such cases, supported accommodation (which provides stable semi-independent accommodation plus additional preparation for full independence) could provide an important 'middle way' between care and independence, particularly for those least well prepared for independent living due to their age, care experiences, life skills or emotional or mental health.

A rounded approach to preparation and support

In reviewing the variety of measured outcomes among care leavers, Dixon et al found significant 'clustering' –the association of one negative outcome with one or more others.[152] For example, over a fifth of young people were experiencing two or more difficulties at either baseline or follow-up and there was a significant correlation between substance misuse and emotional and behavioural difficulties and offending. Those with such difficulties often faced further problems across life areas such as housing, career, occupation and general wellbeing.

This clearly supports Stein et al's grouping approach to children in care, where sets of negative and positive before and during care experiences can be associated with different groups of care leavers. Dixon et al show that this same grouping tendency occurs post care.[153]

These academic findings suggest a holistic approach to preparing children in care for their transition (looking at practical, emotional and social skills in the round) is likely to be effective. Similarly, supporting care leavers once they have left care also needs to be carried out holistically. This means dealing with not just 'symptoms' (eg poor educational outcomes) but also the causal reinforcing factors, which may be poor accommodation (as research suggests this is a key variable in a range of other outcomes) or mental health. Dixon et al found that even care leavers enrolled in low level courses or routine forms of work that might not seem particularly rewarding had a more positive outlook. This may be to do with the fact that all forms of education and work provide important additional benefits – stability and routine, the opportunity to make new friends, manage relationships and responsibility, and provide an avenue for achievements. All of these help build self-esteem, self-efficacy and a sense of control.

Dixon et al conclude:

Equipping young people with the practical, interpersonal and emotional resources needed for adult life should be a central feature of corporate parenting. Given its importance, it is surprising that very few studies have focused on what makes for effective preparation. To date, best evidence suggests that preparation should begin early, occur naturally but in a planned and thoughtful manner and take place in the context of a stable placement allowing for the gradual development of rounded skills and competencies.[154]

Cameron et al's 2007 study surveying care leavers and young people 'in difficulty' found holistic services, multi-agency leaving care teams and third sector 'one-stop shops' were identified by care leavers and in difficulty groups as the most helpful they dealt with. This was because they could access a range of support – practical, health, emotional, etc – from one agency or set of people.[155]

Stability and attachments

As outlined above, there is a large and well-established body of evidence which demonstrates that stability and the maintenance of attachments with adults are vital factors in a positive care experience. Leaving care can represent an abrupt ending of a stable placement and break in attachments. However, the very nature of being 'looked after' (where a child in care is temporarily looked after by the state) means this outcome will be somewhat inevitable.

The key, therefore, is to reduce the negative impact of leaving care as far as possible. This requires a smoother and more transitioned exit, and a rounded package of support. However, Jim Wade's 2006 study also suggested that it was vital to maintain attachments where they can be maintained, and encourage new post-care attachments to replace those that may have been lost.[156]

Several of the care leavers we interviewed spoke positively regarding the relationships they had with their birth families – one had moved back in with his family for a while after leaving care and another had found the support from her older siblings vital when she became pregnant. Wade's study also reflects these findings, concluding that relationships with birth families that had been difficult in the past often remained problematic for care leavers, but contact with birth families was highly valued. The sense that young people had someone to whom they could turn, even if they would not contemplate living with them, was very important.

Citing Marsh and Peel's work, which found that the majority of family members of care leavers were prepared to assume some responsibility for providing support, Wade commented:

Given the value of positive family support (and the time-limited nature of professional help), there is a need for continuing counseling and mediation [with birth families].[157]

The importance of attachments with key care staff, and the impact of inconsistent relationships, was demonstrated in Cameron et al's 2007 study for the DCSF.[158] The team found that the popularity of care leaving teams tended to hinge on there being a good relationship with an individual leaving care worker. The absence of a dedicated worker, or the abrupt ending of that relationship (eg if the member of staff left) was seen very negatively – something which was a consistent theme in our own interviews, and an issue we explore in more detail in section 3. As such circumstances are often unavoidable, encouraging family attachments where appropriate seems to be a vital component of more long-term leaving care support.

Wade also found that while 'staying on' with foster families post-18 provided some valuable breathing space and an opportunity to make a planned transition, it rarely provided young people with a stable home base into adulthood, as the majority of care leavers still leave their foster homes in the year of their 18th birthday. Nevertheless, stability and continuity for young people could also be provided through continuing contact with carers, even once young people have moved out. Even infrequent contact (occasional phone calls, birthdays and Christmas) could act as an important touchstone with their 'previous life' for care leavers and generate a sense of security.

Section 3
Areas in need of reform

The previous section of this report considered 'what works' for children in care. While every child going into care has different needs, and requires very different things from care (everything from lifelong nurturing from early childhood through to brief stays during adolescence), certain requirements remain the same for all children – stability, continuity, a sense of being cared for and about, and an opportunity to form attachments with adults. In this section, we will consider the areas where the care system is not being used effectively to achieve these outcomes, across three phases of care – entry to care, the care placement itself, and then transition from care. It ought to be borne in mind at the outset that given the diversity of the care population, there is no 'typical' care journey – not *all* children will have experience of *all* of the issues outlined below. However, in bringing together the statistical data and evidence from our own primary research, we show that some poor care experiences are all too common and need to be addressed.

Box 3 | **What do the numbers say? Children's experiences according to national indicators**[159]

> **NI 58: Emotional and behavioural health of looked-after children**
> *The average score on the Strengths and Difficulties Questionnaire (SDQ) for children aged 4 to 16 who had been looked after continuously for at least 12 months at 31 March was 13.9. For SDQs completed by primary carers (which this indicator uses), a score of 0–13 is normal; 13.9 is in the 'borderline' category.*[160] *As 2009 was the first year of data collection for this indicator progress cannot yet be measured.*

NI 61: Timeliness of looked-after children's placements for adoption following an agency decision that the child should be placed for adoption

In 2009 more than three-quarters (75.8 per cent) of children who were adopted during the year were placed for adoption within 12 months. This was about 4 percentage points less than in 2005.

NI 62: Stability of placements of looked-after children: number of placements

More than one-tenth (10.7 per cent) of children had three or more placements during 2009. This figure has decreased steadily from 13.7 per cent since 2005.

NI 63: Stability of placements of looked-after children: length of placement

More than two-thirds (67.0 per cent) of children who had been looked after for two and a half years or more had in the past two years to 31 March 2009 lived in the same placement or their combined adoptive placement and preceding placement. This percentage has increased gradually since 2005, when the percentage was 62.9 per cent.

NI 66: Looked-after children's cases which were reviewed within required timescales

Most (90.9 per cent of) children had their cases reviewed within the required timescales during 2009. This percentage has increased from 78.9 per cent in 2006 but there has been little change compared to last year (90.0 per cent).

NI 147 (PSA 16): Care leavers in suitable accommodation

Most (89.6 per cent of) former care leavers, with whom the local authorities were in touch during 2009, were considered to be in suitable accommodation around the time of their 19th birthday. This compares with 83.9 per cent during 2005 and 88.4 per cent last year.

NI 148 (PSA 16): Care leavers in education, employment or training
In the past four years the percentage of former care leavers, with whom the local authorities were in touch and who were in education, employment or training around the time of their 19th birthday, had increased from 58.4 per cent in 2005 to 64.9 per cent in 2008. However, in 2009 the percentage dropped to 63.0 per cent.

7 Delay in entering care

Pre-care experiences

The nature of a child's care journey is partly shaped before he or she enters care. While the previous section shows that care can and frequently does have a positive impact on children's mental health, academic attainment and other outcomes, the pre-care experiences of children are so critically important to their emotional, mental and physical wellbeing that what occurs *before* a care decision is made is perhaps the single largest determinant of what subsequently happens to a child once in care.

Of course, there are many cases where children come into care for reasons that are beyond the control of local children and family services – for example as a result of a parent dying, or in the case of unaccompanied asylum seekers. But if we consider children who come into care for reasons of family neglect or abuse, it is clear that the type of support provided to the family to address those problems *before* care is needed and the timeliness of the decision to take that child into care if necessary are both vitally important to that child's long-term wellbeing. We will consider each in turn.

Following on from the white paper *Care Matters* in 2007, central government has continued to promote pre-care family support services. The national roll out of 'Think Family' is designed to identify families at risk from the earliest opportunity, and from 2009/10 the DCSF provided £80 million for funding family intervention projects and the Think Family reforms.[161] There are now ten multi-systemic therapy site pilots, aimed at families with young people aged 11–17 who are at risk of entering care or custody. The DSCF aimed for family intervention projects to be working with 10,000 families a year by 2011/12, though of course this commitment may change in light of a new government.[162]

Unfortunately, and in spite of this investment, evidence suggests that provision of early family support remains patchy and dependent on the culture of individual local authorities. In 2008 the director of Children's Rights reported on the views of parents and found that 59 per cent said there had been no support to help stop their children going into care.[163] The Future of the Care Population working group noted that in 2005/6 local authorities spent a total of £2.05 billion on looked-after children compared with £687 million spent on family support services – a ratio of 3:1.[164] Meanwhile, the Commission for Social Care Inspection highlighted similar concerns in a recent analysis, which reported that 'high eligibility in response to resource pressures are limiting the range of services to assist families of children in need'.[165]

Given that the level of pre-care family intervention is discretionary at a local level, we might expect to see variations in the number of children who subsequently come into care – the Future Care Population Working Group found this to be the case, discovering that in 2008 there were 20 in 10,000 children in Wokingham in care compared with 151 in 10,000 in Manchester.[166] Such a postcode lottery would suggest that there are very different interpretations of the 'right' amount of support a family should be afforded before their child should be placed in care, and, indeed, the 'right' moment at which a child should be taken in care. This is problematic as it suggests that local authorities are not basing such decisions on what would achieve the best outcomes for children, but on how open (or indeed closed) they are to the concept of care – an issue we deal with below. Yet striking the right balance between providing family support and making a care decision is a vital one – providing too little family support would lead to many children going into care when this might have been easily avoided. But *providing it too late* could simply delay the inevitable. We address this issue in more detail below.

The point of entering care – delays in the process

Several of the experts we consulted as part of this project expressed concern about the delays that could occur in taking a child into care and securing a stable placement. Taking a child into care is a complex administrative and legal process, and delay can occur at a number of stages: within social work teams, who must gather evidence to present to the court, securing a court time, and then during the hearing with the appointment of guardians and witnesses, reviewing evidence, hearing appeals from parents, and so on and so forth.

For those children coming from situations of abuse or neglect, such delays may result in them staying with their birth families and being exposed to physical risk or developing mental health or emotional and behavioural problems. However, as outlined in section 2, even for those who come into care for other reasons, there is evidence to suggest that delay at an early stage can undermine their chances of being adopted or securing a stable placement. Experiencing a period of uncertainty and temporary placements during the court proceedings is likely to damage the chances of children coming into care at an older age forming attachments and maintaining a stable placement later on.[167]

It is slightly concerning, therefore, that of all the national indicators outlined earlier, the delay in adoption indicator is the only one which is getting worse, with fewer children adopted within a year now than in 2005. As we explain in the following chapter, a recent freedom of information request suggests that adoptions may be breaking down more frequently than in the past. There may be many reasons for this, but we cannot underestimate the role that the delay in placing children on the adoption register may have: children may be older by the time they are adopted, making it harder for attachments to form and increasing the chances that behavioural and emotional problems have already been created. This in turn may make the adoption more difficult to sustain.

In 2005 Selwyn et al reviewed the cases of 130 children for whom adoption had been recommended 10 to 15 years earlier. The team found that 68 per cent of the children had been known to social services for more than one year, and some had been known by the authorities for up to eight years, before they were removed from their birth families. They determined that for 53 per cent of these children, the delay in been taken into care or adopted had been the result of lack of social work assessment, planning and action: for 22 per cent care criteria had not being met, and for 12 per cent there were lengthy court proceedings.[168]

The Department of Constitutional Affairs' (DCA's) review of child care proceedings in 2006 found that the average length of time of a court proceeding was 51 weeks.[169] At the time of the initial implementation of the Children Act 1989 in 1991, it was estimated that child care proceedings cases would take an average of 12 weeks in the courts.[170] As a result, many children are left in a transitional phase for nearly an entire year. Since this review, within-court delays have grown worse – in particular since the Baby Peter case of 2008, which has led to an increase in workload. Latest quarterly figures from Cafcass, the Children and Family Court Advisory and Support Service, showed that the courts received 2,185 section 31 care applications from October to December 2009, up 21 per cent on the same quarter in 2008.[171]

This increased workload has, in particular, led to a shortage of guardians,[172] which in turn delays court hearings. A survey by Nagalro, the guardians' professional body, found 40 per cent of 300 cases allocated to children's guardians since January 2009 had to wait more than two months for assignment.[173] However, the DCA's review found that some significant drivers for delay were not related to the courts, but rather social work teams, who gathered incomplete evidence and were unable to identify expert witnesses.[174]

The role of our philosophical approach to care

This problem may well be partly explained by our view of care, based on the British cultural attitude to children and the family. In other countries children are seen as 'social goods' – part of society and its responsibility. In contrast, Britain sees children as 'private goods' – the responsibility of the family and the individual unit.[175] Coupled with the resource implications, this means placing children in care is normally only considered when all other options have been exhausted. A recent study published by DCSF suggested that this may lead to a philosophy of 'last resortism' within children's services and the courts, which could leave children 'unprotected or delay their inevitable entry into care'.[176]

The DCA's findings link this philosophy of last resort to administrative delay, in that they found one reason why care proceedings were progressing slowly was because social work teams were attempting to prove beyond all reasonable doubt that a child had to be removed from their birth family. They concluded that: 'the pursuit of an unattainable level of certainty is a major factor in court delay and therefore a cause of avoidable harm to children'.[177]

This may well be a result of a system which views the act of taking a child into care as a radical, draconian step that must only be used when absolutely necessary. It is understandable in such an environment that social work teams may err on the side of caution and delay, perhaps indefinitely, the decision to take a child into care. For some, this may mean providing family support (mentioned above), to keep children 'bumping along the bottom' in situations of neglect[178] – that is, just beneath the threshold of requiring a care order. Children in such situations are likely to have very poor outcomes.

Martin Narey, chief executive of Barnardo's, has been an outspoken critic of this reticence to take children into care. In an article written in the *Guardian* in 2009, he stated we had 'gone too far' in reducing the numbers of children in care:

There has long been an absolute conviction among social workers, statutory and voluntary, and politicians local and national, that taking a child into care is to be avoided almost at all cost. The unchallenged philosophy is that we should do everything possible to deflect children from the dreadful consequences of being looked after.[179]

He also gave evidence to the Children and Families Select Committee in 2009, and stated that during his investigations as head of a working group for the Care Matter white paper, he:

was struck by the number of professionals who told me that if the system moved more quickly and if we intervened earlier, some children would be taken into care at a much earlier age and might be adopted and have their long-term future guaranteed, but that the system was cautious and slow, so often by the time the in care decision was made the adoption route, for example, was pretty much closed.[180]

Although his comments have been divisive, some senior figures have been broadly supportive. Wes Cuell, director of children's services at the NSPCC, responded to Narey's comments by stating:

We should not be keeping children out of care just because we don't like what care represents. If children need to be in care, they should be, and we should find the right sort of care for them which is not based on traditional beliefs about care based in families.[181]

Forrester et al's 2007 review for the Welsh Assembly was equally critical:

Increasingly, public care has been treated as a choice of last resort. This leads to children being kept in their homes when they should not be. This error looks likely to be compounded by the Care Matters recommendations. The fact that a reduction in children entering care was seriously considered as a government performance indicator is bad enough, but Care Matters continues to take this crude and unhelpful approach to preventing care. For instance, it is argued that only senior managers should be able to authorise care entry and that greater attempts should be made to 'gatekeep' this threshold. It is difficult to see a child welfare justification for this recommendation, and it seems possible that it will lead to managers refusing entry for children who should enter care. This is a crude exposition of the 'care is bad' philosophy of Care Matters.[182]

Research by Judith Masson et al from the University of Bristol seems to confirm this theory. On reviewing nearly 400 care application cases in 2004, the team found that nearly half of the cases had been known to children's services for five years or more, and in many instances, court proceedings were only triggered following a sudden event or emergency.[183]

Another study that interviewed social workers and legal staff involved in child neglect cases also found that a decisive event, what it labelled a 'catapult', was often needed to trigger court proceedings.[184] It was extremely rare for social workers and their managers to decide 'enough was enough' on the basis of an accumulation of long standing concerns about child neglect. This finding is supported by a study of emergency protection cases which found that social workers had sought to bring proceedings earlier but managers and local authority legal departments had refused to endorse it until there was a crisis.[185] This phenomenon, often called 'drift' has been recognised as a problem since the 1970s and 1980s, where social work becomes 'immune' to cases of neglect.[186]

We should bear in mind, however, that this is not always an issue originating in the social work field. Social workers are not actively preventing children from coming into care, but the reality of social work practice, combined with the views of the public and policy makers and the role of the media, often creates a recipe for delay and indecision. Social work, by its nature, deals in uncertainty, the weighing up of risk and different outcomes, and the use of professional judgement. Difficult decisions must be made in complex cases and there is often no obvious 'right' answer. But this is inherently incompatible with a political environment and public that demands certainty and, moreover, a care system which gets it 'right' 100 per cent of the time. Under such circumstances, often the safest option may be to 'fire fight' – deal with the more urgent and life threatening cases, or 'catapults' which may have clearer solutions, while remaining cautious and seeking interim measures for others.

Overall, we can see that a combination of administrative, resource and philosophical factors all play a part in some children being taken into care too late, when significant problems have developed, and when chances of a stable placement have all but disappeared. We know that as children grow older their chances of not just being placed for adoption, but also achieving a stable placement, decrease.

As such, even for children for whom adoption is not a realistic or desirable option, and for those children who may only be coming into care for a short period, delay in being taken into care and placed with a suitable family (or indeed in a suitable residential placement) can still set them on a path of unstable care, which may, in turn, undermine their emotional wellbeing.

8 Instability in the care journey

Multiple placements

Much of the evidence outlined in the previous section points to the fact that good quality, stable, long-term care placement generate the best outcomes for children and create opportunities to develop attachments with adults. Even those children who might be entering care for a brief period do best if their time is spent in a stable environment with consistency of carers.

However, DCSF data shows that in 2009 10.7 per cent of children had three or more placements moves in a year, while 67 per cent were in a long-term placement (defined at more than 2.5 years). Care Matters also reported on local variation on placement instability, with 15–19 per cent of the children in nine local authorities experiencing three or more placements in a year.[187] Furthermore, there are still significant numbers of children with very large numbers of placements. Figures obtained by Earl Listowel in September 2008 showed that children experienced more than ten placement moves in almost three-quarters of English local authorities.[188] The 2007 project What Makes the Difference similarly found that 40 per cent of the 265 looked-after children interviewed had moved more than five times during their time in care and that 6 per cent had been moved more than 21 times.[189]

These statistics were brought to life by our own primary research, particularly in our interviews with children in care and care leavers, many of whom reported having experienced up to ten placement moves, short term, emergency placements and sudden unexpected moves. One young person we spoke to said 'they moved me by force and they didn't even say, come on pack your clothes. They just move you by force.' Asked to explain what had led to him being moved, he replied, 'Nothing, they just said you've got to go.'

Another issue that arose during our interviews was the frequency with which social workers changed. Many of the children we spoke to assured us that this was just as disruptive as a placement move, as it required a new relationship to be formed, repetition of case details and circumstances, and a general loss of continuity in support. One young person we spoke to explained how she had had a new social worker, who started and left before he had even met her for a review. Another explained how he had been called by his new social worker without having been told his previous one had left:

I had like a thousand and one social workers, they would start today and resign tomorrow.

Social workers change quite a lot. As you're getting used to one, they leave and you have to get used to another one.

In one local authority where we carried out interviews, only one of the nine young people we spoke to had kept a social worker for more than a year. The prevalence of this issue is confirmed in a study by Ward, where 17 per cent of the children and young people in the sample experienced four or more changes of social worker during the three to four years they were studied.[190]

Ward contrasts the normal experience of children, who on average move home three times before adulthood, and children in care, who can commonly experience this level of disruption in one year. Her study examining data of 242 children over a period of at least 3.5 years in six local authorities found that the median length of placements in foster care was 4 months and in residential care it was 3.5 months.[191] Although the numbers of placements varied according to children's ages and attributes, Ward noted that even very young children with no additional support needs experienced frequent moves – 17 per cent of those children between 0 and 4 years old had had more than five placements during the study period. Overall, only 19 per cent of the children in the study remained in the same placement during the study period, 41 per cent had had one or two placements, 22 per cent had had more than five, while 4 per cent had 10 or more. One had had 29 placements.

Furthermore, it seemed that the majority of placement moves are not made at the request of the children involved, and arguably are not carried out for the child's own wellbeing. Ward found that 43 per cent of placement moves were initiated and planned by the local authority, and often resource or practice-led, 'occasioned by a shortage of suitable placements, a lack of choice or appropriate planning'.

Planned moves were the single most common reason not only for ending first placements, but also for ending second, third, fourth, fifth and sixth placements. Such planned moves were undertaken for a range of reasons, including to reunite siblings, to match children to carers of the same ethnicity, moves to and from temporary placements when foster carers went on holiday and moves from a short term to a longer-term foster placement once it became clear a child could not return home quickly. Only 21 per cent of placement disruptions were at the request of the carer and only 11 per cent were precipitated by children who refused to stay in placements where they were unhappy.

Attempts at family reunification

Another important driver of unstable care journeys, which can also be viewed as a 'planned' disruption, is repeated attempts at reunification with birth families. During our focus groups with foster carers, we were told many children returned to the system after reunification. One carer described one child she had fostered the previous year:

Before he came to me, he was in the system with another foster carer, and he was only 4. After he'd been in my house for a year, then he went back to his mother. A year later, I found out he was back in the system. Each time he comes into the system he's with a new foster carer, which must be really upsetting. That's why he's collecting all this baggage.

Indeed, evidence suggests a large proportion of children in care experience at least one failed return to their family, while

Farmer et al found that 16 per cent of the children they studied had experienced *two* failed family reunifications.[192] Nina Biehal estimates that between one-third and one-half of children who return home may subsequently re-enter care or accommodation. Sinclair et al's 2004 study found 48 per cent stayed with their families for less than 22 months.[193]

The reasons why these reunifications fail may well be due to a lack of assessment and support. A study commissioned by the DCSF found support after a return home often discontinued without any assessment of whether the families' problems had diminished. This led to a failed return, with children unable to stay with their families but at the same time their prospects of adoption had been delayed and permanently undermined.[194] More recently, a study carried out by the University of Bristol about care leavers' experiences of reunification identified similar problems:

· Family concerns that led to the original entry to care had often not been addressed when the decision was made to return the child to the family; there was no standard assessment to make this decision, no targets and no monitoring.
· There was little support to deal with parents' and children's difficulties before and during the return, such as treatment for alcohol and drug misuse, assistance in cases of domestic violence and parental mental ill health, mentoring and practical help.
· Access to treatment for parental substance-misuse was poor, and practitioners had little understanding of how to work with substance misusing parents.
· Standards of child care and developmental progress during the return needed to be agreed and regularly reviewed.[195]

It is unsurprising, therefore, that many reunification attempts fail after a short period of time, and many children who return to their families are re-abused or neglected before returning to care – the Bristol study found this was the case for 46 per cent of the children in their sample. In 2010 Farmer and Lutman reported on a five-year study of children who had returned to their parents,[196] and found that 65 per cent of the returns home of 138 children in the study had ended. In addition, at the two-year follow-up, 59 per cent of the children had been abused or neglected after reunification and during the next three years, half of the children (48 per cent) whose cases were open were abused or neglected. After the children were returned to their parents, children's social care services received referrals expressing concern about the safety and welfare of almost three-quarters (73 per cent) of them. After such referrals, Farmer and Lutman found, on reviewing the case files, that insufficient action was taken to make children safe in three-fifths of the families. The study concluded:

In half (51 per cent) of the cases a clear focus on important issues in the case had not been maintained at times by children's social care services and in a considerable number of families key problems had not been addressed, in particular parental alcohol and drugs misuse, domestic violence, mental health problems and lack of parenting skills. Decisive action in cases of neglect often awaited a trigger incident of physical or sexual abuse or severe domestic violence.[197]

This particular finding is very similar to those studies looking at children being taken into care for the first time (above), which also found that social workers would react to a crisis event or 'catapult' rather than the steady escalation of ongoing problems.

Under-assessed and unsupported reunifications not only expose some children to further abuse and instability. We should also bear in mind that a child who returns to care following a failed reunification will rarely if ever be able to return to their former foster family, creating yet more new and unfamiliar situations for a child returning to care.

This is likely to have an impact on their chances of securing a stable placement in the longer term. Selwyn et al found, for example, that 29 per cent of the group of children they studied who had been 'successfully adopted' had had previous reunification attempts, compared with 44 per cent of the group who subsequently went on to experience unstable care journeys.[198]

One underlying factor which could be driving repeated attempts at family reunification is the philosophy, outlined above, that care is a last resort and keeping a child in their family should always be a priority. Judith Masson, Professor of Socio-Legal Studies at the University of Bristol, told the Children and Families Select Committee:

There is a kind of rule of optimism. Many people in the system have low expectations and take the view that taking children into care is so draconian an intervention that merely neglecting children is insufficient to justify... taking children away.[199]

This law of optimism may, therefore, be a cause not only of delay in taking a child into care, but also in indecisiveness once a child goes into care, regarding their long-term placement with a family other than their own. Ward's analysis of care plans does seem to suggest that social workers were optimistic about the chances of reunification: of those children who had stayed in care for a year or more, 22 per cent had been expected to remain with their birth families or return within six months, and a further 33 per cent had been admitted for assessment only. Ward reasoned that as a result of the expectation of family reunification, many of these children would have been placed with short-term carers and then would have had to have moved when it became evident that family reunification was not viable and they required longer placements – creating multiple moves early on.[200]

We can see, therefore, that the majority of children in care have multiple placements, and for nearly half, at least two separate periods in care punctuated by a failed attempt at being reunited with their birth families. With each move, a child endures a period of instability and uncertainty, a potential loss of existing attachments, possibly a move of school and entry to a new unfamiliar environment with strangers. Of those who return home, the majority re-enter care, and a large proportion suffer further abuse in the intervening period. Of course, some moves are beneficial (for example if a child is deeply unhappy where they are). However, statistics suggest that moves precipitated in this way are by far the minority. What is most concerning, therefore, is that in most cases, such upheaval is actively planned by social services.

A lack of placement support

However, we cannot discount the fact that many placements end in an unplanned way, and this breakdown may well be due to a lack of support, in particular, mental health support. As we mention in chapter 7, the number of adoptions – once seen as the most stable, 'gold standard' of care placement – which are breaking down seem to be on the increase. Although local authorities do not collect official statistics on how many of their adoptive placements fail, a recent freedom of information request sent to all local authorities by More4 News found that the number of adoptions which have broken down, and children have been returned to care, had doubled between 2005 and 2009.[201] The increase in breakdowns comes despite a fall in the number of children being adopted. During the year ending 31 March 2008 3,200 children looked after were adopted. This represents a 5 per cent decrease from 2007 and a 16 per cent decrease from the 2003/4 figure of 3,800.[202] Adoption UK estimates that as many as one-third of adoptions break down, while the British Association for Adoption and Fostering (BAAF) estimates that one in five fail even before an adoption order is granted.[203]

One possible explanation is that the delays in placing children on the adoption register lead to a period of instability, temporary care, or possibly prolonged exposure to abuse or neglect within their birth families. This, in turn, may lead to greater risk of emotional and behavioural problems, thereby making the adoption more challenging. However, another related explanation is that post-adoption support for families is not sufficient given the potential needs of the children being adopted. A recent survey by Adoption UK and BAAF found that there were no established protocols in local authorities to keep in touch with adopted children and their families, as adoption is a private arrangement.

Perhaps more importantly, the survey found that CAMHS support for children in care and adopted children was patchy, with many local authorities having no teams in place dedicated to helping children in care or those who had been adopted. More than one-third (36 per cent) of the CAMHS clinics surveyed had no established referral process between them and the local authority to ensure the mental health needs of children in care were being met. The research we carried out with foster parents for this report suggests problems were widespread:

It can take a year for you to get an appointment with CAMHS.

You've got to push for it [mental health support]... It's not the social worker... It's you who has to do it if you want that child to get help.

CAMHS said they couldn't work with the younger boy because he wasn't cooperative.

The new care planning guidance and regulations[204] stipulate that looked-after children must receive a full health assessment, including an assessment of their emotional and mental health, either before the child is first placed with the local authority or within the first month of their entry to care. This is certainly a welcome development. However, the 2009 statutory guidance on promoting the health and wellbeing of looked-after children admitted that although the rate of assessments is improving, there is still significant work to be done to ensure that the plans which follow the assessments are implemented.[205] The 2009 guidance, like the BAAF survey, also found 'substantial local variation in the availability of mental health services'[206] for looked-after children and issued guidance that dedicated CAMHS services had to be made available in every area.

This lack of coherent mental health support is particularly concerning when we consider that several studies have established poor mental health as both a cause *and* result of children having unstable care journeys. Children with poorer mental health tend to have a larger number of placements and more unstable placements, and, conversely, those with larger numbers of placements also have poorer mental health.[207]

Given the extent of instability in the current care system, it is perhaps unsurprising that Meltzer et al found that among children in care aged 5–17 years, 45 per cent were assessed as having a mental disorder: 37 per cent had clinically significant conduct disorders; 12 per cent were assessed as having emotional disorders – anxiety and depression; and 7 per cent were rated as hyperactive.[208] However, we cannot discount pre-care experiences here – Sempik et al found that even larger numbers of children (72 per cent) had mental health problems (rather than disorders) when they *entered* care.[209] This may well be the result of prolonged exposure to neglectful or abusive home lives, precipitated by a delay in taking that child into care. It is clear that this can create a vicious circle, where those children with poor mental health on entering care may have less chance of having a stable placement (because of their challenging behaviour), and their subsequent instability exacerbates their mental health problems.

Children placed in residential care settings are particularly likely to have emotional and behavioural difficulties. In one study, 72 per cent of children in residential care were assessed as having a mental disorder.[210] Another study found that children who entered care with either a conduct problem or an emotional or behavioural problem had a higher likelihood of being placed in residential care.[211] Given the particularly high level of need among this group, it is particularly concerning that mental health support is not always accessible in this context either. Interviews with residential care staff conducted in the course of our research identified a number of barriers: some young people were not eligible for help from CAMHS if their placement was not stable and their circumstances were likely to change.[212] Others who are given an emergency psychiatric review experienced waiting lists of one to two years for long-term therapeutic work. Some young people who failed to attend several appointments had their therapy withdrawn and others were unwilling to engage with CAMHS as they found the 'mental health' label stigmatising or had had negative experiences with mental health services in the past.

A recent report by Ofsted evaluating the provision of mental health services for young people in residential care confirmed our own findings, concluding that mental health support in children's homes was inconsistent, with some young people 'severely disadvantaged' by the level of mental health provision that was available to them.[213]

There may also be a problem of a lack of mental health training among care staff, as this does not form part of the NVQ in caring for children and young people. Without a formal expectation of training in responding to mental health issues, residential staff are reliant on ad hoc arrangements (for example one day or short courses), and in a quarter of the children's homes visited by Ofsted, staff had received no additional training in mental health.[214]

A lack of choice

Challenging behaviour and complex support needs are not the only cause of placement disruption. Some placements may also break down primarily because they were poorly matched to begin with. There is a well-documented national shortage of foster carers; the latest survey statistics from the Fostering Network estimate there is a shortage of 10,000 foster carers in the UK, of which around 8,400 are needed in England. Furthermore, 82 per cent of local authorities saw a rise in the numbers of children needing foster homes in 2009/10, and 58 per cent of local authorities said they have found it even more difficult than usual to find suitable homes for children.[215] This shortage of foster carers will, inevitably, mean that some children do not have an adequate choice of placement and that social workers will need to place children where there is availability, rather than with the most appropriate family. This can drive instability in two ways: an unsuitable placement is at higher risk of breaking down, and a social worker may place a child in a short-term placement before making a planned placement move when a more suitable carer becomes available.

Another possibility that should be considered is that for some children, *all* foster placements will be unsuitable. This may particularly be the case for young people entering care in adolescence, who may be experiencing problems with their own family and want to avoid replicating a family environment. For such children, residential care settings may be more suitable. However, the way in which residential care is used at the moment – as an option of last resort, rather than being a first choice –

means that very few children will be considered for a residential placement unless they have already experienced a number of disrupted foster care placements. Such an experience is both costly and damaging to a child's emotional wellbeing, but could be inherently avoidable if residential care was considered as a viable placement option earlier on. We consider this issue in more detail below.

Instability in residential care

Residential care in England and Wales tends to be viewed as an 'end of the line' option for children and young people whose previous placements have failed. As a result, children in care homes tend to be older, with only 14 per cent of children now in homes under 13 and 40 per cent over 16.[216] This has been described by Deloitte as a 'ladder of care', with a sliding scale of increased intervention and increased costs from family intervention, to foster care, to in-house residential care, to outsourced residential care.[217] This means that young people placed in residential care are likely to have already experienced several failed placements, a significant degree of instability, and are more likely to demonstrate severe emotional and behavioural problems.[218]

This use of residential care is in marked contrast with most other European countries, where residential care is used as a mainstream service for children in care, and often a first choice option. Denmark and Germany have over 50 per cent of looked-after children in residential homes, Netherlands just under 50 per cent and France just over a third.[219] The outcomes for these children are far better than those in residential care in England and Wales, although there is disagreement as to whether this is simply because of the concentration of children with the most serious problems in English and Welsh homes, or whether the different management practices and approaches used in these countries achieve better outcomes (see section 2).

Nevertheless, the last-resort approach to residential care has been widely criticised for discounting residential care as a viable care option in and of itself.[220] As we explain in section 1, children in care are a hugely diverse group, with a variety of needs and preferences. To assume a 'one size fits all' style of placement (foster care) is suitable for all of these children is particularly short sighted, and may mean children for whom foster care is simply not a suitable option will have to endure multiple failed foster placements, and the turmoil this entails, before they are placed in a residential home.

The New Economics Foundation (NEF), in explaining that the cultural attitude to children and the family in England and Wales is that of 'private goods' – the responsibility of the family and the individual unit, makes it clear that the 'state run' care homes for children would appear 'soviet' in such a context.[221] Certainly this underlying philosophy that 'family is best' is one reason why there is such a strong bias towards foster care placements in England and Wales. However, another reason why social workers avoid using residential care must certainly be that outcomes for children in such homes are poor, even by looked-after children's standards. Many describe this as a vicious circle, or 'self-fulfilling prophesy', in that the most troubled children are sent to care homes, achieve the worst educational and longer term outcomes, which in turn makes local authorities reticent to send any child but the most troubled (and troublesome) to such homes.

In reality, it may be that for children for whom foster care is not suitable nor welcome, residential care placements are a valuable source of stability and opportunity to develop peer relationships. Certainly some of the care leavers we interviewed for this project said they had enjoyed their time in residential care, saying that the other children there had felt like family.

However, it is clear that current residential care system is not fulfilling its potential in this regard. Indeed, its use as a measure of last resort can undermine its potential as a source of stability in several ways. First, there is a lack of continuity in staffing. Several of the young people we interviewed who had had experience of residential care raised this as an issue:

In a residential place, it's a lot difficult because it is carers as staff so they have shifts on and shifts off so you don't get that kind of bond like people do in good foster homes.

When you are in foster care, it's actually the foster carers looking after you but in residential care, you've got so many different faces.

Harriet Ward et al have recently concluded that residential care placements can provide young people with less stability and fewer opportunities to develop close attachment relationships due to the high level of staff turnover, shift working patterns and shorter placements.[222] Deloitte suggests that recruitment and retention problems are driven by a lack of career progression, low pay and negative perceptions of the job. This in turn means care homes see high staff turnover, over-use of agency staff, and lack of consistency in the care being provided.[223] It may be, therefore, that the 'last resort' perception of this service is undermining homes' ability to provide consistency of staff, so critical if children there are to maintain stable attachments.

Second, with a decline in demand for residential care, there has been a decline in the number of care homes, as well as a consolidation in the market and a shift towards smaller care homes, which can emulate a 'family' feel and have higher staff-to-child ratios.[224] While these smaller, more personal homes might be a welcome trend, they are certainly less efficient. To reduce costs, therefore, care homes are increasingly filling their beds to capacity, rather than leaving a proportion of spare beds for emergency admissions or to give children a choice of different homes when entering the system. Unfortunately, this means children are more likely to be placed where there is space, rather than being given a choice of placements or identifying a placement that suits their needs. This is likely to increase the chances of a mismatch between the child's needs and the home selected, which increases the risk of placement breakdown or a series of planned temporary placements.

Erratum

Page 135 paragraph 1

Reads:
'89.6 per cent of 19-year-old care leavers were not in employment, education or training (NEET) in 2009'

Should read:
'26 per cent of 19-year-old care leavers were not in employment, education or training (NEET) in 2009'

9   An abrupt exit from care

The transition from care to independence is a critical period for young people, and needs to be handled carefully to prevent a traumatic break from the stability and attachments formed during care. However, the experience of many young people falls far short of the gradual, supported transition that is proven to be the most effective. It is unsurprising, then, that key adult outcomes for care leavers are so poor – for example, 89.6 per cent of 19-year-old care leavers were not in employment, education or training (NEET) in 2009[225] compared with 16.6 per cent of 18-year-olds[226] in the general population (DCSF did not collect NEET statistics for the general population at age 19). Just 7 per cent of care leavers go to higher education.[227] Of course, experiences *during* care are critical too, and leaving care teams may be able to effect little improvement among children who have already endured poor, unstable care journeys. Nevertheless, the following section describes in more detail how a poorly managed transition to independence can serve to reinforce these earlier disadvantages.

An abrupt and compressed transition

Although the Care Leavers Act 2000 created a duty for local authorities to create pathway plans and provide personal advisers to all care leavers until they are 21 (with the Care Matters white paper extending this to 25 if they are in education[228]), the reality is that all children in care must, under normal circumstances, leave their residential or foster home on or before their 18th birthday. Every year, around 6,000 looked-after children leave care for good; 21 per cent are 16, 17 per cent are 17 and 61 per cent are 18. The average age at which young people leave home in the general population is 24.[229]

This means a significant proportion of young people are still leaving care prematurely to live alone in private accommodation, ill prepared for the realities of adult life. Even those who 'stay on' in their foster families tend to do so for only a short time: Jim Wade's 2006 study found that while 24 per cent of his sample had remained with their foster families at 18, this had dropped to 8 per cent nine months later.[230] This suggests that the majority of care leavers still leave their foster homes in the year of their 18th birthday.

This is a significant concern for campaigners and policy experts including the Care Leavers Association, Barnardo's, Fostering Network and Rainer. Several organisations have stated that 18, and even 21, is too early for some young people to leave care.

Interviews with care leavers carried out for this project suggests that those who had left care at 16 had regretted the move – some described how leaving care and living with 'too much freedom' at an early age led to them dropping out of education, drinking and wrecking their accommodation with parties. Some had felt pressured to move out at this age:

Social services keep pressuring us to leave care...they kick you out into your own place when you get to 16.

One young person described how once he reached 16 he experienced frequent visits from his new social worker in the leaving care team, and he felt under pressure to move out of his placement and leave care. He described how the social worker kept saying, 'I'm here to talk to you to see if you want to move out of care.' And he would reply that he still wanted to live with his carer. In his own words, he said that 'I kind of hated her because she put pressure on me.'

Our findings have been echoed in several other consultations with care leavers, whose participants have tended to agree that 16 is too young to leave care; many feel 18 is also too young, and all feel they should only leave care when they were ready and prepared.[231]

In addition to the departure from care being premature for many young people, the process itself is compressed (transition happens rapidly). A study from the ESRC found care leavers were experiencing several key milestones (eg leaving school, going to college, finding a job, leaving home) *simultaneously*, whereas other young people might encounter and deal with them in succession over a period of months or even years. The ESRC found that the sample of care leavers they spoke to:

were attempting to juggle a range of responsibilities and challenges at the same time which had come about overnight on moving to their own accommodation. The impact and difficulty of these coinciding challenges had often not been anticipated.[232]

Stein describes this phenomenon as 'an accelerated and compressed transition to adulthood'[233] and explains how this means care leavers do not experience the all-important 'liminal phase', which allows other young people to transition and gain confidence in a safer environment before enjoying full independence. For many care leavers, there is the expectation of instant adulthood on leaving care. Many care leavers we spoke to also described their experience of leaving care in this way:

One minute they said you're ready, now we don't, then yes we do and you're moving out next week.

It comes on quite fast though, doesn't it? They say, ok you've got to this point, and they move you out.

Dixon et al's study also found that for almost all care leavers, leaving care is final and irreversible.[234] Young people often have little contact, let alone further support, from their carers and social worker after they leave care. Although Wade found that 46 per cent of care leavers were still in touch with a foster-carer, frequency of contact diminished sharply over the nine-month follow-up period, declining from 42 per cent with at least monthly contact at baseline to 14 per cent at follow-up.[235]

As one care leaver we interviewed put it:

Foster parents in their own right are your parents but when you leave, all of a sudden they're not like your parents no more. In real life situations, when you leave home, your parents are always there for you.

Once children leave care, responsibility for their wellbeing is transferred to the care leaving team in a local authority and a personal adviser, and it is almost unheard of for a care leaver to move back into a care placement once they have left, even if their support needs change radically. Barnardo's describes children at this stage as 'having no interim status':

[They] are either 'in care' or they are living independently and supported under the provisions of the Children (Leaving Care) Act 2000. This should be contrasted with the experiences of most young people who do not 'leave' home as a single act – the normal transition is graduated and characterised by frequent returns to the family home and continuing support from parents/carers.[236]

The process of moving from 'looked after' to 'care leaver' status might be compared to being released from prison in the suddenness with which a person's life changes, and certainly reminds the young person (if they had ever forgotten) that they are very much part of a 'system'. The speed with which a young care leaver finds themselves 'independent' has been reported to be traumatic for many, as they are ill prepared practically and emotionally for what this transition entails.

A lack of transition support

The 'cliff edge' style of transition from care is all the more worrying because of the lack of support care leavers are subsequently provided with – practical, emotional and financial.

A survey by the Care Leavers' Association found that the financial support provided to care leavers in the form of the care leaver's grant (specified in the Care Leaver's Act 2000 to help care leavers set up a new home) varied from £500 to £2,200, as local authorities have discretion to set this figure themselves. The Care Leavers' Association looked at the average cost of furnishing and essential household items, and suggest a realistic figure for the grant ought to be around £2,000.[237]

Money was a common subject of concern in our interviews with children in care and care leavers. When asked to suggest one thing that would have made their transition from care easier, a large number said more money to help them move into their own homes.

They don't think about things like, if my 16yr old was living by themselves what would they need? They just give you the basics to cover the basics.

If you put them in the flats they put us in the way they are, they wouldn't live there themselves.

You just get flung into a flat and get given £30 for electricity and gas. I had to start from scratch.

The Children and Young Persons Act 2008 introduced a minimum grant of £2,000 for care leavers, although this was only for those who go on to higher education. Furthermore, a survey of university students who had been in care in 2005 found that this group was still significantly disadvantaged financially and succeeding in spite of their difficulties. For example, their average level of debt was found to be £11,235, compared with the national average of £9,210. Most were obliged to take jobs in supermarkets or bars throughout every vacation, many did too much paid work, and this conflicted with academic demands.[238]

A number of surveys carried out with care leavers found that many are in unstable and poor quality housing. Dixon's study of care leavers found that 35 per cent of those interviewed had been homeless at some point during the nine months, and care movement was strongly associated with a risk of homelessness ($p<0.001$, $n=101$). Over two-fifths (43 per cent) of those who had experienced homelessness at some stage had made four or more moves since leaving care compared with just 5 per cent of those who had not.

Evidence from Ofsted also found that rural areas in particular were increasingly short of housing and dependent on the private sector for provision. Bed and breakfast accommodation was also being used as a short-term measure to accommodate asylum-seeking young people and those whose behaviour is described as 'chaotic'.[239]

Rainer's 'home alone' survey in 2007 of 1,244 young people found that:

- 16 per cent of care leavers assessed were not in suitable supported accommodation
- 32 per cent of the care leavers felt that their accommodation did not meet their needs
- almost one in six care leavers assessed were not receiving appropriate support with their housing needs[240]

A number of the case studies and interviews showed young care leavers being housed in buildings known for drug dealing and prostitution, in rooms with no cooking facilities, where care leavers with children were in unsecure buildings with no lifts or lighting, and so on.[241] The Children, Schools and Families Committee commented that housing care leavers in such run down areas where social problems were rife meant their 'inherent vulnerability is compounded by proximity to problems such as substance abuse, exploitation and crime'.[242]

The survey No Place Like Home 2006, carried out by A National Voice with 581 people (half care leavers, and half either leaving care or housing professionals), similarly found that:

- 50 per cent felt they had no real choice in the accommodation offered to them on leaving care
- 29 per cent did not feel safe in their accommodation
- 32 per cent felt it did not meet their needs
- 12 per cent were living in bed and breakfast accommodation[243]

The Frank Buttle Trust reports that care leavers' choice of course and institution was severely limited even for those care leavers who go to university, as they were stuck in council accommodation they had been allocated on leaving care. Those living at a distance from campus had restricted access to facilities such as computers and libraries, and found making friends harder.[244]

The importance of mental health support

Although much research focuses on the poor and locally variable quality of financial and housing support for care leavers, a growing concern is that care leavers living on their own display a range of emotional and psychological problems. Several of the care leavers we spoke to described leaving care as an emotional experience:

The isolation of it all was just strange. Coming from a foster placement into a flat is like, from a family setting into living alone, so I was like, wow!!

The ESRC described this as 'malaise' among care leavers, related to their earlier life traumas but which is exacerbated by the prospect of living alone and burdened by multiple responsibilities. They found a significant minority of care leavers they interviewed were being prescribed anti-depressant medication and 'longer-term non-participatory lifestyles' were being established.[245] Centrepoint has also noted that apart from care leaver's concerns about their safety and welfare in inappropriate accommodation, a major reported problem was loneliness, with many finding it hard to adapt to coming home from college or work and having no one there. They found that loneliness could turn into depression, which had a negative effect on education and work.[246]

However, research suggests that local authorities tend to overlook the need for emotional and psychological preparation for those on the verge of leaving care and living independently, focusing instead on practical issues such as cooking and budgeting to pay rent. Dixon et al's 2004 study of 106 care leavers found that when it came to preparation for leaving care, hobbies and interpersonal skills were the least well delivered and assessed (table 2).[247]

Table 2 **Preparation support for care leavers in life skills areas**

Life skill	Enough	Some	None
Health and lifestyle			
Personal hygiene	62	9	28
Healthy diet	70	15	15
Keeping fit	53	21	26
Safe sex	81	11	8
Hobbies	57	24	20
Alcohol use	79	12	9
Drug use	82	9	9
Smoking	79	9	11
Practical skills			
Cooking	48	29	23
Shopping	58	17	26
Budgeting	45	31	24
Interpersonal skills			
Making friends	44	14	42
Personal and sexual relationships	47	14	39
Dealing with official people	37	21	42
Finding help or information	58	25	17

Source: Dixon et al (2004)

This was certainly confirmed by some of the experiences care leavers shared with us during interview. One care leaver, who left care at 16, felt she had no emotional support and in her own words,

As long as I could budget to be able to do my shopping, cooked, ate and I could survive, that's all they cared about.

Cameron et al also found that leaving care teams were not integrating well with health services – particularly mental health services – and care leavers often struggled to access this.[248] The research team concluded:

*Leaving care services had often made housing a priority, and had
committed resources to supporting young people in education, training and
employment, but very few practical steps had been taken to improve the
health of care leavers... A similarly energetic approach is required to expand
access to services that address emotional issues at different levels of
specialisation, such as counselling, psychotherapy and psychiatry.*

It seems unsurprising, then, that given the lack of
emotional preparation before and support after leaving care,
young people's mental health can deteriorate. Dixon et al's study
showed that at baseline interview, 38 per cent of young people in
the study reported having a physical or mental health problem or
a disability which affected their daily life, while 61 per cent
reported problems at follow-up.[249] Most notably, more young
people reported mental health problems (24 per cent at follow-
up compared with 12 per cent at baseline). This was largely
reported in terms of stress and depression, although at least four
young people had made suicide attempts over the previous nine
months. There was also increased reporting of 'other health'
problems (44 per cent at follow-up compared with 28 per cent at
baseline). These included asthma, weight loss, allergies, flu, joint
pains and illnesses related to drug or alcohol misuse. Also, more
young women had become or were currently pregnant and
reported problems such as morning sickness and miscarriage.

The decline in mental health over time among a large
proportion of care leavers is a particularly concerning finding
from Dixon's study. This suggests that there is a definite gap in
care leaver preparation and subsequent support, which is either
exposing care leavers to increased emotional distress or stress, or
not adequately dealing with existing emotional and mental health
issues. The transition to independence from care can be a stressful
and challenging experience for care leavers, and although for
some this may be eased by a range of practical and emotional
support and a more gradual transition thanks to supported
accommodation, this is clearly not the case for everyone.

Section 4
Care journeys and costs

In the last section we described some of the weaknesses in how the current care system is used at entry, during and when leaving care. However, we must be clear that the care system certainly does not deliver poor experiences universally, but that it is *patchy*. Children's experiences vary hugely, and not just between local authority areas. Dozens of separate decisions and events, made by several different individuals, may fundamentally change a child's care journey and future outcomes. And of course, the intrinsic characteristics of the child themselves and their needs will influence the path they take through the care system. It is for these reasons that the same care system is able to produce successful, university educated adults, as well as some of society's most disadvantaged and vulnerable young people.

To illustrate the full scale of this variation, the following section models the costs of caring for two children who have contrasting but realistic experiences at the two extremes of the care system, from the time that they first enter care, until age 18. We then go on to compare the costs to the state of the later life outcomes they might go on to experience in adulthood.

10 The cost of care journeys

We originally sought to explore whether care journeys that are poorly planned, initially under-resourced and increasingly unstable work out to be more expensive as a result of the poorer later life outcomes with which this is often associated.

Unfortunately, a lack of publicly available longitudinal data linking looked-after children's experiences in care to their later life outcomes makes it extremely difficult to establish this relationship of cause and effect between good care and good later life outcomes and poor care and poor later life outcomes.

However, a number of small-scale academic studies have demonstrated that there is a correlation between a child's:

· age of entry to care and their level of emotional and behavioural difficulties
· level of emotional and behavioural difficulties and potential for a stable or unstable experience of local authority care
· experience of instability in care and a higher risk of poor behavioural outcomes, poor educational outcomes and early exit from care
· age of exit from care (and level of support in transition to independence) and educational attainment and employment outcomes

But as the majority of these studies lack controls, and the different factors of age of entry to care, stability in care, and age of exit from care tend to be interrelated and mutually reinforcing, it is not possible to isolate the impact of these individual factors from one another and identify a causal relationship in each case. It is important to note that we have, therefore, limited our analysis to variables for which we can find a *correlation*.

Purpose and scope of illustrative care journeys

In order to negotiate these data limitations, we have drawn upon the national statistics on looked-after children published by DCSF, and a number of small-scale academic studies, to construct two exemplar care journeys that demonstrate how a child's age of entry to care, experience of stability or instability, and age and type of exit from care are interrelated and often mutually reinforcing.

The first care journey illustrates how a 'good' care journey, characterised by entry to care at an early age (associated with lower mental health needs), a stable and high-quality placement in long-term foster care, and a supported transition from care at 18, is frequently associated with the young person experiencing better mental health outcomes and educational attainment.

The second care journey illustrates how a 'poor' care journey, characterised by entry to care at a later age (associated with higher mental health needs), a number of unstable and low quality placements and several unsuccessful returns to her birth family, and a premature exit from care aged 16½, translates into escalating costs to social services and is often associated with that young person experiencing worse mental health outcomes and poor educational attainment.

It is important to establish at this point that this study does not purport to prove that one particular type of care journey has an inevitable impact on young people's outcomes. Studies consistently show that young people's personal characteristics, level of resilience, and opportunity to draw on the support of secure attachments, determine how well they are able to cope with challenging life experiences.[250] Equally, it is important to establish that this research does not attempt to identify a 'one size fits all' recipe for a good care journey. As the first chapter of this report demonstrates, children come into local authority care for a variety of reasons, at different points in their lives, and with a variety of different needs. We cannot, therefore, recommend child A's care journey (below), entering care at age 3, for the many children whose family situation dramatically changes in later childhood, which then necessitates them going into care. Nevertheless, for many children who experience a history of abuse and neglect from early life, child A's care journey represents something to work towards.

The 'good' care journey: child A

When constructing child A's care journey, we sought to establish:

- an aspirational care journey for a child who is looked after away from home in the long-term (from age 3 to 18), but is not adopted
- a realistic care journey, representing the current experience of between 5 per cent and 10 per cent of looked-after children
- a care journey that facilitates stability and permanence and provides the opportunity for a secure attachment
- a care journey that would be most likely to produce 'good' outcomes such as good mental health and good educational outcomes

Box 4   **Journey outline – child A (female)**

One period in care and two stable placements

- *enters care aged 3*
- *care proceedings to obtain a care order*
- *short-term foster care placement for 1 year*
- *long-term foster care placement for 14 years*
- *leaves care aged 18 with good mental health and with good qualifications*

Child A's care journey (box 4) was constructed on the basis of several data sources, which can be found in more detail in appendix 1. These data, including academic studies and DCSF statistics, were used primarily to establish a 'realistic' care journey for child A, and where possible to bring her care experience in line with between 5 per cent and 10 per cent of the current care population in relation to age of entry, number of placements and periods of care she experiences, and age of exit.

We also used these sources of information to explain why child A's stable care journey could be associated with good educational attainment and mental health. Although causality cannot be proven, we drew from various studies which demonstrate a clear correlation between stable care journeys and better mental health and educational attainment. These include UK studies, such as Biehal et al, and academic evidence from the US which found that children who had a stable care experience had a lower probability of experiencing behavioural problems (controlling for pre-care experience and other characteristics).[251]

The 'poor' care journey: child B

When constructing child B's care journey, we sought to demonstrate:

· a flawed and poor quality care journey for a child who is looked after away from home from age 11 to age 16½
· a realistic care journey, representing the current experience of around 10 per cent of looked-after children
· a care journey that is characterised by disruption and instability and does not provide opportunities for the child to develop a secure attachment with a carer
· a care journey that is therefore more likely to produce 'poor' outcomes such as emotional and behavioural problems, poor mental health and poor educational attainment

Box 5   **Journey outline – child B (Female)**

Three periods in care and ten placements

· *enters care aged 11 (voluntarily accommodated)*
· *emergency foster care placement (1 week)*
· *short-term foster care placement (12 months)*
· *reunified with family (6 months)*
· *emergency foster care placement (1 week)*

- *short-term foster care placement (6 months)*
- reunified with family (6 months)
- *re-enters care and legal processes are undertaken to obtain care order*
- *three foster care placements over 12 months*
- *placement with agency foster carer (12 months)*
- *short-term residential placement (1 month)*
- *residential placement (11 months)*
- *exits care at 16 ½ and lives in independent accommodation until 18*
- *has poor mental health and no qualifications*

Again, we used several data sources to compile child B's care journey. We used data, often from DCSF, to ensure the age of entry and exit, number of placements and types of placement reflected the experience of around 10 per cent of children currently in care.

We also used studies such as Sempik et al and Dixon et al[252] to establish a negative escalation in child B's experiences; from late entry to care, leading to greater risk of instability, leading to emotional and behavioural problems, which in turn gives rise to a greater numbers of placements. We also used various studies to establish a correlation (again, causation was not established) between child B's journey and poorer outcomes on leaving care –poor mental health and educational attainment. The full range of data and studies we used can be found in appendix 1.

Calculating the cost of child A and child B's care journeys

To estimate the total costs of the care journeys experienced by child A and child B we have worked in partnership with Harriet Ward, Jean Soper and Lisa Holmes from the Centre for Child and Family Research (CCFR) at Loughborough University, who have developed a cost calculator for children's services. This tool is able to calculate and aggregate the cost of children's care journeys by bringing together data on the children's character-istics, their placements and other services they receive with the unit costs of social care activities.[253]

The methodology underpinning the cost calculator is outlined in Ward et al's book *Costs and Consequences of Placing Children in Care*.[254] As an earlier study by Harriet Ward and Lisa Holmes explained:

It is possible to cost children's pathways through care, first by identifying and developing unit costs for the specific social care processes, and then by identifying the numerous variations and their causes. The frequency and duration of processes incurred over a specific period can then be calculated and the cost of each one aggregated to build up a cost pathway covering all or part of the care episode.[255]

Ward et al calculated their eight 'process costs' in consultation with staff from social service departments in six different local authorities.[256] The table in appendix 2 outlines these processes and the estimated costs attributed to each one.

The cost calculator for children's services is able to aggregate the costs to social services that would be incurred by child A and child B's care journeys, according to the social service activities that would need to take place:

· deciding that child A and child B needed to be taken into care and finding suitable placements
· initiating legal proceedings at the appropriate times for each child
· maintaining their placements in foster care, residential care or independent accommodation
· finding any subsequent placements that are necessary
· undertaking the necessary review and care planning activities (with the frequency prescribed in the Children's Cases (Amendment) (England) Regulations 2004[257])
· exiting care on the two occasions when child B returns to her birth family
· the transition to leaving care services, which is undertaken by child A at 18 and by child B at 16$\frac{1}{2}$

In addition to the process costs outlined above, we believe it is likely that child B would need to receive some form of mental health support during the later phases of her care journey. At the time when child B is placed with an agency foster carer for 12 months (from age 14 ½ to age 15 ½) we have therefore factored in the cost of a weekly session with a clinical psychologist for 12 months.[258]

Using the cost calculator to match the costs of the above processes to the two care journeys outlined above, we found that in total:

· the cost of child A's care journey over 15 years, up to age 18 is *£352,053*, which translates to *£23,470 each year*
· the total cost of child B's care journey over 7 years, up to age 18 is *£393,579*, which translates to *£56,226 each year.*

Total costs of the care journeys of child A and child B

As these figures demonstrate, higher expenditure alone does not necessarily generate a better care experience. Indeed, as Harriet Ward and Lisa Holmes have observed of similar types of care journey, child B experiences 'an inverse relationship between costs and outcome'[259] in that the points at which child B's costs escalate (when she has three local authority placements in one year, when she is placed with an agency foster carer and when she is placed in residential care) are also the points at which her emotional and behavioural difficulties become more severe and her chance of achieving stability in care recedes (figure 4).

Mapping costs in this way demonstrates that care journeys built around earlier intervention, stability and gradual transitions are not only better for children's wellbeing, they are also likely to be less expensive to the state. This is not to understate the sheer difficulty of 'getting it right', which should not be underestimated in the case of child A. There is no doubt that the involvement of skilled practitioners would be necessary, along with all of key decisions and processes being undertaken swiftly in order to lead to such a care journey; something which is not always easy to achieve in practice.

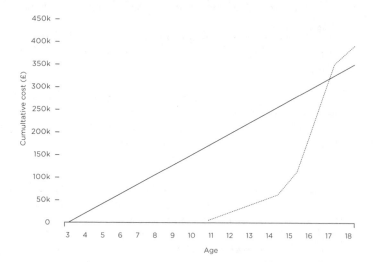

Figure 4   **Care journey costs for child A and child B**

The next section of the report will go on to consider example cost implications for child A and child B's later adult lives, taking into account their educational attainment and mental health on leaving care.

11   Later life costs: the cost of outcomes to age 30

As we have seen with our example care journeys, 'child A' leaves care at 18, following a stable placement, with good qualifications. 'Child B', on the other hand, leaves care at 16½, has no qualifications, and has mental health problems.

Rather than starting their adult costs at different points, the following analysis begins at age 16½. This is because although both children are still technically in care at this point, their costs to the state (as separate from their care costs) begin at 16, as this is the end of their compulsory schooling. The choice of child A to stay in school means she will be eligible for education maintenance allowance. The choice of child B to leave school means she is at a high risk of being NEET. Both of these scenarios represent costs to the state which are not included in the care costs outlined in the previous section, but which are included in the following calculations.

Child A

Assumptions

We assume child A lives in Coventry, where she stays at school to 18, then attends a university (not in Coventry, but outside London) to age 21, living away from home. On graduating, she finds a job and, between graduating and age 30, we assume she earns in the top 30 per cent of average salaries for her age. We take this to be a reasonable and conservative estimate given the lack of data regarding average adult earnings linked to qualification levels. Our assumption is supported by two broad reference points: analysis by the Institute for Fiscal Studies in 2002, which found that 55 per cent of the Labour Force Survey's top decile earners in the 25–34 age range were graduates; and DCSF analysis of the Labour Force Survey in 2008, which shows that women working fulltime with Level 4 qualifications, equivalent to a degree or higher degree, had gross hourly earnings 28 per cent higher than the average for all women working full-time, and 55 per cent higher than those with Level 3 qualifications.[260]

Additional costs associated with a care leaver with this life course
Having a low household income, child A may well be eligible for education maintenance allowance at the highest rate (£30 per week), but will not be claiming housing or other benefits as she is still living at home with her foster family at this point.

At 18, on entering university, all students are entitled to a range of loans and grants. These include student loan, maintenance loan, maintenance grant and bursaries, which should cover child A's accommodation costs. Coventry also pays for the accommodation of care leavers during university vacations so they can return to Coventry during these periods.

In appendix 4 we have presented the full range of costs associated with going to university outside London. These demonstrate that in total child A would cost the state £40,480.10 from age 16 to 21, if she chose to continue her education, or around £8,096 per year (table 3).

Table 3   **Total costs of child A ages 16–30**

Education age 16–18 (education maintenance allowance)	£3,120.00
Student grants	£12,818.00
Student loans	£20,361.00
Accommodation support	£4,181.10
Total costs child A age 16–30	£40,480.10

After 21, we can assume that child A's costs are in line with the average working population, recouped by government from income and other taxes. Child A has no *additional* costs associated with her path beyond age 21.

However, we should bear the following points in mind:

1 £20,361 of this sum is a repayable loan, which child A will be paying back through her working life (although in practice this is not necessarily entirely cost free to the state because of the subsidised interest). The remaining £20,119.10 is non-recoupable, so in reality, child A would actually cost the state £6,706 per year while at university.

2 A large proportion of these non-recoupable funds are given to *all* low income students. Overall, £12,838 is provided to other students who may have low incomes or caring responsibilities, or are lone parents.

3 Therefore, only £7,281.10 of the total £45,872.50 costs would be generated *specifically* because child A is a care leaver, and not just because she was from a low earning family or vulnerable in some other way. This cost would be made up of £2,000 care leaver grant plus £4,181.10 in housing costs to the local authority, and £1,100 bursary cost to the university (figure 5).

Gains of child A

Having graduated, child A can potentially generate gains for the government, thanks to her increased earning potential. She might well start work at 21 on an average starting salary of £19,677 per year,[261] which is substantially above the median salary for 18–21-year-olds in full-time work.[262]

As outlined above, we have assumed that throughout her working life child A will earn in the top 30 per cent of salaries between graduation and age 30, given her level of qualification. We believe this is reasonable and conservative, using a 2002 IFS analysis of the Labour Force Survey as a broad reference point.[263]

So, if child A were to be in the top 30 per cent of earners, the government would receive more in income tax and national insurance contributions (NICs) on this higher salary. These gains are calculated in box 5, but are an underestimate of true gains as

Figure 5 **Child A's costs ages 16—30**

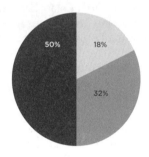

- Grant care leavers only
- Grant all low income students
- All students repayable loan

50% 18% 32%

we exclude employer NICs and focus on the gains provided directly by child A.

Box 5 **Increased tax and national insurance contributions above national median**

The average salary of a 22–29-year-old female, working full time in the 70th percentile of earners, is £24,920.[264] The overall average for this group is £21,008.[265]

The difference between the income tax and NICs received by the government of these two salaries is £1,212.72 per year, therefore:

- Child A would pay the state £52,209 in tax and NI contributions between the age of 21 and 30 (based on an average salary across all years).
- This means she would pay £10,914.48 more in tax and NI contributions over these nine years than if she were on average wages.

Child B

Assumptions

We assume child B also lives in Coventry. She leaves school at 16 with no qualifications, and moves out of her care placement at $16\frac{1}{2}$. We know from her care journey (described above) that she is likely to have mental health problems. Based on a range of national data, we are able to estimate the risks of child B being unemployed during her life, and a range of costs associated with this.

Additional costs associated with child B's life course

We considered three main variables in child B's life – unemployment, underemployment and mental health problems. Using various data sources including the International Labour Organization (ILO), Annual Survey of Hours and Earnings, Labour Force Survey and others, which can be found in more detail in appendix 3, we were able to estimate the length of time child B might be NEET between 16 and 24, and unemployed between 25 and 30, based on the fact that she left school with no qualifications. As she also has mental health problems, however, we believe our calculations may well be an underestimate. We then calculated how much these periods of inactivity would cost the state.

We also considered the average salary of adults with no qualifications compared with the average, and calculated child B's 'underemployment' costs – the cost to the state of child B not fulfilling her potential (or at least, not being able to earn an average wage). Finally, using data on costs of mental health from the King's Fund,[266] we were also able to add child B's costs for being treated for depression. Appendix 3 provides evidence to justify our choice of depression as child B's principle mental health problem.

Total costs – summary

We have calculated the costs of each of the variables above, which can be found in detail in appendix 4. A summary of the costs for child B's life course are shown in table 4.

Table 4 **Total costs of child B ages 16–30**

Unemployment– welfare benefits	£25,172.86
Unemployment –foregone tax and NIC revenue	£20,208.61
Housing benefits during periods of inactivity	£35,493.12
Underemployment – foregone tax and NIC revenue	£26,984.90
Mental health treatment costs	£4,064.50
Total costs child B age 16 to 30	£111,923.99

What haven't we included?

We should bear in mind that the costs for child B are likely to be a significant underestimate. We have only included direct welfare costs and tax revenue and NIC loss resulting from child B's lack of qualifications. Even then, we have underestimated welfare costs – for example, we have assumed, perhaps optimistically, that child B will be employed full time when she is employed. In reality, she may well work part time, which could make her eligible for income support. We have not included tax credits because of the complexity of calculating their interactions with other benefits.

We have also excluded a range of additional costs that might arise from child B becoming pregnant. We know female children in care are 2.5 times more likely to become teenage mothers than average,[267] and low educational achievement and social exclusion also increase the risk of teenage pregnancy.[268] However, we considered pregnancy to be a cost associated with a large proportion of the population and so therefore not an 'additional' cost associated with child B's life course specifically.

We have also excluded the possibility of other, more costly, mental health problems in addition to depression, and the potential costs associated with the higher risk of offending behaviour of child B, which could be associated with having poor educational attainment, and low income is also associated with this. Again, this would substantially increase child B's costs to the state.

Table 5   **The total costs of child A and child B ages 16–30**

Child A	
Education support age 16–18	£3,120.00
Student grants	£12,818.00
Student loans	£20,361.00
Accommodation support	£4,181.10
Total child A costs 16–30	£40,480.10
Child B	
Unemployment – welfare benefits	£25,172.86
Unemployment –foregone tax and NIC revenue	£20,208.61
Housing benefits due during periods of inactivity	£35,493.12
Underemployment – foregone tax and NIC revenue	£26,984.90
Mental health treatment costs	£4,064.50
Total child B costs 16–30	£111,923.99

Comparing the costs of child A with those of child B

The difference between the additional costs associated with child A and child B up to age 30 is £71,443.89 (table 5). This does not take into account gains in tax revenue and NICs made by the state as a result of child A's better salary, which at £10,914.48 over and above a median earner, would reduce her additional costs to the state.

However, it is clear that additional costs associated with child A's life course (going to university) end at 21. After this age, her net costs to the state are in line with the average tax payer (or perhaps slightly less given that she will pay slightly more in tax and NICs as a graduate, and assuming she has no underlying health conditions).

Child B, on the other hand, will have ongoing *additional* costs over and above the 'normal' tax payer for the rest of her life (though we only illustrate these up to age 30).

We can see from figure 6 that child A's line stops at 21 as we have no additional costs to calculate. Child A's life course *appears* to have considerable 'up front' costs. However, we should bear in

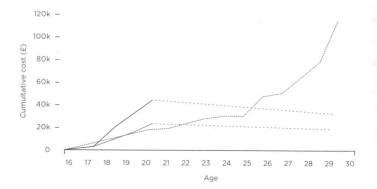

Figure 6 **Costs of child A and child B over a lifetime**

— Child A

— Child A (Grant only)

···· Child B

mind that only the lighter shaded line actually counts – the darker shaded line includes student loan costs, which are paid back by all graduates who then earn a salary of more than £15,000 per year (although subsidised interest rates may mean the government does not recoup full costs of these loans, we are assuming full repayment over a lifetime here). As we have seen, child A is likely to pay her student loan off at a rate of £900 per year immediately after graduation. Looking at the green line, even by the age of 20, child B's costs have almost met child As.

Furthermore, from 21 onwards, the government will have nothing but 'gain' from child A – her costs will be in line with the national average, but she will be paying more tax thanks to her increased income, and paying off her student loan. This also does not count other potential gains that have been associated with higher education levels (eg lower risk of offending behaviour and improved mental health).

This possible onward life cost journey is reflected in the dotted lines on the graph, continuing the darker and lighter shaded lines, which suggest that in child A's active year (before motherhood or old age) child A may well be cost neutral, or indeed a net contributor to the state. This is slightly more apparent with the darker shaded line, as we include child A paying off her student loan here. Child B's life course, on the other hand, sees escalating costs, because of the cumulative costs of unemployment and underemployment throughout her working life. We would not expect these to decrease particularly beyond age 30.

Child A and child B - conclusions

In attempting to cost two young people's care journeys and subsequent adult outcomes up to age 30, we have made some interesting discoveries:

1 It is possible to model a care journey which is both more beneficial for the child, *and* more cost-effective. In contrast, a poorer care journey seems, at points, to be correlated with increased cost due to higher levels of instability. Although time in care is longer for child A, her overall costs are lower – as intervening early is usually associated with more stable journeys, fewer costly placements and a reduced risk of needing specialist intervention or mental health support.

2 Decisions at the outset of a care journey can set in motion a domino effect of positive or negative outcomes, with costs accumulating over a lifetime. Although, of course, making the 'right' decision when a child or family is first known to social services is easier in theory than in practice.

3 Stability has cost benefits at any stage, even for those who only need to enter care at adolescence. It is important to note that these journeys are not intended to 'prove' from a cost perspective that children should necessarily enter care earlier – clearly this is not appropriate in many cases. However, stability or permanency will have benefits at all ages.

A comparison of total costs and costs per year is given in table 6 and figures 7 and 8 these figures combine costs to the state *and* costs to children's services. Note that the difference in annual costs for child A and B during care is larger than the total costs, as the time child B spends in care is significantly less (7 years compared to 15 years for child A), so total costs are spread over a shorter period.

We should also bear in mind that as child B entered care later, overall annual costs are also compressed in a shorter period – 19 years, compared with 27 years for child A. So child A's combined costs to children's services and the state is on averagee £13,784.15 per year for 27 years, while it is £26,605.42 per year for 19 years for child B. As a result of the nature of child B's outcome costs (see above), we would expect her costs to continue accumulating throughout her life, so the difference between child A and child B would grow larger with each year.

The difference between the total care journey costs of child A and child B is £41,526, even though child A's care journey is

Table 6 **A comparison of total costs and costs per year for child A and Child B**

	Child A	Child B	Child A average cost per year	Child B average cost per year
Total care journey cost from entry to exit	£352,053.00	£393,579.00	£23,470.20	£56,225.57
Total outcome cost from 16 to 30	£20,119.10*	£111,923.99	£1,437.00	£7,994.57
Total costs from entering care to age 30	£372,172.10	£505,502.99	£13,784.15	£26,605.42

*excluding student loan

Figure 7 **Total costs from entering care to age 30**

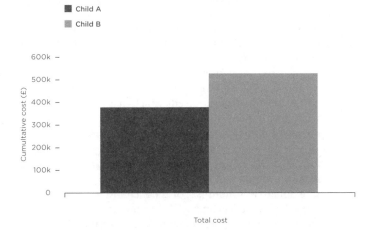

Figure 8 **Average annual costs from entering care to age 30**

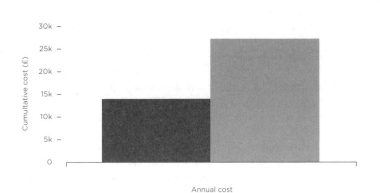

longer. And ultimately the difference reaches £133,330.89 when the total costs to the state are included up until age 30. Although these are only examples and we have not proved that the respective care journeys caused these outcomes, they point to the existence of real potential cost savings for local authorities in the short term, and to the state in the long term, of investing in high quality care journeys for children.

Of course, all children are different, and enter care with specific characteristics and needs which may have costs associated with them (for example a disability). And it is important to note that many children enter care in later childhood not as a result of delay or indecision, but rather because care was simply not needed before that time (eg if they entered care after a parent died). Others may only need to stay in care for a matter of months. For these children, lifetime costs associated with indecision and delay may not be relevant. Nevertheless, even in these circumstances, local authorities should strive to avoid some key elements of child B's journey. Stability, timely decisions and effectively supported transitions can benefit *all* children in care – regardless of when they come into care and how long they need to stay for.

The difference in costs between a stable and unstable care journey should be borne in mind in section 5, where we present our recommendations. We are aware that we are entering a period of unprecedented fiscal constraints. Children's services are likely to experience substantial reductions in funding, and as local authorities must meet their statutory safeguarding commitments, cuts will have to be made elsewhere. In such circumstances, it is understandable that local authorities may 'firefight' to deal with child protection cases and urgent needs, rather than invest in approaches that may save costs over the long term.

However, we hope that by costing an unstable journey, we have demonstrated that timely care decisions along with stability and better mental health can reduce *immediate* costs to the local authority by reducing social work time, use of expensive agency and residential placements, and therapeutic support. These are not distant cost savings beyond the budgetary cycle, but amount to an average of £32,755.37 in the difference between the two journeys, which could be saved each year while that child is in care.

With this in mind, we should consider again the range of adult outcomes that are experienced by young people who come into contact with the care system at some point, from those who have a positive care experience and are in the minority that ultimately go on to university,[269] through to those who become more or less dependent on the state and health services into early adulthood. Combining both the costs of the care journey and the outcomes, the difference could be £133,330.89 *per child* from entering care to age 30. Given the current care population is nearly 61,000 children, the contrast between the two creates a powerful argument to invest to save in both the short term and the long term.

Section 5
What next for care?

12 Recommendations for systemic reform

Over the past decade the care system has been the subject of almost continuous reform. Although there have undoubtedly been real achievements, lasting improvements have been slow to materialise. There have been major legislative and policy interventions and we may not be able to assess the impact of these for a number of years to come. However, the most intractable problem still confronting the care system is how to deliver real change on the ground, and by extension to children's day to day lives. This can only be achieved by focusing on relationships and attachments that will enable these children to thrive.

In most cases the care system exists to supplement, or sometimes replace, the care children receive from their parents. Recent reforms have done much to improve the framework and legislation surrounding the care system, but they have not gone nearly far enough in tackling the parenting deficit in the lives of many looked-after children. To build the long-term relationships children need, local authorities need to assume the role of parent much more proactively and earlier than they do today.

What must care achieve?

As we have seen in section 2, a wealth of evidence indicates that for children to flourish, they must have security, stability and continuity in their lives, and the opportunity to form long-standing attachments with those who care for them. This must clearly be accompanied by good quality and appropriate care (as stability in an unsuitable care placement will not necessarily be beneficial – 56 per cent of children surveyed by the director of Children's Rights believed their care plan should seek to keep them in placements for as long as possible, *assuming everything was going well*, and another 34 per cent felt that this goal should be in all care plans regardless[270]).

Although children come into care for different reasons, at different ages, and for different periods of time, there is no reason why all children, when living away from their families, should not benefit from warm relationships and sense of stability. It is for this reason that we differentiate between *permanence* (which would imply a permanent care solution or adoption) and *stability*. Although the latter may be delivered effectively through the former, we should also bear in mind that when a permanent care solution such as adoption is not viable, stability can and should still be sought.

The following recommendations, therefore, all seek to reinforce permanency (where appropriate), stability of good quality placements and continuity of support. These can be achieved in very different ways at each phase of a care journey, from entry, during care and at exit from care. Given the current fiscal climate, we have avoided a number of recommendations which would have been more costly, and have instead focused on changes that we believe would be high impact relative to cost. In some cases recommendations are almost cost-neutral. Given the escalating spending associated with poor care journeys we believe that the relatively modest investment we propose in particular areas makes economic sense, and will help to make the care system more sustainable in the future. However, before addressing these targeted recommendations in detail, we must first consider the system as a whole.

Systemic reform

Throughout this report we have alluded to the prevalent philosophical approach to care, which treats it as a radical step of last resort. This conceives of family life as a private sphere, which ought not to be interfered with by the state unless all avenues have been exhausted. This philosophy may be an underlying factor in a number of areas of poor practice: the delay in taking children into care; the 'law of optimism' and 'drift'; the repeated attempts at unsupported reunification; using residential care as an 'end of the line' option; and perhaps even the conditional nature of support beyond 18. This poor use of public care can be linked, in part, to society's belief that the care system is destined only ever to be a poor second to the quality of care by any birth family.

This points towards a self-fulfilling prophecy. A lack of confidence in the care system to generate positive outcomes leads to poor use being made of it, which is associated with poor outcomes. Poor outcomes reinforce the underlying lack of confidence in the system. Of course, the care system certainly is not perfect, and we have outlined many of its weaknesses in this report. But compared with the alternative (remaining in an neglectful or abusive home environment), and in spite of popular misconceptions, the care system as it currently stands *can and does* create stable, nurturing environments. The next sections of this report suggest specific reforms to the care system that would help to make this a more widespread occurrence, but Demos believes our practical recommendations will have limited impact unless the wider philosophy of the state as parent is reviewed.

Demos believes it is necessary to shift our approach through:

· making more pro-active, positive use of care
· destigmatising care as family support and carrying out early intervention projects
· providing improved data on children in care
· having a better understanding of placement and care journey costs

A more pro-active, positive use of care

Policy makers within the DfE and government more widely must start to acknowledge that the state can provide good quality care, and should be confident in making this view clear to the public and practitioners. In other public spheres, we are increasingly viewing children as young citizens and recognising the state's role and ability in helping to build the resilience and promote the wellbeing of young people. This same view must be applied to a modern interpretation of corporate parenting. Demos urges the government to adopt a more confident stance on the capacity of the care system to achieve positive outcomes. We should strive to create a new virtuous circle – one where care is used earlier and *more effectively* and in turn becomes *more effective*.

Care as family support and the provision of early intervention projects

'Corporate' parenting and birth parenting should not necessarily be seen as mutually exclusive. The state should be recognised as being capable of acting as a 'parallel parent' for children and families who need such ongoing support. Although the principle of 'partnership' between parent and state was enshrined in the Children Act 1989, its current practical application is very far from what might have been intended. The government must therefore embark on a concerted effort to destigmatise care as a form of family support, and promote the concept of parallel parenting. We set out in our specific recommendations below an example of how parallel parenting might work in practice for some families with packages of support care.

Although this report has focused on the care system itself (with reference to family services for those on the 'cusp' of care), it is self-evident that today's policies on early intervention and prevention will also have a tremendous impact on the care system of tomorrow. In particular, well-targeted prevention services could dramatically alter the characteristics of the care population in the future. Such services could help to identify problems in families or among parents-to-be early on, before children have been exposed to neglect and abuse, rather than after they have developed emotional and behavioural difficulties. Tackling these problems 'upstream' will be key to the success of the care system in the future.

One example of this approach is the Nurse–Family Partnership Programme, an evidence-based nurse home visiting programme that was developed by Professor Olds at the University of Colorado. The purpose of the programme is to improve the health, resilience and quality of life of vulnerable parents and their children. Young first-time mothers taking part in the programme receive home visits from a specially trained family nurse from the first few weeks of their pregnancy, until their child is two years old.[271] The programme has been trialled in three sites in the USA: in Elmira, New York in 1977, Memphis in 1987 and Denver in 1994. Successes of the programme, verified by randomised controlled trials, have included a reduction in child abuse and neglect by 50 per cent (in the Elmira study) and 75 per cent fewer hospitalisations for injuries with non-accidental causes (in Memphis).[272]

In April 2007 the programme was initiated in England in ten local authority areas and it has subsequently been expanded to a further 20 sites. Results from the second year evaluation suggest that the programme is having a positive impact on participants' parenting skills and confidence. There was also evidence that early referrals were being made to other agencies (around three-quarters of the clients had been referred to another agency; almost one in ten had been referred for substance abuse issues and social care referrals were divided mainly between domestic violence and safeguarding). Further outcomes and the cost-effectiveness of the Nurse–Family Partnership Programme will be investigated more fully as part of the randomised control trial that was initiated in April 2009.[273] However, it was estimated that the US programme will produce savings that exceed its costs four times over (£4 saving for every £1 spent), as a result of lower reliance on welfare, fewer convictions and higher tax contributions over the lives of the children who took part in the intervention.[274]

The positive impact of early intervention or prevention will be highly dependent on developing and using sophisticated tools to assess parental characteristics and difficulties, to ensure that interventions are targeted at those who are realistically able and willing to meet the needs of their children within a particular timescale. But, were the UK to move towards a more preventative model of family intervention for children at risk, this would free up resources downstream for those children who do eventually enter the care system.

Our first two recommendations have called for a cultural shift in how the state and the public view the purpose of care. We are aware such a shift does not come about on its own, but Demos believes that if policy makers and the public had a *clearer view* of the outcomes achieved by the care system, this cultural shift would be much easier to achieve. This is because our lack of confidence in the care system is in part philosophical, but is also justified by the 'evidence' of the poor outcomes among children in care. The way in which we interpret those outcomes is fundamentally flawed. Demos therefore also proposes that the data on children in care should be improved.

Improved data on children in care
Demos recommends that those producing outcomes data relating to children in care adopt a 'value added' approach to take into account children's backgrounds; and publish longitudinal analyses of the data it collects from local authorities.

We currently compare children from backgrounds of deprivation, neglect and abuse with children from stable family backgrounds, and attribute the difference in outcomes to the care system (in which those children may only have stayed for a matter of months.) By failing to take into account or controlling for background characteristics, we generate a fundamentally flawed picture of the care system. As we explain in section 1, those few studies which have attempted to compare like with like (children in care with other vulnerable children not in care) have in fact shown that children in care can do as well or better than their peers from similar backgrounds. It is important therefore that children in care and care leavers are compared with those from similar peer groups to better take into account their disadvantaged backgrounds.

This does not mean promoting a poverty of aspiration, but evaluations of the outcomes for children in care should be based on a comparison of like with like, using a value added approach, rather than a 'snapshot', which benchmarks against national averages. Children who have severe emotional problems on entering care may never achieve five A*–C grades at GCSE, but if they have improved mental wellbeing after coming into care, this must be captured.

We also believe the publication of *annual snapshots* of the SSDA 903 data, which records a range of outcomes, also contributes to a skewed perception of the care system. The SSDA 903 does, in fact, track children over time, and this data would enable the public and researchers to see how children's outcomes may be improving while in care. However, the DCSF (now DfE) has not published longitudinal analysis of this data. Instead, annual snapshots are published, which, given the mobility of the care population, means we are comparing the outcomes of *different* populations year on year. Such data cannot show any improvement in children's outcomes over time, and it is vital that we move to this system in order to evaluate the 'impact' of care properly.

A better understanding of placement and care journey costs

Demos recommends that local authority budgets for children's services move away from perceived costs and break down actual costs of each placement type and intervention.

Value-added and longitudinal measures of children's outcomes may help change perceptions of the care system, but will not drive real reform unless spending decisions at local level change. To achieve this, local authorities need both a better understanding of the outcomes of different types of care placement (which could be provided by the SSDA 903) *and* the costs associated with these placements. We deal with this latter issue here. Currently, local authority budgets do not have a transparent breakdown of costs associated with each placement, but rather rely on perceived costs. This makes it difficult to establish which placement types, and which actions, are cost-effective.

We suggest local authorities look to the cost calculator for children's services (CCFCS)[275] to break down their costs more accurately. The calculator, developed by the Centre for Child and Family Research as part of a DfES funded research study, is a computer software application and costing methodology designed to calculate the costs to the public purse of providing services to children in care. The cost calculator aggregates costs from actual placements and all the associated costs of each child in a local authority. It does this by using data which local authorities already collect on all the placements of looked-after children for the SSDA 903 annual return to the DfE. By analysing the dates of placement changes, children's age milestones, reviews and key services, the CCFCS can identify all the services actually required and delivered for each child as they pass through the various processes involved in being looked after by the local authority. The reports produced by the cost calculator allow users to compare the costs of the care histories of different groups of children, for example children who achieve particular outcomes or who have particular needs.

In attributing costs to different children's care pathways, the CCFCS could prove a highly effective tool in enabling local authorities to better understand the relationship between timeliness or type of placement and cost, and ultimately (with the right longitudinal data being collected regarding outcomes – see above) between cost and outcome. Our own exemplar journeys of two children are extremely informative in demonstrating how early placement decisions are related to later costs, but we were limited in our analysis by the availability of data. By combining a CCFCS model with longitudinal outcomes data, such care journeys could be used as powerful tools to demonstrate the cost-effectiveness of more timely interventions and more stable care journeys.

However, annual budgeting may make it difficult to take into account longer term outcomes or attribute cost savings to them, and may also make it difficult for authorities to under-stand how placement delays generate costs over time.

There are reports that some children's services departments have already shifted to multi-year spending plans (in line with the comprehensive spending review) allowing annual budgets to be carried over from year to year. Multi-year spending plans are an important step in the right direction, and where appropriate other Local Authorities should use these to manage annual budgets more flexibly for looked-after children.Some placement costs clearly need to be carried over through a number of years based on evidence that savings will be made later on via improved outcomes. Although this would be a complex change, it could alter the culture of decision making in a way that could give rise to real long-term benefits for looked-after children.

Targeted recommendations

Changing the philosophy behind our perception of the care system will go far in promoting more positive outcomes – as we outline above, many of the flaws in the current system are a result of a system which is poorly *used*, not poor in and of itself. That said, there is certainly room for improvement. The current system suffers from local variation and a patchiness in outcomes which is difficult to defend.

In these next chapters, we present specific recommendations aimed at delivering more stability and continuity for children in care, and promote secure relationships which take account of birth family ties. This should be the goal for all children in care, regardless of age, placement type, or length of stay. The current system is already capable of creating such experiences, so a foundation of good practice already exists. Our recommendations take this into account by drawing on many examples of good practice as inspiration.

Recommendations for early intervention and less delay

1　Demos recommends there should be a government audit of local authority policies on managing their care populations and research into associated child outcomes.
2　Demos recommends the 'tapering' of the care system for families in need of occasional support, for example by local authorities making 'support care' arrangements matching foster carers and families more widely available.
3　Demos recommends there should be a statutory duty on local authorities to offer family group conferencing.

4   Demos calls for the government to provide seed for concurrent planning in local authorities wishing to pilot the service.
5   Demos calls for a renewed government focus on adoption timeliness and a DfE review of the 12-month target.
6   Demos recommends that all local authorities consider establishing permanency planning tracking panels.

Recommendations for stability

7   Demos recommends that the DfE makes mental health assessments of children entering care mandatory, using a standardised multi-disciplinary measure.
8   Demos calls for the Children's Workforce Development Council (CWDC) to include mental health training in training standards for foster and residential care workers.
9   Demos recommends that primary care trusts commission on-site CAMHS support for children in residential care and residential staff.
10 Demos recommends that local authorities make short breaks and placement support workers available to foster carers on request.
11 Demos proposes introducing social pedagogy training in CWDC standards in order to spread existing good practice in residential care work.
12 Demos calls on the DfE to amend care planning guidance to ensure there are fewer failed reunifications, and to introduce better resourced and time limited reunification plans.

Recommendations for supported transition to independence

13 Demos recommends that looked-after children teams and 16 plus teams shadow one another before and after transition.
14 Demos calls for local authorities to use personal advisers at an earlier age and for CWDC to outline specific training requirements.

15 Demos urges the government to raise the care leaving age to 18 and asks the DfE to support flexible approaches to allow young people to stay on in placements to 21.

16 Demos recommends that DfE amends transition support guidance to prioritise emotional and mental health support.

17 Demos recommends that DfE guidance explicitly applies the resilience model to transition planning, and independent reviewing officers are trained accordingly.

18 Demos calls for the wider availability of supported accommodation through commissioning and active promotion by government and local authorities.

19 Demos recommends floating support services are made more readily available by local authorities, and calls for the government to create a statutory 'right to return' for all care leavers.

13 Recommendations for early intervention and less delay

Time is a crucial element in work with children and should be reckoned in days and months rather than years.[276]

With this set of recommendations we look at the steps that could be taken to improve the beginning of a child's care journey. In earlier chapters we outlined the established body of evidence on the damaging impact of delay, drift and impermanence. We also argued above that the care system should be used more proactively as a form of destigmatised family support.

Consequently, these recommendations emphasise strategies, services and approaches that facilitate earlier intervention. Not all are immediately cost neutral, but in light of the escalating costs associated with intervening late we believe they will be cost-effective in the longer term. They are specifically targeted at addressing local authority variations in the use of care, increasing the use of earlier, targeted family support and reducing drift after entry into the system.

> ### Case study – Concurrent planning
> *As part of our research into ways of minimising delay for children when they first enter the care system, Demos profiled three concurrent planning projects and reviewed the research literature on this approach. We interviewed staff from local authorities in Brighton & Hove and Devon with a member of staff from the concurrent team at Coram in London. We also interviewed a consultant who had advised several of the projects in England.*

The objectives of concurrent planning

Designed to combat drift and delay in the care system, concurrent planning is a form of case planning for young children, which pursues the goals of adoption and reunification simultaneously. Reduced to its essential elements, the concurrent planning process asks the social worker to manage intense and targeted outreach to engage birth parents in the reunification process, along with the participation of foster parents who are approved as foster carers and adopters, and who are willing to be 'potentially permanent' adoptive parents.[277] Concurrent planning was originally developed by Linda Katz and her colleagues at Lutheran Social Services in the USA in the 1980s. Some of the key elements were as follows:

· *early assessment of the likelihood of reunification between birth parents and infant*
· *the simultaneous development of reunification and adoption plans*
· *placement with foster families who are approved to adopt the child*
· *a new goal of 'timely permanence', with reunification as the objective*

Assessment of potential cases was based on a standardised assessment tool known as 'differential diagnosis'. This was designed by Lutheran Social Services to gauge the likelihood of reunification. Katz argued that concurrent planning should be applied where the prognosis for reunification is poor – as in cases where the parents have child or substance abuse histories – and is more effective for younger children.[278]

Concurrent planning in the UK

In mid-1990s the first concurrent planning projects were introduced in the England. Five concurrent planning teams have since been set up in the UK, two within voluntary adoption agencies – Goodman and Coram – and three embedded within local authorities – Brighton & Hove, Devon and Kent. All the British services have adopted different approaches with varying outcomes, but the majority of placements have ended in adoption rather than reunification with birth families. In our research we focused on the approaches of teams at Coram, Brighton & Hove and Devon.

The concurrent planning service at Coram was launched in late 1999, originally funded by the Department of Health with grants from two local authorities (via money from the government's 'Quality Protects' initiative). Today, Coram supports the concurrent planning service using fees paid by the local authority for concurrent planning placements (which are higher than the interagency adoption fees). To a large extent this arrangement is dependent on the adoption agency receiving referrals from social workers, for which there need to be high levels of awareness in the participating local authorities about the project.

The Brighton & Hove service was also established in 1999, also with the help of Quality Protects funding. Originally the concurrency team was 'embedded' in the local authority, with the advantage that the team can develop a more 'complementary role' with field social workers. A decision was recently taken to change the structure of the team. Now assessment work with the birth families (which was previously undertaken by the concurrency team) is undertaken by the area social work teams as in all care proceedings, with the assessment and supervision of concurrent carers remaining within the Adoption and Permanence Service.

Devon has developed its concurrent service similarly to the way Brighton & Hove now operates, creating a small 'team' around each case or referral. Devon is also operating on a smaller scale with one case ongoing and only three placements so far (two of which went to adoption with the third baby about to be returned to the birth mother). In this case the local authority did not access a distinct stream of funding; the money for the service was found in the existing budget.

Does it work?

Our research would seem to indicate that concurrent planning is a resource intensive, but effective way of reducing delay in adoption processes and at the same time working intensively with birth parents to explore the possibility of reunification. This is supported in the literature; by using mainstream adoption services as a comparison group Monck et al performed an evaluation of three of these projects. Monck et al concluded that 'on the basis that policy-makers need to know "what works", it is possible to say with confidence that concurrent planning worked well for the children in this study'.[279] As they explain: 'concurrent planning was not seen as a perfect solution to the problems surrounding the placement of children in care, but it was a solution that put the child's needs at the centre of the social work decision-making'.[280]

Monck et al's evaluation also shows that the concurrency services compare very favourably against national performance in terms of minimising delay. The children in concurrency placements were considerably younger than those placed in mainstream adoption placements, so to control for selection bias the pilots were also compared against the national cohort of adoptees under 1 year old. Against the national cohort (adopted during the year ending March 2001) the concurrency children waited on average less than half as long for their adoption order to be granted.[281]

In a study published in 2009, which focused on the contact experience of babies and toddlers in the Coram concurrent planning project, Kenrick concludes that on the principle that the approach 'aimed to prevent "drift" and achieve early permanency for very young infants and children within the care system, the [concurrent planning] project must be judged a success'.[282] Kenrick found that concurrently cared for children 'do not appear to have had difficulties with attachments'.[283] Positive though Kenrick's conclusion is, it must be taken with caution: the sample size considered was small and the majority of children were placed before 5.5 months of age.

Limitations

The success of concurrent planning is of course, predicated on children and families being identified early enough and on a sufficient number of willing carers being found. Of the 219 referrals in the Monck et al study, 43 per cent were rejected for want of suitable concurrency carers. Carers are asked to make a considerable time commitment to ongoing contact sessions between the child and the birth parents, in the knowledge that adoption is far from a certain outcome. Our own research confirmed that staff felt foster carers are asked to take on considerable risk in this respect, both because the child may be reunified with birth parents and because some infants may be suffering from the effects of a maternal dependency on drugs or alcohol so developmental outcomes were uncertain.

But it is notable that difficulty recruiting in carers was not a problem in all of the projects, some projects did not find this to be problematic. And it is also worth noting that the staff interviewed also identified some benefits of the intensive contact sessions for birth parents and carers:

Ultimately carers are generally able to relate to families and work with them. They can feel strong empathy when they meet the birth parents who are struggling with a number of personal problems.

If the child was ultimately adopted, some staff suggested this early relationship helped to ensure that positive contact with the birth parents could continue for the child.

Concurrent planning also presents challenges for social workers. In our interviews almost all of the services reported difficulties in keeping social workers fully informed and engaged in referring possible cases to them. This is reflected in the literature on concurrent planning, which points to misapplication of the assessment tools, and some misunderstanding of the concept.[284]

In our interviews one of the most consistent barriers identified to establishing successful concurrent planning projects was the perception (among social workers and the judiciary) that it represented a form of 'adoption by the back door'. It was felt that this confusion had been exacerbated by the fact that the majority of placements had ended with adoption rather than reunification. In two interviews it was said that courts preferred to delay taking a more permanent step in favour of the 'safer option' of mother and baby placements. It was often suggested that judiciary was under-estimating the importance of establishing long-term attachments in the first six months to a year of a child's life. At present, stable placements for infants are by no means guaranteed in the care system, which can result in a number of broken attachments in infancy.

In particular the 'Munby judgment' was described as being as a key obstacle to achieving court approval for concurrent planning. In February 2008, Mr Justice Munby ruled against Nottingham County Council for removing a baby from an 18-year-old mother with a mental health history.[285] The case has proved to be a landmark in increasing the burden of proof on social services to separate mother and child, proving that 'imminent risk' is particularly challenging in concurrent planning cases, because the assessment of risk is often based on the history of the birth parents.

What improves the chances of successful projects?

All of the services profiled in this project were clear about the importance of having a senior champion in the local authority who could act as an advocate of concurrent planning from the outset. Training for social workers and the dissemination of information on the aims of the project to the courts and judiciary were also crucial to generating a sufficient number of referrals and court approvals. Working with foster carers who were emotionally resilient and prepared to take on the risks involved was of course essential.

Given the additional contact that needs to be facilitated between birth parents and the child, social workers with small caseloads and considerable expertise made it possible to manage cases successfully. Whether the service was embedded or operating from a voluntary agency, engagement with the project needed to span child protection, adoption and fostering teams.

What next for concurrent planning?

This potential of concurrent planning has already been acknowledged by the government in the Care Matters white paper and in the new care planning and review regulations. But this endorsement has not resulted in significant practical support. Most of the services we profiled owed their existence to one-off streams of funding such as quality protects, or to committed managers in local authorities reorganising their budgets. Successful concurrent planning projects depend on specialist professionals, who can invest considerable time in supporting contact with birth parents and children. Although the outcomes (reunification or adoption) are likely to be cheaper and swifter with concurrent planning, the funding cycles of local authorities are often too short term for the benefits to be fully realised. The Goodman project is already in the process of closing owing to financial difficulties of its parent organisation, Manchester Adoption Society; previously this was the only project offering concurrent planning outside the south of England.[286] Kent local authority's concurrent planning project has also closed recently.

It should be noted that while concurrent planning 'frontloads' the costs, it is very likely to minimise delay and sequential placements at a crucial stage – which is likely to result in cost savings later on. However, the pressure on local authority budgets, along with the challenges of securing court approval for concurrent planning, means that this approach in England faces an uncertain future without active government support and promotion.

1 Demos recommends there should be a government audit of local authority policies on managing their care populations and research into associated child outcomes

Demos believes that the government should work towards greater consistency in local authority approaches to managing their care populations, and ensure that these policies are evidenced based. Although this may be counter to a move to devolve control over public services to local level, Demos believes that the quality of the parenting the state provides is one area where a nationally consistent approach is vital.

Far too little is currently known about the reasons behind the variation in the size of the care populations in different local authorities discussed at the beginning of this report. This variation, it has been argued, cannot only be explained by socio-economic local trends but could also be attributable to a range of different factors such as the approach of professionals, variation in thresholds, the approach of managers or the budget constraints of individual local authorities.[287]

The government should therefore undertake an audit to investigate the reasons behind this variation across England and, more importantly, assess the outcomes associated with approaches that aim to 'prevent' entry into care. We would recommend commissioning longitudinal research on child outcomes in local authorities that prioritise 'prevention' approaches, to establish how and if this form of support can be effective. Local authorities that opt to have smaller care populations should be doing so in the knowledge that this strategy will be the most effective in promoting positive outcomes for children. Children and their families should not be exposed to a postcode lottery in family support services or thresholds to entering care.

2 *Demos recommends the 'tapering' of the care system for families in need of occasional support, for example by local authorities making 'support care' arrangements matching foster carers and families more widely available.*

Based on the audit of local authority policies outlined above, Demos recommends that local authorities make family services such as 'support care' more available for children on the edge of care in families that require more intensive support, where permanent placements are not appropriate. Support care is short-term, foster care. It aims to support families in crisis and it is time-limited, typically no longer than one night a week or a couple of weekends a month over a six- to nine-month period.

As children's services budgets are squeezed, the investment in family support after Care Matters should not be regarded as an optional add-on to the care system, but as a core part of the service offered to vulnerable children. We do not, however, support the view that family services should be used with the sole objective of 'preventing' entry into care. Family support is the right option only when it can be shown to be in the best interests of the child.

Currently, ratios of spending on looked-after children compared with family support services range from 2:1 in some local authorities (where a greater proportion of their budget is dedicated to supporting children to remain their families) to 10:1 in others.[288] This variation was evident during the course of this research, with some local authorities making family support available much earlier and more consistently.

For example, we visited Merton local authority, where family support services are deployed early and proactively in families whose children might be at risk of going into care. Support packages vary, from funding day care for children (providing parents with a break and also to support children's early development), to offering intensive daily support or home visits from a support worker one or two times per week. Parenting interventions are tailored according to the level of need and are time limited (after six months a decision is normally taken on whether continued support is appropriate). Some of the support will be provided by universal services, for example, in Sure Start centres.

In the future Merton plans to investigate the option of providing 'support care' between a foster parent and the birth parents, with each caring for the child for a portion of time during the week. While recognising that such an approach would not be appropriate for families where safeguarding was an issue, Demos believes that using care as a form of family support in this way could have real potential for those families who need occasional (rather than ongoing and intensive) support. In a review of literature on the impact of care on children's welfare, Forrester et al also suggest that for children who need periodic care local authorities could explore 'matching' families with a foster family or specially recruited family to provide ongoing support and short breaks.[289] This would clearly have benefits for children who could build a relationship with just one foster family over a period of time.

We tested this idea in our focus groups of foster carers. Many of the participants could see the benefits of this approach, if it was carefully targeted at the right families, in tapering the edges of the care system and creating stability for a particular group of children who can oscillate in and out of care at an older age.

3 *Demos recommends there should be a statutory duty on local authorities to offer family group conferencing.*

Demos believes family group conferencing should be made available in the following circumstances: in advance of care proceedings being initiated (except in emergencies) in order to find out whether family support should be offered; before family reunifications to establish the extended support networks that might help the reunification and also as a means of discussing the reunification 'action plan' (see the reunification recommendation below); and as part of preparations for leaving care to help care leavers reinitiate contacts (where appropriate) and establish what support might be in place to ease transition to independence.

In recent years local authorities have begun using family group conferences more frequently. In England, 69 per cent of local authorities now have some form of family group conference project (in house or commissioned) or are in the process of setting one up.[290] In *Care Matters* it was announced that the government would 'fund a programme of regional training events to equip managers and practitioners with the necessary skills to develop and sustain the Family Group Conference model'.[291] In 2008 the Public Law Outline introduced a requirement that a record of discussions with the family (which could include a family plan arising out of a family group conference) is filed by the local authority when proceedings are issued. The best practice guidance on PLO13 reiterates the importance of planning in partnership with whole family and seeking alternative potential carers in pre-proceedings stage as appropriate.[292]

The increasing uptake of family group conference services or in-house provision is promising, but the availability of this service still varies considerably between local authorities and it is not automatically available at key moments. Of course the priority for every local authority will be safeguarding, and family group conferences do not in any way eliminate the need for child protection conferences. However, as a relatively low cost strategy to reduce delays associated with identifying kinship carers and to target family support before crisis point, family group conferences should become standard in local authorities.

4 *Demos calls for the government to provide seed funding for concurrent planning in local authorities wishing to introduce the service.*

Although concurrent planning can be resource intensive, it is also extremely successful at minimising delay and uncertainty for a specific group of entrants to the care system who are at high risk of drift. The cost benefits of targeting support for this group could be substantial. The scope for using concurrent planning with older groups of children, whose care costs also often escalate over time, also remains under-explored. It is important that central government invests in approaches such as this, which shift the risk of uncertainty experienced by children entering the care system to the adults involved. The care planning, placement and review guidance of March 2010 states that:

For children who are unable to return to their birth or wider family, adoption offers a lifelong and legally permanent new family. Twin track or parallel planning, including concurrent planning, may provide a means to securing permanence at an early stage for some children.[293]

Given this recognition, Demos recommends that DfE should support local authorities to make concurrent planning part of their 'adoption offer'. This could be provided through voluntary adoption agencies servicing more than one local authority or through in-house 'embedded' teams of practitioners. The necessary upfront investment should be made available to establish the service and target it towards those families who could benefit from intensive support towards reunification or children who need permanency in their early years.

To have the best chance of success, the introduction of concurrent planning should be accompanied by DfE investment in training for social workers in the aims of the projects and the necessary assessment criteria, as well as targeted recruitment of carers willing to enter into such arrangements. This could be supplemented by information dissemination for the courts and attachment training for judiciary about the implications of delay and placement movement in infancy.

5 *Demos calls for a renewed government focus on adoption timeliness and a DfE review of the 12-month target.*

Adoption should be one of the first options for the group of children in need of long-term permanence. As outlined in previous chapters, adoption is associated with better outcomes for children, although it may only be appropriate for the minority of children. For those children for whom adoption is identified as the best course of action, the evidence proves that timeliness is essential – delays have significant implications for a child's chance of being successfully placed for adoption. Research shows that rates of adoption breakdown increase from 10 per cent for children placed under the age of 10 to 20 per cent to 40 per cent for those placed when over 10.[294]

Demos recommends that the government initiates a renewed push on the use of adoption, focusing on the root causes of delay, and reviews local authority performance against the 12-month target. In this review consideration should be given to the possibility of introducing a shorter timeline or target for young children or infants who need to find permanency as quickly as possible.

Such a step would be relatively low cost to undertake, but could reap significant benefits, as evidenced by the previous political drive led by Tony Blair to increase the use of adoption. At that time, a target was set in England for 2004/5 to increase by 40 per cent the number of looked-after children who were adopted and to aim for a 50 per cent increase in these adoptions by 2006. To begin with this policy initiative was effective, and about 1,000 more children were adopted from care in 2005 than in 2000, a 37 per cent increase in just five years.[295] However, we have now lost momentum on this issue: latest figures show that in 2008/9 only 3,300 children were adopted from care.[296] Although this was a slight increase on the previous year, there has been a decline of 13 per cent since 2005.

As the same time, delays in the adoption process have also been on the rise. Recent performance on the National Indicator 61 (which measures the timeliness of placements of looked-after children for adoption following an agency decision that the child should be placed for adoption) demonstrates that initial momentum has been lost. In 2009 75.8 per cent of children who were adopted during the year were placed for adoption within 12 months. This was about 4 percentage points less than in 2005. Moreover, a significant proportion of children with adoption recommendations are still never actually placed – estimates suggest this is now 25 per cent at any one time.[297]

6 *Demos suggests that all local authorities consider establishing permanency planning tracking panels.*

There is currently a requirement for a permanency plan to be considered four months after a child becomes looked after. The plan can be for a return to the parents with support, through special guardianship, fostering or adoption, or remaining in residential care until they leave care.

Some local authorities have already introduced 'permanency tracking panels' to enable them to identify where these plans are being delayed as soon as possible, for example in Harrow and Cardiff.[298] Demos recommends that this practice is extended to other local authorities and is acknowledged as best practice in care planning guidance. Tracking panels would be tasked with taking an overview of planning and delay in the local authority, rather than in individual cases.

Demos believes this is necessary as in spite of the introduction of clearer planning guidance[299] and new statutory guidance for independent reviewing officers[300] in overseeing permanence in *individual* cases, on *overall* performance on permanency planning local authorities still have a great deal of improvement to make and should be subject to greater scrutiny.

Although some costs would be associated with establishing these panels, the commensurate reduction in delay (improving the chances of more stable care careers) would generate significantly larger and ongoing cost savings. Swifter adoption processes would also save children's departments substantial immediate costs: Selwyn et al found that of the 130 cases they reviewed, in four out of every ten cases (41 per cent), children waited longer than a year before the making of a permanency plan. For these children the average delay was 2.7 years. For those children who were adopted quickly, care costs amounted to an average of £8,904, with time spent in foster care around 26 weeks. Conversely, those children who waited longest to be adopted cost children's departments £94,551, due to a wait of more than five years in care.[301]

14 Recommendations for stability during care

In this report we have reviewed a substantial amount of evidence that demonstrates the importance of stable, good quality care journeys. Stability is vital in allowing children to form warm and secure relationships with those who care for them, and in building routines and consistency, which improve their emotional resilience, allowing them to stay at the same school and in the same friendship groups. Fewer, longer-term care placements have been associated with more positive outcomes, including improved emotional and mental health and educational attainment. In the light of these findings, we have considered carefully the factors which are likely to prevent placements from breaking down in this section and built our recommendations around this objective.

Case study – Essex County Council Social Pedagogy Project

This process is not just about training or altering practice. It's about changing the culture and ethos of residential services. We are inviting our whole residential workforce to become actively involved in constructing an English social pedagogic understanding and approach.[302]
Essex county council case study interviewee

Demos visited Leverton House residential care home in March 2010 to meet Essex County Council's children's residential services development manager, four residential care workers and the project's internal researcher, to discuss how the social pedagogical approach is being implemented across Essex.

Why social pedagogy?

Social pedagogy can also be seen as 'just good residential care work'. Many residential workers who have never come into contact with social pedagogy already work with children in a way that is child-centred, creative and reflective. However, the important benefit that social pedagogy can bring to English residential care is that it provides a coherent theoretical framework for articulating effective residential care practice. As recent studies have shown, many English residential workers feel inhibited from developing personal relationships with the children they care for 'due to increasing procedure, policies, time spent on risk assessment and allegations from the young people'.[303] *Social pedagogy can provide English residential care workers with a coherent set of values and techniques they can use to challenge the 'institutionalisation' that has dominated English residential care in recent decades and prioritise building positive relationships between staff and children.*

Essex launched their three-year project to introduce social pedagogy into their children's residential services in September 2008. The project is being delivered in partnership between Essex's residential services department, all 12 of Essex's residential children's homes and ThemPra, which is providing training in social pedagogy to residential staff teams and working directly with staff teams and children to support them in adapting to a pedagogic way of working. The project is being evaluated independently by the University of Lincoln and an internal researcher has been appointed to help staff and children feed their learning and reflection back into the project as it develops.

Progress

Over a third of Essex's residential care workforce has undertaken the initial six-day course in social pedagogy. Residential workers from the 12 children's homes have set up a practitioner's network that meets every two months. Staff use this forum to share the challenges and successes they have experienced in introducing a pedagogic way of working. It has also been used to engage and provide additional support to staff who have not yet received training in social pedagogy.

Thirty residential staff have undertaken an additional two-day residential course to prepare them to work as social pedagogy agents. These staff will take a lead role in supporting and inspiring other residential care workers to develop their practice and create a pedagogic culture in their residential care home.

How social pedagogic principles are changing residential care workers' practice in Essex

Several social pedagogic principles are changing the practices of residential care workers in Essex, including:

- *approaching each child as an individual*
- *using shared activities to build relationships and create new learning opportunities*
- *introducing a new approach to assessing risk*
- *emphasising the shared life space*
- *emphasising continuous learning through reflective practice*

Approaching each child as an individual: *social pedagogy emphasises the importance of developing personal relationships between child and carer. This principle has enriched a previous emphasis on the need for consistency, enabling residential care workers to develop individual relationships with the children they care for.*

Using shared activities to build relationships and create new learning opportunities: *children have been very receptive to this approach and have particularly enjoyed having the opportunity to teach staff something new. One residential care worker commented:*

It's shared learning really. It's very much doing things with the young person that they want to do and that the member of staff wants to do rather than doing it to the young person. So learning a new skill or craft together rather than dropping the young person off at the swimming pool and saying 'pick you up in twenty minutes'.

A new approach to assessing risk: *the pedagogic approach encourages staff to balance risk with opportunity before making a decision on whether an activity is in a child's best interests. This has made staff feel more empowered and confident in judging risks for themselves, without only relying on guidelines. One residential care worker commented:*

Social pedagogy allows you to recognise that there are boundaries, you have to be accountable for your actions.

The shared life space: *social pedagogy emphasises the fact that the residential home is the staff member's workplace, but the child's home. People want flexibility in their own home, so rules should not be imposed on young people arbitrarily or without discussion.*

An emphasis on continuous learning through reflective practice: *each residential worker now keeps a reflective diary, which they use to consider what they have done with children that has worked well and what could be improved. In some of the residential homes a 'reflective handover' has been built into the 45-minute handover time between staff to provide an opportunity to consider what they did in their shift that worked well and what could be improved.*

Benefits
Staff have reported a new spontaneity and sense of fun in their relationships with the children they care for, as one residential care worker commented:

Within a five or ten minute interaction whilst roller-blading she approached me completely differently.

Training in social pedagogy is providing residential workers with a stronger professional identity and a confidence in their work that was sometimes lacking previously. This improved professional status is already contributing to improved relationships with other agencies including social work teams and CAMHS.

Lessons from implementation

To achieve a culture change on this scale, the workforce needs to be engaged as widely and inclusively as possible. Residential workers were more likely to resist changes to their practice if they had not yet received the social pedagogy training. The changes in working methods that are required to embed social pedagogy may be quite far-reaching, therefore there will be an ongoing need to support staff in achieving these changes.

Each residential home will have its own culture, so staff will want to implement their training in different ways. Essex County Council has found that the staff practitioners' network is a useful way of sharing good practice between homes.

Next steps

The project team aims to move towards applying social pedagogy across the board; their vision is to use social pedagogy to provide a coherent theoretical framework for bringing together the perspectives of all agencies that work with children and young people in Essex.

To help realise this goal the project team are developing an action plan to engage Essex County Council with social pedagogy more broadly (including schools, social work teams and CAMHS).

Case study – Kensington and Chelsea 'life skills' project

The on-site Life Coach CAMHS worker has undoubtedly increased access for both young people and staff to a mental health resource and has gone, in some way, to reduce the stigma associated with accessing mental health support.[304]

Whistler walk case study interviewee

Demos visited Whistler Walk residential unit in November 2009 to meet the unit manager and the CAMHS child clinical psychologist who is delivering the life skills project.

The life skills project was set up to address the problem of a high level of unmet need for mental health support among young people in residential care. The project was initially piloted for a year at Whistler Walk, which is a long-term residential unit, and has expanded in its second year to also include St Marks, which is a shorter stay residential unit in the borough.

The problem to address

Whistler Walk residential unit had experienced a longstanding mismatch between residents' emotional and psychological needs and successful engagement with CAMHS. Research has shown that young people in residential care are particularly likely to have emotional and behavioural problems; however, residential care staff at Whistler Walk and St Marks found that young people were not always eligible for help, particularly if their situation was unstable. Young people could also be resistant to receiving support from CAMHS as they found the 'mental health' label stigmatising. This meant that young people were more likely to turn to residential support workers for help with their problems, and staff did not necessarily feel equipped with the right skills as many had only received very basic mental health training.

Purpose and set-up of the project

The name 'life coach' was chosen to avoid the stigma associated with mental health services. The life coach is a CAMHS child clinical psychologist who has been funded by a grant from CAMHS to work with young people and staff onsite at Whistler Walk and St Mark's residential homes. The project was initially funded for one year but has since been extended for a second year.

Three frameworks were selected for the project:

- *life skills, which include cognitive skills, interpersonal skills and emotional coping skills*
- *a solution focused approach, which works from the perspective that young people are best placed to identify solutions to their problems*
- *social pedagogy, which focuses on the conscious use of relationships between staff and young people*

Young people have either weekly or fortnightly sessions with the life coach and are encouraged to focus on their achievements and the progress they are making, as opposed to dwelling on their problems.

The life coach also works with staff, attending staff team meetings and providing training on mental health issues, such as understanding the symptoms of depression, and techniques to improve their practice such as reflective learning and parenting styles. The life coach is working with staff to help them work in a way that is more child-centred and to focus on the emotional as opposed to practical side of caring for young people. As she is based onsite, the life coach is able to offer staff informal support with addressing young people's emotional and behavioural issues as they arise, making assessments and offering support on the spot. However, as an employee of CAMHS, the life coach is also able to retain a degree of independence. This helps build trust with young people as their sessions are kept confidential.

Benefits of the project

The life coach has been able to provide young people with emotional support as well as mental health support. The majority of young people at Whistler Walk have now engaged with life skills sessions and over the period of the project the number of incidents of physical threats and verbal assaults has reduced. One young person has used her sessions to address her barriers to engaging with her education and has since successfully completed a term at college.

Staff have reported that the project has helped them to contextualise difficult and challenging behaviour by taking mental health issues into consideration. They have also learnt new tools to manage young people's behaviours and feel more able to influence these behaviours.

The life coach has also worked with other agencies such as education staff to increase their awareness of young people's mental health issues and how this may influence their behaviour and attendance.

Challenges

The project has expanded so that in the second year of the project the life coach also works with young people and staff at St Mark's Children's Home, which is a short-term unit. It continues to be challenging to provide mental health support to young people who are in a short-term or emergency placement as they might not feel it is worth engaging over such a short period of time.

The project is currently being funded by grant funding from CAMHS; there is therefore a need to investigate more sustainable sources of funding to ensure that the residential homes can continue to offer integrated mental health support for young people in the long term.

Case study – East Sussex placement support service

East Sussex County Council originally set up a 'special placement scheme' to provide intensive support to eight young people in foster care who had complex needs and would otherwise have needed to go into residential care. When this service was up and running, it soon became apparent that a larger number of young people in foster care with complex needs could benefit from the support of placement support workers. Therefore, from 2001 East Sussex County Council developed a more universal placement support service, which is now working with over 75 young people in foster care. A further 20 young people receive intensive support from the 'special placement' scheme, which is limited to young people with the highest needs.

Placement support workers

Placement support workers offer practical and emotional support to young people and their foster carers to promote placement stability. The practical side of the role may mean taking out the carer's own child, so that the carer can spend one to one time with the young person they care for, or give the young person more opportunities to participate in extracurricular activities and providing their carer with short breaks from caring.

Placement support workers also provide an important source of emotional support to young people in foster care. They are often involved with the same young person for years and can maintain a continuous relationship despite changes of social worker or placement, providing a much-needed source of stability. Placement support workers undertake long-term individual work with young people in foster care to work on building their self-esteem and positive attachments, developing their social skills through group activities and managing challenging behaviours. The service is particularly targeted at young people as they enter adolescence, to provide foster carers with additional support when it is needed, and prevent placements from reaching crisis point.

7 *Demos recommends that the DfE makes mental health assessments of children entering care mandatory, using a standardised multi-disciplinary measure.*

Demos recommends that the government amend the statutory requirement on general health assessments to include the use of a standardised mental health assessment framework, which should be implemented as a discreet and stand-alone element of general health assessments. This assessment should include the Strengths and Difficulties Questionnaire (SDQ), and where possible should be completed with input from a member of the child's birth family or another adult who has a relationship with the child such as a teacher, to ensure that any emotional and behavioural difficulties the child has are correctly identified.

The government is making some progress in ensuring that looked-after children's mental health needs are identified and met. There is now a statutory requirement that looked-after children's mental health is assessed as part of their initial health assessment when they enter care, to form the basis of their health plan.[305] However, the evidence suggests that there is a great deal of variation in how health assessments are conducted and who they are conducted by. A research study informing the 2009 guidance *Promoting the Health and Well-Being of Looked After Children* found that 'there is no consistency and considerable variability in what is covered in initial health assessments', and many of the stakeholders consulted felt that insufficient attention was given to children's mental health and wellbeing.

Furthermore, once any emotional or behavioural difficulties are identified, it is essential that this assessment is acted on and that adequate support and an appropriate placement are provided to meet the child's emotional and mental health needs, as outlined in the Care Planning Regulations.

Although this will come at an additional cost to local authorities, unmet mental health needs are such an important factor in placement breakdown, and behavioural and emotional problems are so common among children in care, that it very difficult to justify such assessments *not* being mandatory and standardised.

8 *Demos calls for the Children's Workforce Development Council (CWDC) to include mental health training in training standards for foster and residential care workers.*

The specialist role that CAMHS play in supporting looked-after children's mental health does not exist in isolation; foster and residential carers also play an important role in promoting looked-after children's wellbeing and good mental health at the front line and this should not be overlooked.

This is supported by a recommendation that was made in the final report of the 2008 National CAMHS Review:

There is a need for better basic knowledge of child development and mental health and psychological wellbeing across the children's workforce. The Government should ensure that all bodies responsible for initial training provide basic training in child development and mental health and psychological wellbeing.[306]

The CWDC's Training, Support and Development Standards for Foster Carers currently include recognition of the need for the foster carer to 'Know what "healthy care" means for the physical, mental, emotional and sexual health of children and young people'.[307] But we believe this needs to be developed into a more explicit recognition of the need for basic mental health training, given the prevalence of mental health needs in the looked-after population. The CWDC is also currently developing new professional practice standards for residential child care workers, and we urge the CWDC to also specify that residential care workers receive mental health training as part of their basic training.

In addition to this basic training, Demos also recommends that where looked-after children's health assessments identify more serious emotional or behavioural problems, or such problems become apparent over time, foster carers should have access to specialist training courses to help them understand and meet the child's daily needs. Similarly, residential care staff should also have the opportunity to receive training in the specific mental health problems that affect the children they work with.

As with some of the other recommendations we present, there will be a cost implication to this step. However, we must consider the numerous studies that have shown that children who have emotional and behavioural problems have an increased risk of placement disruption.[308] Carers who are better prepared to deal with these issues will not only increase the chances of maintaining that placement (and preventing all of the costs associated with a placement breakdown), but may also help prevent the escalation of more serious mental health problems by being better able to identify and address problems earlier on.

9 *Demos recommends that primary care trusts commission on-site CAMHS support for children in residential care and care staff.*

Demos recommends that where there is identified need, children and staff in residential care homes should have onsite access to a CAMHS worker. This resource would be commissioned by the PCT and could be shared between a number of residential children's homes that needed additional on-site support. The CAMHS worker would deliver this support within the residential home to remove some of the barriers to young people accessing the service. Mental health support sessions could be presented to young people as 'life coaching' to remove the stigma of engaging with the service.

Given the particularly high level of mental health needs experienced by many young people who are placed in residential care, it is concerning that these children tend to have the poorest access to CAMHS support. Residential care staff we spoke to through the course of the project described difficulty in accessing CAMHS support and long delays. The frequency of placement moves also contributed to this, particularly if children were placed outside the local authority before returning. More than one-third (11 out of 27) of the children's homes recently visited by Ofsted reported experiences of delays of between three and twelve months before young people were able to receive a service from CAMHS. Ofsted observed: 'In these situations, staff were left to manage young people's needs and difficulties without direct support or guidance.'[309]

Informed by the approach taken by the Whistler Walk residential home, the on-site CAMHS worker would work with young people and staff to increase their awareness of mental health issues. This would provide an additional source of emotional and practical support to staff who are coping with young people who display very challenging behaviour, and would address the need for a stronger working relationship between residential staff and CAMHS.

10 *Demos recommends that local authorities make respite support and placement support workers available to foster carers on request.*

Demos recommends that local authorities invest in providing short breaks for foster carers caring for children with challenging needs to reduce the likelihood of placement breakdown, particularly in the early stages of a placement when the task can seem particularly overwhelming.

A survey by the Fostering Network in 2003 found that foster carers' access to short breaks from caring was very mixed, with a number of foster carers rating the provision by their fostering service as poor. The Fostering Network's October 2009 policy recommendations specify that an effective support services for foster carers must include 'the availability of short breaks for those foster carers that need it and ask for it'.[310] The multidimensional treatment foster care model, which provides placements for young people with challenging behaviour and complex needs, is an example of good practice in providing foster carers with respite; this programme specifies a recommended minimum of one respite carer to seven foster care placements.[311] In our focus groups, foster carers who were caring for children or young people with particularly challenging support needs spoke of the importance of receiving respite care to their ability to continue with the placement:

When I was at the end of my tether, they offered me respite – I had to go in and ask for it, mind you. I now take it once every two weeks. It makes a real difference.

However, they also felt it was important to avoid introducing too many unfamiliar people into looked-after children's lives. Several commented that they would be unwilling to leave a child with somebody who was unfamiliar to them:

I wouldn't want to put my boys with somebody they don't know, who they haven't been around a lot.

Ideally, therefore, respite care should be provided by a carer who is already familiar to the child, and the same respite carer should be used each time to enable the child to develop a relationship with that person. Demos recommends that authorities look to the introduction of *placement support workers* as one method of providing a consistent source of short break support, as well as a source of practical help and emotional support for children in care and their foster parents, following East Sussex's approach. East Sussex's decision to increase the provision of placement support workers, in spite of additional costs, suggests that these are cost-effective in preventing placement breakdown and providing hands-on support for front line foster carers.

11 *Demos proposes introducing social pedagogy training in CWDC standards in order to spread existing good practice in residential care work*

Care Matters has sought to pilot and evaluate the effectiveness of social pedagogy in the context of English residential care. Given that the evaluation of the national pilot is not yet complete, it is too early to speculate on the successes of this programme. However, our research has led us to believe that many of the principles of social pedagogy are very much intuitive to the care workforce already. Therefore social pedagogy's greatest value will be in articulating these principles to allow for a greater recognition and replication of existing good practice.

Our discussions with Essex County Council, which has implemented training for its residential care workforce in social pedagogy theory and practice, 'in constructing an English social pedagogic understanding and approach', independently of the national pilot, leads us to support a recommendation first made by the Children, Schools and Families Select Committee:

We urge the Government to think broadly and creatively about the possible future applications of the social pedagogy approach in the care system rather than looking to import wholesale a separate new profession.[312]

With this in mind, Demos recommends that training in the social pedagogic approach should be included in the new qualification framework for residential care workers being developed by CWDC. We consider that this embedded approach has a greater chance of spreading good practice than the creation of a separate role of 'social pedagogue' to work alongside other members of the children's workforce.

12 *Demos calls on the DfE to amend care planning guidance to ensure there are fewer failed reunifications, and to introduce better resourced and time limited reunification plans.*

Given the negative effect that failed family reunifications can have on children in care, Demos recommends that care planning guidance, which now already seeks to improve reunification planning and assessment,[313] is further amended to stipulate that reunifications *cannot* be attempted if the problems that had originally instigated the child's need to be looked after have not been resolved. Where possible, local authorities should aim to make fewer, yet better resourced reunification attempts.

This would mean that where reunification is deemed appropriate and viable, a reunification plan for children should begin with support being provided to the family *before* reunification to address the underlying causes of their child being taken into care. Only once sufficient progress is made in this respect should a child be returned. The plan would then need to include a clear list of actions, which specified how change would need to be sustained and improvements built on once a child was home, a timeframe within which these must be achieved, and the course of action that will be taken if they fail to make these changes. This approach would guard against 'drift' and introduce greater transparency into the care planning process that would both highlight parental failure to comply and motivate more proactive case management. To prepare for the event that the parent may not be able to demonstrate that they have taken the actions required, an alternative plan for permanence for the child would also need to be specified at this early stage.

Although a reunification such as this would become more resource intensive, it also has a higher chance of being successful. It is clear that one successful reunification will be far less costly than several failed attempts leading to greater support needs once the child returns to care.

15 Recommendations for supported transition to independence

It is far from inevitable that a transition from care should represent an abrupt experience which disrupts existing attachments and sense of stability. Indeed, through the course of this project, we have seen how this transition, when undertaken sensitively, can provide opportunities for developing attachments that may not have been experienced during care.

The review of academic literature, case studies, interviews with academics and experts and then consultation with children in care, care leavers and foster carers have enabled us to develop a series of recommendations which we believe could improve young people's transitions to independence. These recommendations seek to ensure:

- that young people are ready, emotionally and practically, to leave care
- that stability and consistency is maintained during and after transition, including the maintenance of attachments formed during care
- that transition is gradual and responsive to a young person's needs, emulating more closely the natural experiences of young people leaving their birth families

Case study – Transition to independence in Northern Ireland

Northern Ireland's care leaving framework is guided by the Care Leaving Act 2002, which was implemented from 2005. It is based on England's Care Leavers Act 2000 but the resulting system is different in several key ways. The In Loco Parentis team visited Northern Ireland in November 2009 to explore these differences.

Before leaving

Northern Irish care leaving teams are invariably called '16 plus teams'. They engage with looked-after children (LAC) teams from when a child in care is 15 ½, getting to know the child's circumstances and needs, and planning for the young person's transition to 16 plus services. Their objective is to ensure the case transfer is undertaken in as seamless a manner as possible, thereby improving continuity across the transition and supporting a single pathway through care for each young person. The concept of seamless planning and positive interfaces with services that young people may need is being further developed through establishing agreed transition protocols for those young people who require continuing support to adult disability services.

Planning for the appointment of personal advisers commences also from age 15?to ensure that appropriate arrangements are in place for when the young person reaches 16 years of age. The Personal Adviser Service in the first instance seeks to identify with the young person and the LAC social worker or carer if there is anyone in the young person's existing network whom they would wish to assume the role of the personal adviser, for example, a previous carer, former residential worker or key worker, youth worker, mentor, significant adult and so on. Known as 'young person specific personal advisers', trusts have arrangements in place to satisfy themselves as to their suitability and availability to support the young person. Through the Personal Adviser Service, young person specific personal advisers receive induction and training and are paid per session for the support they provide to individual young people. Personal advisers also have their own manager, separate from the 16 plus team, who is a qualified social worker.

Between the ages of 13 and 15, children in care in Northern Ireland also work with a transition support worker. They work with teenagers on life and social skills, with the aim of supporting carers and the young people in care to better integrate 'preparation for adulthood' into the daily life experiences and routines of young people. Their remit is to ensure children in care are afforded experiential opportunities to develop skills and learning that will better equip them for the adult world. Such opportunities encompass personal development, health initiatives, social and community links and practical skills development such as learning about cooking, going to the bank, shopping, and so on. The language of 'leaving care' is replaced with an emphasis and focus on preparing for adulthood – the goal is to better equip adolescents for life during their earlier care career in the way the average teenager would learn about things at home. Transition support workers are also engaged in group work – and plans are in place to train looked-after children to hold educational and life skills classes for their peers, which have a fun and social element, to help build self-esteem, resilience, and so on.

At leaving

Northern Ireland care leaving teams use the 'Going the Extra Mile' (GEM) scheme, which allows foster children to stay at home with their foster families after 18 and until 21 with financial support given to foster carers. England is still at the pilot stage, but the GEM scheme has been in all regions since 2006, with 200 children out of a total care population (aged 18–21+) of 771 now staying on past 18.

With GEM, the Department of Health, Social Services and Public Safety[314] *simply continues foster payments after the fostered child turns 18. The amount paid can vary if the child only stays with his or her foster family part time, for example on weekends. Retainers are also paid to foster families so that children can go to university and have somewhere to come home to during the holidays. The scheme costs £1.4 million a year.*

The Health and Social Care Board also monitors any moves from care among 16-year-olds. Health and social care trusts[315] *must fill in a regionally agreed notification form if a 16 or 17-year-old child moves from a care placement to an alternative living arrangement in the community which is not family. Notification reports collate information on the reasons* and circumstances of such moves and provide an important means for monitoring placement moves and assessing needs.

Case study – Barnardo's Leaving Care Project, Northern Ireland

The Leaving Care Project NI provides a range of accommodation and support services across two trust areas in Northern Ireland to young people who are leaving the care system.

Accommodation comprises two units in different geographical areas, each with five and six self-contained flats respectively, and three houses in the community, each facilitating two young adults sharing. This part of the service can therefore accommodate 17 placements at any one time. The project also provides a floating support service to up to four young adults who are leaving project accommodation and moving into their own tenancies.

Levels of support vary in each location, with a higher level of staffing and an overnight staff presence in the units. There is no overnight staff presence in the houses; however, the project operates a 24/7 on call service for its young people for planned support, emergency support and monitoring of risk.

Former residents can receive 'aftercare' from the project, in the form of casual contact, professional befriending, outings, and crisis intervention.

As a condition of placement, all residents must enter into agreements with the project to work on their needs. An initial assessment helps the young adults and project to decide what accommodation would be most suitable, and what outcomes the care leaver wants to achieve. This directs the work that they will undertake with the project through, for example, individual sessional work, group work and so on. Young adults' needs range from very practical life skills training– cooking, cleaning, budgeting, sustaining tenancies, neighbourliness, self-care and so onto requiring emotional support in order to work through past life experiences. The project will help young adults address and manage risk behaviours impacting on their lives.

Outcomes are measured against the six high level outcomes as set out in the Governmental Children's Strategy, Our Children and Young People: Our pledge,[316] *which are based on the five Every Child Matters outcomes.*

Young people are reviewed regularly during their stay (usually every six months) and then on leaving, to monitor progress and identify any areas requiring continued work which the after-care social workers can help with when they visit former residents in their own homes.

The service is based on the resilience model, aiming to build resilience by ensuring a safe home (base), promoting good attachments through relationships with the project workers, and encouraging interests and talents. Maintaining routines and attendance at school, work or training is also a priority to maintain consistent, stable, reliable life styles.

There is low staff turnover, the work was described as vocational and many former residents stay in touch with their project workers and come back to visit in their 30s and 40s.

Case study – Hackney's social pedagogy pilots

The pedagogues are a flexible, floating resource in Hackney, and are involved in the journey to independence between ages 16–17 (not after the young person is 18). They carry out a variety of activities with young people, including going to the young person's house and cooking together, shopping and working on other practical life skills, as well as budgeting and managing money, and thinking about careers, friends and family. They are made aware of other interventions that might be needed and can arrange this. Social pedagogues provide a distinctive resource because they work outside the traditional social work team structure.

Case study – Horizons Centre, Ealing

The Horizons Centre in Ealing is a resource for those aged 13–25 plus, providing rounded support for children in care and care leavers – educational, emotional, social and practical.

This support takes the form of classes, sessions, social events, trips and drop-in support from staff. As the centre is open six days a week until 7pm, young people can come and go as they please, to see staff or meet friends, and use it as a 'safe' space. A typical week of activities might include after school study support and homework help, which is available every day from a team of six teachers, health sessions (eg on substance abuse or emotional health); music and arts classes; cooking classes; or a trip to a gallery or museum. In addition to formal activities, there are also study suites with PCs, a kitchen, a laundry and showers, aimed at young people who may be living on their own without adequate facilities.

Horizons is also a centre for peer mentoring, with young people in years 10 and 11 and those who have moved on to university acting as mentors for others who are still in school. In addition to direct benefits of advice and support for mentees, this scheme builds social networks, enables mentors to contribute and give something back, and encourages them to stay in touch with the centre well into their 20s.

In Ealing, 18 per cent of care leavers were offered university places in 2009. Across England, only 7 per cent of care leavers go on to university.

13 *Demos recommends that LAC and 16 plus teams shadow one another before and after transition.*

Demos asks local authorities to ensure their 16 plus teams shadow LAC teams and carry out joint reviews and visits after children in care are 15, following Northern Ireland's approach. We would also seek to ensure that social workers of children in care attend joint visits and reviews with the personal adviser for a year after the social worker has formally passed case responsibility to the personal adviser and leaving care team (so to age 19). This creates an extended period of handover to reinforce continuity at such a critical point of change.

By doing this, a phased transition from care to independence can be achieved by maintaining key relationships across the transition period. Maintaining these relationships is a vital component for a young person's sense of stability and emotional wellbeing, but we must recognise that 16 plus and leaving care teams have a distinct set of skills and areas of knowledge (eg regarding housing, benefits and employment), which LAC teams and social workers do not have. Without a complete overhaul of the social work function, it would be very difficult for social workers to maintain the same level of support and contact for children in care as for those who are leaving or who have left care. Demos believes this overlapping approach is a cost-effective alternative to achieving a less abrupt handover.

14 *Demos calls for local authorities to use personal advisers at an earlier age and for CWDC to outline specific training requirements.*

In order to maintain continuity of attachments across the transition to independence, Demos proposes that personal advisers begin working with children in care from age 14, carrying out functions similar to Northern Ireland's transition support workers and Hackney's social pedagogues, providing adolescent life skills and emotional support in a way that is not associated with leaving care, and which remains independent from LAC and care leaving teams at this age. At 18, the personal adviser should replace the young person's social worker as their key worker, a transition that should be eased thanks to the familiarity and relationship built early on.

Latest DCSF guidance on personal advisers states that personal advisers need to 'provide the young person with advice and support (this will include direct practical help to prepare them for the time when they move or cease to be looked after and also emotional support)'.[317]

Demos believes very strongly that personal advisers should fulfil this wider role of emotional support, and be trained accordingly. No specific training is associated with the personal adviser role, though the Children (Leaving Care) Act 2000 does state the personal adviser should have significant experience in youth mentoring, social work or other related field. We would ask CWDC to outline specific additional training requirements related to emotional support, resilience, attachment theory and social pedagogy to reflect the more holistic role personal advisers should fulfil.[318]

The Children and Young Persons Act 2008 stipulates that all young people in education should have a personal adviser until they are 25. However, there does not seem to be any particular reason why young people in education would be in greater need of a personal adviser than their counterparts in work or NEET. Indeed, it may be that providing personal advisers for those in education is actually concentrating support on the highest achievers among care leavers. We therefore add our voice to those who have already called for personal adviser support be provided to all young people up to 25, if they want it.

These recommendations would mean that personal adviser support could last up to ten years overall, spanning both sides of the transition and into adulthood. The form of support is likely to be quite different in adulthood, but may still include acting as a gateway to specialists within the care leaving team or adult social services, employment, benefits and so on. Personal advisers may also help negotiate the young person's 'right to return' to supported accommodation at this age (see below).

15 *Demos urges the government to raise the care leaving age to 18 and asks the DfE to support flexible approaches to allow young people to 'stay on' in placements to 21.*

Demos believes that the care system must move with the times, and raise the leaving care age to 18. The latest DCSF (now DfE) guidance seems to agree that allowing young people to leave care at 16 is wholly inappropriate:

Very few 16-year-olds will have the resilience, emotional maturity and practical skills necessary to make a successful move to independent living... a young person should not be expected to move from his/her care placement at least before legal adulthood, until they have been sufficiently prepared and are ready to take this significant step.[319]

The first objective of an effective transition to independence must be to ensure that young people are ready, emotionally and practically, to leave care. Although care orders last until a young person is 18, we know that 21 per cent of children in care left their last placement at 16, and 17 per cent at 17 in 2008/9. During the course of this project, we have been convinced that even with the most intensive support structures in place, children of this age will not be adequately prepared and ready to live independently.

As a society, our expectations of children, childhood and parenting have changed fundamentally. The number of unskilled jobs has halved from around eight million in 1960 to 3.5 million today,[320] so it is harder for young people with few qualifications to find employment. Subsequently, fewer young people leave school at 16 to enter the labour market; more move into further and higher education and stay at home during this period. A steady increase in house prices has also led to more young people staying at home for longer before they move on to the housing ladder (the average age of leaving the family home has increased to 24[321]) and nearly 40 per cent of all young people go on to university. Reflecting these wider societal changes, the government has announced that it will raise the compulsory education participation leaving age to 17 by 2013 and to 18 by 2015.

Our interviews with care leavers suggested that those who had left care at age 16 had, in retrospect, regretted this decision. Many others agreed that they had wrongly believed they had been ready to leave care:

I should have had more help. I wasn't able to make decisions for myself and they just let me make them. They shouldn't have let me make them.

I don't think that at the age of 16 you are ready to cope with all that freedom.

By raising the care leaving age to 18, the confusion of those aged 16 and 17 who might be tempted to leave to gain more freedom will be eliminated, and leaving at 18 will truly become the norm. This will also clarify the entire transition process as care placements will naturally end with looked-after status and the support that entails at 18. It will also align the care system to the increased age of compulsory schooling. Having all three fixed at 18 provides a clear message to children in care and practitioners about expectations of childhood and parental responsibility.

Demos also believes that all children should have the option to stay in care longer, up to 21 if they want to. Several organisations have already called for the government to skip the pilot phase of the Staying Put Pilots, which are exploring how foster children might stay with their families until they are 21, and simply roll this out to children in care nationally.[322] Demos would like to add our support to others and urge the government to implement this scheme as a matter of priority. However, in addition to the option to stay to 21 becoming standard, Demos also recommends part-time placements and retainers be offered where viable. Part-time foster payments would allow those over 18 to spend some of their time with their foster families and some in their own accommodation, for example. Retainers would allow those at university to come home to their foster families during the holidays. This may have implications for the legal status of foster carers in that they may need to maintain their status as guardian (rather than landlord in a supported lodging) of a young person in care post-18. Demos suggests English policy makers look at the experience of Northern Ireland – where these foster payment options are already on offer as part of the GEM scheme – to establish how these might be implemented.

There may well be additional costs of implementing this proposal, but the longer-term savings could be substantial. There is early evidence from the USA which suggests that those young people who stay on to 21 were more likely to have access to transition and mental health support, were economically more secure, and less likely to have been in contact with the criminal justice system, and young women were less likely to be pregnant. The study also found that those who had the option to stay in care to 21 were 3.5 times more likely to have completed at least one year of college than their counterparts who had to leave by 18.[323] However, in the study the evidence that this advantage continues into later life is weaker – an issue we come to below.

16 *Demos recommends that DfE amends transition support guidance to*
    prioritise emotional and mental health support

Given the evidence (outlined in chapter 9) that many care
leavers' mental wellbeing deteriorates on leaving care, that
mental health correlates with academic achievement and housing
stability, and that many children in care already have underlying
mental health problems, Demos recommends that emotional
wellbeing and mental health are central to transition support and
viewed as the foundation stone of all other outcomes.

Although pathway planning guidance stipulates that care
leavers must be assessed and plans made for practical and
emotional issues during the transition, the implementation of
these assessments and plans tend to favour practical skills over
emotional or interpersonal preparedness.[324] Our own interviews
with care leavers corroborated this. The newest (2010) regulations set out areas that must be addressed by the pathway
plan, including emotional and mental health, and developing
social relationships. However, the majority of the guidance
is still dedicated to practical skills, accommodation and
education.[325]

A study of care leavers and care leaving teams by the
National Foundation for Education Research in 2009 found that
not all teams had a mental health specialist and communications
with CAMHS could prove problematic.[326] There is also a
potential gap and disruptive transition between CAMHS and
adult mental health services, which have very different ways of
working and needs thresholds.[327] Demos therefore recommends
that there must be a designated mental health specialist in each
care leaving team, who works closely with personal advisers to
identify early warning signs of escalating need and acts on them.
This specialist should also have a duty to act as liaison with a
named CAMHS specialist in the authority. Both should have a
specific duty to ease the transition of care leavers to adult mental
health services, should they be required, including information
sharing and briefing adult services of a young person's specific
situation, and joint visits with the young person during the
transition period.

17 *Demos recommends DfE guidance explicitly applies the resilience model to transition planning, and independent reviewing officers are trained accordingly.*

Demos believes that care leaving teams have a specific duty to provide seamless, integrated support for young people, with personal advisers acting at the gateway and first point of contact. All authorities should also have an external local presence representing this integration, in the form of a care leaving centre at which all needs can be addressed and all members of the care leaving team can input their expertise. Ealing's Horizon centre, which encapsulates multi-agency, multi-dimensional support, is a highly successful model that could well be replicated more widely.

Mike Stein's work, described in section 2, clearly demonstrates that considering care leavers' overall resilience, rather than a specific skill set, is a useful way of assessing their ability to live independently and do well in later life.[328] A resilience framework could therefore be an effective and relatively cost neutral means of delivering this integrated support. Resilience is already implicit in guidance which states that the independent reviewing officer must maintain stability and attachments wherever possible in a young person's transition to independence.[329] However, Demos recommends that the independent reviewing officer should also be trained specifically in resilience theory, so that the objective of resilience in later life is ingrained in the review of the planning process and nature of transition. This would ensure that not just accommodation, education and employment opportunities, but also interpersonal skills training – encouraging self-esteem and dealing with adversity and isolation – and developing interests and pursuits outside work or school, were considered.[330]

18 *Demos calls for government and local authorities to make supported accommodation more widely available through commissioning and active promotion of supported accommodation.*

Demos would like to see the government and local authorities actively encourage more care leavers to use supported accommodation, and introduce a strategy to stimulate this market. Although all care leavers are different, we have been convinced during the course of this project that supported accommodation is an extremely valuable 'middle way' between care and independence, particularly for those least well prepared for independent living as a result of their age, care experiences, life skills or emotional or mental health. These young people are less likely to be able to maintain an independent tenancy (for example they may have problems with budgeting and paying rent), and so are more at risk of unstable accommodation and homelessness. Supported accommodation, in being easier to maintain, provides stable accommodation for young people, additional preparation for full independence, plus the chance of ongoing attachments with support staff – combating isolation and loneliness, which can be so prevalent among those living alone.

In spite of the benefits, it seems that supported accommodation is a service enjoyed only by the few.[331] From the latest government statistics, we can see that only around 18 per cent of 19-year-old care leavers use some form of supported accommodation (excluding those living with their relatives), with nearly a half already living independently at this age.[332]

The latest (2010) sufficiency guidance already stipulates that local authorities 'systematically review the current situation in relation to securing accommodation which meets the needs of looked-after children and care leavers' and commission 'a range of provision to meet the needs of care leavers including arrangements for young people to remain with their foster carers and other supported accommodation'.[333] However, we would like to see the government go further and implement a strategy of active promotion. While supported accommodation may be more expensive than, say, independent living, encouraging those least able to live independently to use supported accommodation will clearly save costs in the longer term by reducing the risk of homelessness and other negative outcomes associated with unstable accommodation.

19 *Demos recommends floating support services are made more readily available by local authorities, and calls for the government to create a statutory 'right to return' for all care leavers.*

In order to fully taper the transition to independence, Demos believes young people who have engaged in a period of supported accommodation should be offered the option of 'floating support' for a further year from staff who would visit them in their homes.

In addition, Demos proposes that all young people leaving care should have a 'right to return'. A young person who finds themselves with too much independence too soon should be able to request a return to supported accommodation up to age 24 or, potentially, to a foster placement up to age 21. Ideally this would be the foster family they had left, although this may not always be possible. While the Children (Leaving Care) Act 2000 guidance states that care leavers may well fail in their first and second attempts at living independently, and local authorities should have contingency plans for this (including a return to more supported accommodation),[334] this does not seem to be a widespread practice. The Children, Schools and Families Committee agreed with this view, and recommended in its 2009 report that the government's Staying Put pilots 'should be used to explore how more flexibility can be built into the process of leaving care, so that young people who find they are not yet ready for independence are able, and encouraged, to revert to a higher level of support'.[335] By introducing a statutory *right* for young people to go backwards in the transition process, local variation in implementation of this guidance would be removed.

Transition to independence for young people is not a linear experience, nor does it cut off at a given age. As a highly diverse group with varying levels of need and emotional maturity, it is not inevitable that full independence can be maintained at 18, 21 or even 24. Indeed, early evidence from the USA seems to suggest that those children in care who are able to stay to 21 do better initially (by attending college, having a lower risk of teen pregnancy and being less likely to access support from mental and social care services), but this advantage seems to have disappeared by age 24. The research team has suggested that 'staying in care until 21 is important but not sufficient to lead to high educational (and other) outcomes, given that non care-leavers often receive support from family well into their 20s'.[336] By providing this additional optional assistance, resources are likely to be targeted most effectively at those who feel least ready to be independent and who might otherwise have a range of negative outcomes in adulthood.

Conclusion

Every child is different and will need something different from the care system, from a short break away from home to a lifelong adoptive placement. By no means do we underestimate the difficulty of meeting the needs of each individual child, and of making the right decisions at key moments in that child's life. Although we have not been able to address the issues surrounding the social work profession in this report, we are certainly aware that balancing these risks and 'getting it right' in individual cases is no easy task for professionals or for local authorities more broadly.

Nevertheless, we have argued that, where possible, a shift of resources and investment to the beginning of a child's care journey could have real long-term benefits for that child and minimise the costs associated with unstable and unhappy care experiences later on. Of course, intervening earlier through focused family support or placements away from home is not always possible or appropriate, and so we have been clear about the key ingredients proven to make a difference at any stage of a care journey, namely a high quality stable placement and a supported, smoother transition to independence.

We recognise that there are resource implications to this approach and to implementing some (though not all) of our recommendations. Many local authorities will be looking to make sweeping cuts to services, and in the short term there will be little appetite for investing in new approaches from central government. Consequently, the interventions and recommendations outlined in this publication should be seen as part of a long-term, ongoing project to raise standards in the care system rather than a 'quick fix' for the next few years. We also believe that we have shown that the escalating costs associated with poor care journeys and placement disruption have real resource implications for local authorities today. Investing in high quality experiences of care for vulnerable children and young people is not only right from a social justice perspective, it could be less expensive for local authorities in the short term.

As we have seen in this report, the care system serves some groups of children better than others, and so it is not meaningful to state that care does or does not 'work' for *all* children. However, the popular notion that it is the care system alone which generates poor outcomes is simply not grounded in the evidence, and so the view that care somehow fails all children catastrophically is inaccurate. Expanding the evidence base on the impact of care with the use of longitudinal data will be essential in developing a more sophisticated analysis of the impact of different interventions for different groups of children.

Most importantly, we should not doubt the capacity of the system to provide a nurturing, safe haven for many children, and we should be using care more confidently and proactively to provide this when it is needed. In this respect the edges of the care system need to be 'tapered'; entering care should not be seen as an all-or-nothing intervention to be used only when all else fails. We should work towards destigmatising the use of care, so that families and children can benefit from it when they most need to. Recognising that care can, and often does, succeed will enable us to be ambitious for the system as a whole, and by extension for the children and young people who pass through it.

Appendix 1 Data sources to establish a realistic care journey for child A and B

Child A

Child A enters care aged 3

Age of entry is a key predictor of stability.[337] In a study by Biehal et al, the group of children who experienced stable foster care entered care at mean age 3.9. They entered their stable foster care placement at mean age 4.1

Age of entry is also a key predictor of emotional and behavioural difficulties:

- In a study by Sempik et al, 81.1 per cent of children who entered care under age 5 showed no sign of emotional or behavioural difficulties.[338]
- Biehal et al's research also found that the child's age of entry to their current placement was correlated with their mental and behavioural health. Lower scores on the SDQ (less serious difficulties) were predicted by entry to the child's current placement at age 3 or under.[339]

DCSF statistics show that 19 per cent of children who entered care in 2008/9 were between the ages 1 and 4.[340]

Child A has a one-year short-term foster care placement, followed by one long-term stable foster care placement until age 18

One period in care

DCSF statistics on a child's *whole care journey* are not publicly available for 2009. DCSF statistics from 2005 showed that over the course of a child's care history, 75 per cent of children experienced only one period in care.[341]

Sinclair et al's 2007 study found that 6 per cent of those who entered the care system when aged between 2 and 4 were still looked after at the age of 16 and over. They were much more likely still to be looked after at this age than those who entered care aged less than 2 (much of this difference relates to adoption).[342]

Two placements

DCSF statistics on a child's *whole care journey* are not publicly available for 2009. DCSF statistics from 2005 showed that during their whole time in care, 26 per cent of children who left care aged 18 or over had experienced two or fewer placements.[343]

Leaves care aged 18

DCSF statistics for looked-after children leaving care in 2009 showed that:

- 21 per cent left care aged 16
- 17 per cent left care aged 17
- 61 per cent left care on their 18th birthday
- 1 per cent left care later than their 18th birthday[344]

Child A has good mental health outcomes and good educational attainment

Good mental health outcomes

As seen above, children who enter care aged 3 or younger are more likely to have good emotional and behavioural health:

- Biehal et al's study found that, on average, scores on the SDQ showed little change over time. This study found that placement stability was associated with better scores for emotional and behavioural difficulty (and 'significantly worse scores' for those whose placements had disrupted). Two-thirds of those in the study's stable foster care group did not have mental health difficulties.[345]

- Rubin et al's study in America (discussed in more detail in chapter 2 of this report) found that a child who has a stable care experience has a lower probability of experiencing behavioural problems (controlling for pre-care experience and other characteristics).[346]

Good educational attainment

DCSF statistics relating a child's educational attainment to the period of time they spent in care are not publicly available for 2009. DCSF statistics from 2005 show that the educational performance of children in care increased as the time they had been in care increased:

- 66 per cent of girls whose last period in care was eight years or over got at least one GCSE or GNVQ.
- 25 per cent of girls whose last period in care was less than six months got at least one GCSE or GNVQ.[347]

DCSF statistics for 2009 showed that 7 per cent of looked-after children attain at least five GCSEs at grade A*–C.[348]

Biehal et al's study found that the strongest predictor of a child doing well at school was having a low score for emotional and behavioural difficulties on the SDQ.[349]

Child A has a good likelihood of going on to higher education

DCSF data from 2009 shows that 7 per cent of care leavers at age 19 were in higher education (studies beyond A level).[350]

Child B

Child B enters care aged 11

DCSF statistics for the year ending 31 March 2009 show that 36 per cent of children who started to be looked after that year were between the ages of 10 and 15.[351]

Age at entry to care is a key predictor of stability:

· A study by Sinclair found that children under the age of 10 will often experience a stable long-term placement with the same carers, but older children had a much greater chance of disruption;40–50 per cent of teenage placements broke down within three years, even when the placement had already lasted some time.[352]

· Sinclair et al's 2007 study found that children who had had three or more placements in a year were more likely:

  · to be aged 11 or over
  · to enter for the first time over the age of 11
  · to have experienced a repeat admission
  · to have higher challenging behaviour scores
  · to have lower school performance scores
  · to be slightly less likely to accept care[353]

Sempik et al's 2008 study found that age at entry to care was predictive of emotional and behavioural problems. In this study 70 per cent of girls aged 11–15 on entry to care had an emotional or behavioural problem or disorder.[354]

Voluntarily accommodated

DCSF statistics for the year ending 31 March 2009 show that 66 per cent of children who started to be looked after that year were accommodated by voluntary agreement under section 20 of the Children Act 1989.

Sinclair et al's 2007 study found that 57 per cent of those who were first admitted when 11 or over were voluntarily accommodated; 32.2 per cent of children in the sample who were aged 11 or over entered care for reasons of abuse or neglect.[355]

Child B has three separate periods in care and 10 different placements

Three separate periods in care

DCSF statistics on a child's *whole care journey* are not available for 2009. DCSF statistics from 2005 showed that over the course of a child's care history, 10 per cent of looked-after children experienced three or more periods in care.[356]

Sinclair et al's 2007 study found that 44 per cent of the 'abused adolescents' in the study sample (children first looked after when aged 11 or over who had a need code of abuse) returned home at least once; 50 per cent of the 'adolescent entrants' in the sample (children first looked after when aged 11 or over and not abused) returned home at least once.[357]

Farmer and Lutman's 2010 study found that the child's age at the time they returned home was strongly related to the outcome of their return home.[358] Those whose return home remained stable had a mean age of 7.2 years, while those whose return home broke down had a mean age of 11.5 years. In half of the families in the study, children had experienced two or more failed returns home. By the five-year follow-up, 65 per cent of the returns home in the study had ended.

Ten placements

DCSF statistics on a child's *whole care journey* are not available for 2009. DCSF statistics from 2005 about children aged between 16 and 17 who ceased to be looked after that year found that 13 per cent had experienced ten or more placements.[359]

Sinclair et al's 2007 study found that one in six of the sample of 7,399 children (17 per cent) had had six or more placements.[360]

Dixon et al's 2006 study found that there was a negative correlation between the length of time young people had been looked after and placement movement. Those who entered care later and therefore stayed in care for a shorter time tended to have greater difficulty establishing themselves in a settled placement.[361]

Harriet Ward et al's 2008 study found that children with emotional and behavioural difficulties are more likely to 'enter a vicious circle in which frequent movement from one placement to another exacerbates their problems, with the result that the pattern of instability continues. Such children become "difficult to place", and the costs of finding them further placements increase substantially.'[362]

Two placements in residential care

Dixon et al's 2006 study found that those young people in the study who experienced higher levels of placement movement were more likely to have a last placement in a residential setting: 44 per cent of those with a last placement in residential care had experienced four or more placement moves compared with 30 per cent of those whose last placement was in foster care.[363]

Child B has poor mental health outcomes and poor educational attainment

An unstable care experience impacts negatively on child's B's mental and behavioural health

Rubin et al's study in America found that instability significantly increases the probability of behavioural problems for children in care. Regardless of their characteristics and pre-care experiences, those children who did not achieve placement stability in foster care were estimated to have a 36–63 per cent increased risk of behavioural problems compared with those who did achieve a stable placement.[364]

Meltzer et al's 2003 study found that three-quarters of the young people living in residential care (72 per cent) were assessed as having a mental disorder.[365]

Child B has poor educational outcomes – no qualifications

Biehal et al's 2009 study found the severity of children's emotional and behavioural difficulties to be a key predictor of their participation and progress in education. Children in the 'unstable care' group were doing worse on all measures of participation and progress in education. They were more likely to have truanted, to have been excluded from school in previous six months, to show behavioural problems at school and to do worse on measures of educational progress.[366]

DCSF statistics from 2005 show that 43 per cent of females whose last period of care was between two and four years had no GCSEs or GNVQs (the equivalent statistic is not available for 2009).[367]

DCSF statistics from 2009 show that 56 per cent of all

children who ceased to be looked after that year had no GCSEs or GNVQs.[368]

Child B has a high likelihood of going on to be NEET

DCSF statistics from 2009 show that 26 per cent of 19-year-olds who had been in care were NEET and 32 per cent of those with no qualifications were NEET.[369]

Appendix 2 Basic costs to children's social care of case management processes for a looked-after child in foster care (outside London)

Table 7   **Processes used to estimate costs**

Process	Description	Process costs (£)(updated to 2009/10 prices)
Process 1	Deciding child needs to be looked after and finding a first placement	700
Process 2	Care planning (includes education plans and individual healthcare plans)	131
Process 3	Maintaining the placement (per month)* (cost of this process comprises social care activity in supporting the placement and the fee or allowance paid for the placement)	1,846
Process 4	Exit from care or accommodation	288
Process 5	Finding a subsequent placement**	224
Process 6	Review (NB statutory requirement to review all LAC at least every 6 months)	446
Process 7	Legal processes (where the child is subject to a care order or other legal order, this unit cost is added to the full cost of the care episode)	3,026
Process 8	Transition to leaving care services	1,274

Basic costs to children's social care

Notes:
* Monthly unit costs for other placement types: £763 for placed with parents; £1,914 for kinship care; £14,662 for residential unit; £5,951.85 for agency foster care placement within local authority area; £2,848 for independence.
** Unit costs for finding other types of subsequent placement: £506 if a residential placement is sought and £786 if child is placed with agency foster carers outside local authority area. If a child has emotional or behavioural difficulties and also has either a disability or has had three or more placements in the preceding 12 months, he or she is classified as 'difficult to place' and additional costs are incurred in placing him or her of £471 for foster care and £628 in residential care.

Source: Ward, Holmes and Soper, Costs and Consequences of Placing Children in Care[370]

Appendix 3 Evidence to explain child B's outcomes

Outcomes of child B

1 Unemployment

At 16, child B becomes NEET, like many care leavers that age and along with 5.2 per cent of the general population. The latest NEET statistical bulletin from DCSF found that 42.4 per cent of 16–24-year-olds with no qualifications are NEET.[371] The average time NEET in an 18-month period is 9 months for all young people this age, but 13 months for those with no qualifications.[372] Child B would therefore be NEET for 78 months in this 108-month period. As child B has additional mental health problems, this is likely to be an underestimate.

The ILO survey shows unemployment rates for those with no qualifications aged between 25 and 30 was 12.5 per cent in 2008.[373] Gregg also found that the future incidence of unemployment is related to youth unemployment.[374] Conditional on background characteristics, an extra three months of youth unemployment (before the age of 23) leads to an extra 1.3 months out of work between the age of 28 and 33. Based on this and the Labour Force Survey data regarding periods of unemployment, we assume that child B will have three periods of economic inactivity, lasting in total 2.5 years.

2 Poor mental health

The King's Fund estimated a range of costs for each form of mental health disorder based on service and treatment costs and lost earnings.[375] We are assuming child B's main mental health problem is depression, based on findings from Buchanan 1999, which found higher instances of depression at age 33 among care leavers compared with the general population,[376] and Chevalier and Feinstein who found that the probability of depression is higher among those with no qualifications by age 23.[377]

3 Underemployment

When child B is at work, with no qualifications, she will be earning less than the average (just like child A would be earning more as a graduate). This means the government will be gaining less in income tax and NICs from child B than from the average worker. Using data from the ILO, we know that the average weekly wage in 2008 for a person with no qualifications working full time was £350 compared with £536 per week for all full-time employees.[378] The government would earn £2,998.32 per year less in tax and national insurance as a result of this difference.

Appendix 4 The costs of adult outcomes for child A and child B

Table 8   **Summary of adult costs for child A**

Event	Description	Cost
Attends school from 16 to 18 to complete A levels or equivalent	Requires education maintenance allowance	£30 per week for two years = £3,120
Enters university at 18	Care leavers' university grant from local authority	£2,000
	University bursary for care leavers	£1,100 (varies from uni to uni)
	Accommodation in Coventry paid for during vacation (not all local authorities provide this support but Coventry does)	One-bed social rented flat = £63.35 rent per week 3 years' worth of vacations approx = 22 weeks p/a = 66 weeks (including summer vacation of last year, during which child A may be looking for a job) = £4,181.10
	Access to learning fund from university	£1,000
	Government maintenance grant/special support grant	£2,906 p/a =£8,718
	Student loan	£3,290 p/a = £9,870
	Maintenance loan	£3,497 p/a = £10,491

Table 9   **Summary of adult costs for child B**

Event	Description	Cost
Unemployment 16–24	Employment Support Allowance	£16,177.20
NEET for 78 months in that 108-month (9-year) period	Lost tax take and NI take assuming median[379] wages of: £3,375 for age 16–17 £9,648 for 18–21 £18,978 for 22–24 which are foregone in this period	24 months NEET at 16/17 – no lost tax or NIC (wages too low to qualify) 34 months NEET at 18–21 = £3,020.56 lost in potential NIC and tax 20 months NEET at 22–24 = £6,598.30 lost in potential NIC and tax Total lost tax and NI take during 6.5 years inactivity, based on median wages foregone = £9,618.86
Unemployment 25–30 (inactive 30 months in 60-month period)	Employment support allowance (1.5 years)	£1,702.22 short-term ESA cost = £3,404.44 year unemployed ESA cost = £5,106.66
	Incapacity benefit (1 year)	= £3,889
	Lost tax take and NI take assuming median[380] wages of: £18,978 for 22–24, which are foregone in this period.	5 consecutive years of median salary of £18,978 with 2.3 per cent inflationary wage increase = total NIC and income tax take of £21,179.49. Government will therefore forego approx 2.5 years of inactivity = £10,589.75.
Housing costs 16–30	As a low earner, ESA claimant and care leaver, child B will be prioritised for council or social housing and be eligible for council tax benefit. In Coventry, a one-bed council owned flat = £63.35 rent p/w + council tax = £980.72 pa.	When child B is claiming ESA and IB, her rent is paid and she receives £18.81 per week council tax benefit.[381] Total cost for ESA/IB period = £8,125.92 CT benefit + £27,367.20 housing benefit = £35,493.12.

Table 9 **Summary of adult costs for child B** *continued*

Event	Description	Cost
Underemployment costs 16–30	The average weekly wage in 2008 for a person with no qualifications working full time is £350 compared with £536 per week for all full time employees (ILO)	The government will earn £2,998.32 less in NICs and income tax per year on someone with no qualifications compared with an average earner. Child B will therefore generate £26,984.90 less in tax and NICs for the government during her period of active participation in the labour market, compared with an average earner.
Poor mental health between 16 and 30	According to the King's Fund, £1.68bn is spent yearly treating depression in 1.24 million sufferers. This is an average depression cost of £1,354.80 per person per year in treatment and services	Assuming no other mental health problems, we might assume child B is treated for depression for a total of 3 years up to age 30. This would cost £4,064.50 in NHS and service costs.

Notes

1　See www.ccfcs.org.uk/ (accessed 29 May 2010).

2　E Chase, A Simon and S Jackson (eds), *In Care and After: A positive perspective* (London: Routledge, 2006).

3　C Gammell, 'Baby P: social workers admit string of failures', *Daily Telegraph*, 25 May 2010, www.telegraph.co.uk/news/uknews/baby-p/7760374/Baby-P-social-workers-admit-string-of-failures.html (accessed 29 May 2010).

4　A Gentleman, 'Children in care: how Britain is failing its most vulnerable', *Guardian*, 20 Apr 2009, www.guardian.co.uk/society/2009/apr/20/care-system-failures (accessed 29 May 2010).

5　DoH, *Personal Social Services Expenditure and Unit Costs England: 2005–06* (London: Information Centre, Dept of Health, 2007), quoted in M Narey, *Beyond Care Matters: Future of the Care Population Working Group Report* (London: HM Government, 2007).

6　CAFCASS care demand quarterly figures January 2010.

7　S Jackson, 'Care past and present' in Chase, Simon and Jackson (eds), *In Care and After*.

8　Ibid.

9　Children, Schools and Families Committee, House of Commons, *Looked-after Children*, Third Report of Session 2008–09, HC 111-1 (London: HM Parliament, 2009).

10 S Jackson, 'Care past and present' in Chase, Simon and Jackson (eds), *In Care and After.*

11 J Rowe and L Lambert, *Children Who Wait* (London: Association of British Adoption Agencies, 1973); and J Goldstein, A Freud and A Solnit, *Beyond the Best Interests of the Child* (New York: Free Press, 1979).

12 M Adcock, R White and O Rowlands, *The Administrative Parent: A study of the parental rights and duties* (London: British Association for Adoption and Fostering, 1982).

13 Taken from Rowe and Lambert, *Children Who Wait*, quoted in Adcock, White and Rowlands, *The Administrative Parent.*

14 S Jackson, 'Care past and present'.

15 Adcock, White and Rowlands, *The Administrative Parent.*

16 S Jackson, 'Care past and present' in Chase, Simon and Jackson (eds), *In Care and After.*

17 Ibid.

18 Ibid.

19 J Rowlands and J Statham, 'Numbers of children looked after in England: a historical analysis', *Child and Family Social Work* 14 (2009), 79–89.

20 D Forrester et al, 'What is the impact of care on children's welfare? A focussed review of the literature', prepared for the Welsh Assembly Government (2007).

21 Narey, *Beyond Care Matters.*

22 Ibid.

23 Deloitte, *Determining the Optimum Supply of Children's Residential Care* (London: Dept for Children, Schools and Families, 2007).

24 Children, Schools and Families Committee, House of Commons, *Looked-after Children*.

25 DCSF, *Care Matters: Ministerial stocktake report* (London: Dept for Children, Schools and Families, 2009), http://publications.dcsf.gov.uk/eOrderingDownload/Care_Matters_Stocktake.pdf (accessed 31 May 2010).

26 DfES, *Every Child Matters: Change for children* (Nottingham: DfES Publications, 2004), http://publications.everychildmatters.gov.uk/default.aspx?PageFunction=productdetails&PageMode=publications&ProductId=DfES/1081/2004& (accessed 4 Jun 2010).

27 See www.opsi.gov.uk/acts/acts2008/ukpga_20080023_en_1 (accessed 29 May 2010); see also DfES, *Care Matters: Transforming the lives of children and young people in care*, Cm 6932 (London: Dept for Education and Skills, 2006) and DfES, *Care Matters: Time for change*, Cm 7137 (London: Dept for Education and Skills, 2006).

28 L Hunt, 'Children and Young Persons Bill close to becoming law', *Community Care*, 10 Oct 2008, www.communitycare.co.uk/Articles/2008/10/10/109660/children-and-young-persons-bill-last-ditch-amendments-fail.html (accessed 30 May 2010).

29 Narey, *Beyond Care Matters*.

30 Rowlands and Statham, 'Numbers of children looked after in England'.

31 Narey, *Beyond Care Matters*.

32 Rowlands and Statham, 'Numbers of children looked after in England'.

33 Ibid.

34 Ibid.

35 Narey, *Beyond Care Matters*.

36 DCSF, *Children Looked After in England (Including Adoption and Care Leavers) Year Ending 31 March 2009*, www.dcsf.gov.uk/rsgateway/DB/SFR/s000878/index.shtml (accessed 30 May 2010). The figures are based on data from the SSDA903 return collected from all local authorities.

37 Ibid

38 Ibid.

39 NEF, *A False Economy: How failing to invest in the care system for children will cost us all* (London: New Economics Foundation, 2008).

40 DCSF, *Children Looked After in England (Including Adoption and Care Leavers) Year Ending 31 March 2009*. The figures are based on data from the SSDA903 return collected from all local authorities.

41 Ibid.

42 Ibid.

43 DCSF, *Outcome Indicators for Children Looked After: Twelve Months to 30 September 2009, England 21 April 2010*, http://data.gov.uk/dataset/outcome_indicators_for_children_looked_after_twelve_months_to_30_september (accessed 30 May 2010).

44 DCSF, Data Tables (table d5), 'Children who ceased to be looked after during the years ending 31 March by legal status on ceasing, average duration of latest period of care in days and duration of latest period of care', 2009.

45 DCSF, *Children Looked After in England (Including Adoption and Care Leavers) Year Ending 31 March 2009*, (table D6), www.dcsf.gov.uk/rsgateway/DB/SFR/s000878/SFR25-2009Additionalv2.xls (accessed 4 Jun 2010).

46 Ibid.

47 I Sinclair et al, *The Pursuit of Permanence: A study of the English care system* (London: Jessica Kingsley, 2007).

48 Ibid.

49 Ibid.

50 J Sempik, H Ward and I Darker, 'Emotional and behavioural difficulties of children and young people at entry to care', *Clinical Child Psychology and Psychiatry* 13, no 2, (2008), 221–33.

51 H Meltzer et al, *The Mental Health of Young People Looked After by Local Authorities in England* (Office for National Statistics: The Stationery Office, 2003).

52 H Sargeant, *Handle with Care: An investigation into the care system* (London: Centre for Policy Studies, 2006).

53 R Robson et al, *Couldn't Care Less: A policy report from the children in care working group* (London: Centre For Social Justice, 2008).

54 Gentleman, 'Children in care'.

55 The first attempt to complete an SDQ for each child in care in 2008/9 SSDA903 was unsatisfactory. It was completed for only 59 per cent of eligible children and was of doubtful accuracy (a higher than expected proportion of zero scores).

56 Taken from DCSF, *Outcome Indicators for Children Looked After: Twelve Months to 30 September 2009, England 21 April 2010.*

57 DCSF, *Children Looked After in England (Including Adoption and Care Leavers) Year Ending 31 March 2009.* The figures are based on data from the SSDA903 return collected from all local authorities.

58 See A Simon and C Owen, 'Outcomes for children in care: what do we know?' in Chase, Simon and Jackson (eds), *In Care and After.*

59 ONS, *Statistics of Education: Children looked after by local authorities year ending 31 March 2005* (London: Office of National Statistics, 2006), 45.

60 M Stein, 'Wrong turn: the consensus that children in care are failing, and that the system is to blame, is plain wrong', *Guardian*, 6 December 2006, www.guardian.co.uk/society/ 2006/dec/06/childrensservices.guardiansocietysupplement1 (accessed 30 May 2010).

61 Forrester et al, *What is the Impact of Care on Children's Welfare?*

62 Ibid.

63 Ibid.

64 I Brodie et al, *Improving Educational Outcomes for Looked-after Children and Young People* (London: C4EO, 2009).

65 C Cameron et al, *Using Health, Education, Housing and Other Services: A study of care leavers and young people in difficulty* (London: Thomas Coram Research Unit, Institute of Education, 2007).

66 C Pritchard and R Williams, 'Does social work make a difference?: a controlled study of former "looked-after-children" and "excluded-from-school" adolescents now men aged 16–24 subsequent offences, being victims of crime and suicide', *Journal of Social Work* 9 (2009), 285.

67 Ibid.

68 H Ward, L Holmes and J Soper, *Costs and Consequences of Placing Children in Care* (London: Jessica Kingsley Publishers, 2008).

69 J Margo et al, *Freedom's Orphans: Raising youth in a changing world* (London: ippr, 2006).

70 Urie Bronfenbrenner as cited in L Feinstein, J Bynner and K Duckworth, *Leisure Contexts in Adolescence and their Effects on Adult Outcomes* (London: Centre for Research on the Wider Benefits of Learning, Institute of Education, 2005).

71 Ibid.

72 J Lexmond and R Reeves, *Building Character* (London: Demos, 2009).

73 E Monck, J Reynolds and V Wigfall, *The Role of Concurrent Planning: Making permanent placements for young children* (London: British Association for Adoption and Fostering, 2003).

74 Ibid.

75 ID Smith and G Allen, *Early Intervention: Good parents, great kids, better citizens* (London: Centre for Social Justice and the Smith Institute, 2008).

76 Ibid, 64.

77 D Baumrind, 'The influence of parenting style on adolescent competence and substance use', *Journal of Early Adolescence* 11, no 1 (1991), 56–95.

78 Ibid.

79 Ibid.

80 Ibid.

81 Lexmond and Reeves, *Building Character*.

82 R Gwyther et al, *Understanding Children's Well-being: A national survey of young people's well-being* (London: The Children's Society, 2010).

83 M Stein, *Resilience and Young People Leaving Care: Overcoming the odds* (York: Joseph Rowntree Foundation, 2005).

84 J Margo and S Sodha, *Get Happy: Children and young people's emotional wellbeing* (London: NCH, 2007).

85 M Rutter, 'Resilience concepts and findings: implications for family therapy', *Journal of Family Therapy*, 21 (1999), 119–44.

86 M Rutter, H Giller and A Hagell, *Antisocial Behaviour by Young People* (Cambridge: Cambridge University Press, 1998), as cited in M Stein, 'Young people leaving care' in G Schofield and J Simmonds (eds), *The Child Placement Handbook* (London: British Association for Adoption and Fostering, 2009).

87 Monck, Reynolds and Wigfall, *The Role of Concurrent Planning*.

88 Sempik, Ward and Darker, 'Emotional and behavioural difficulties of children and young people at entry to care'.

88 Ibid.

90 J Selwyn, L Frazer and D Quinton, 'Paved with good intentions: the pathway to adoption and the costs of delay', *British Journal of Social Work* 36 (2006) 561–76.

91 Ibid.

92 Ibid.

93 N Biehal et al, *Characteristics, Outcomes and Meanings of Three Types of Permanent Placement: Adoption by strangers, adoption by carers and long-term foster care* (York: University of York, 2009).

94 Ibid.

95 Stein, *Resilience and Young People Leaving Care*.

96 Ibid.

97 Biehal et al, *Characteristics, Outcomes and Meanings of Three Types of Permanent Placement*; and Selwyn et al, 'Paved with good intentions'.

98 Biehal et al, *Characteristics, Outcomes and Meanings of Three Types of Permanent Placement*.

99 Sinclair et al, *The Pursuit of Permanence*, 221.

100 G Schofield and M Beek, 'Risk and resilience in long-term foster care', *British Journal of Social Work* 35 (2005) 1283–301.

101 Ibid.

102 Bowlby, cited in P Petrie et al, *Working with Children in Care: European perspectives* (Maidenhead: Open University Press, 2006).

103 Petrie et al, *Working with Children in Care*.

104 Ibid, 95–6.

105 Biehal et al, *Characteristics, Outcomes and Meanings of Three Types of Permanent Placement*; and Schofield and Beek, 'Risk and resilience in long-term foster care'.

106 Biehal et al, *Characteristics, Outcomes and Meanings of Three Types of Permanent Placement*.

107 S Jackson and A Simon, 'Costs and benefits of educating children in care' in Chase, Simon and Jackson (eds), *In Care and After*.

108 Biehal et al, *Characteristics, Outcomes and Meanings of Three Types of Permanent Placement*

109 Jackson and Simon, 'Costs and benefits of educating children in care'.

110 J Dixon et al, *Young People Leaving Care: A study of costs and outcomes*, report to the Department for Education & Skills (York: University of York, 2006).

111 Children's Rights Director, *Planning, Placement and Review: A report of a children's consultation to the DCSF by the Children's Rights Director for England* (London: Children's Rights, 2009).

112 Ofsted, *Children's Care Monitor* (Manchester: Ofsted, 2009).

113 Selwyn et al, 'Paved with good intentions'; A Rushton and C Dance, 'The adoption of children from public care: a prospective study of outcome in adolescence', *Journal of the American Academy of Child and Adolescent Psychiatry* 45, no 7(2006), 877–83; and H Ward, 'Patterns of instability: moves within the English care system: their reasons, contexts and consequences', *Child and Youth Services Review* 31 (2009), 1113–18.

114 G McCarthy, 'The developmental histories of children who experience high levels of placement instability in the care system', *Adoption and Fostering* 28, no 4 (2004), 60–5

115 Biehal et al, *Characteristics, Outcomes and Meanings of Three Types of Permanent Placement*.

116 DM Rubin et al, 'The impact of placement stability on behavioral well-being for children in foster care', *Pediatrics* 119 (2007), 336–44.

117 Ward, Holmes and Soper, *Costs and Consequences of Placing Children in Care*.

118 Sempik, Ward and Darker, 'Emotional and behavioural difficulties of children and young people at entry to care'.

119 Biehal et al, *Characteristics, Outcomes and Meanings of Three Types of Permanent Placement*.

120 A Rushton, 'Outcomes of adoption from public care: research and practice issues', *Advances in Psychiatric Treatment* 13 (2007), 305–11.

121 Schofield and Beek, 'Risk and resilience in long-term foster care'.

122 Sinclair et al, *The Pursuit of Permanence*, 199.

123 DCSF, *The Pursuit of Permanence: A study of the English care system, research brief*, November 2007, www.dcsf.gov.uk/research/programmeofresearch/projectinforma tion.cfm?projectid=15321&resultspage=1 (accessed 30 May 2010).

124 N Biehal, 'Foster care for adolescents' in Schofield and Simmonds (eds) *The Child Placement Handbook*, 171.

125 DCSF, *Multidimensional Treatment Foster Care in England (MTFCE): Annual project report* (London: Dept for Children, Families and Schools, 2008).

126 Ibid.

127 Ibid.

128 Ward, Holmes and Soper, *Costs and Consequences of Placing Children in Care*.

129 Sinclair et al, *The Pursuit of Permanence*.

130 National Institute for Health and Clinical Excellence (NICE), 'The physical and emotional health and wellbeing of looked-after children and young people, draft guidance', 2010, www.nice.org.uk/guidance/index.jsp?action=download&o=47451 (accessed 4 Jun 2010).

131 Ibid, p14.

132 Sinclair et al, *The Pursuit of Permanence*.

133 J Cashmore, 'Promoting the participation of children and young people in care', *Child Abuse & Neglect* 26, no 8 (2002), 837–47

134 Ibid.

135 J Wade and J Dixon, 'Making a home, finding a job: investigating early housing and employment outcomes for young people leaving care', *Child and Family Social Work* 11, no 3 (2006), 199–208.

136 Dixon et al, *Young People Leaving Care*.

137 I Sinclair et al, *Foster Children: Where they go and how they get on* (London: Jessica Kingsley, 2005); M Stein, *What Works for Young People Leaving Care?* (Barkingside: Barnardo's, 2004); M Stein, *Living out of Care* (Ilford: Barnardo's, 1990); and Dixon et al, *Young People Leaving Care*.

138 Stein, *Resilience and Young People Leaving Care*.

139 M Stein, 'Research review: young people leaving care', *Child and Family Social Work* 11, no 3 (2006), 273–9.

140 J Coleman and L Hendry, *The Nature of Adolescence* (London: Routledge, 1999).

141 ESRC, *Tracking Care Leavers as They Move to Independence* (Swindon: Economic and Social Research Council, 2003).

142 A Hart, 'Resources for transitions from care' in *Leaving Care – Where?*, conference report (London: National Association of Young People in Care, 1984).

143 Now Catch 22.

144 Barnardo's evidence to the Children, Schools and Families Committee, 2009.

145 Ibid.

146 Dixon et al, *Young People Leaving Care*; Stein, *Resilience and Young People Leaving Care*; Wade and Dixon, 'Making a home, finding a job'; Cameron et al, *Using Health, Education, Housing and Other Services*; and A Simon, 'Early access and use of housing: care leavers and other young people in difficulty', *Child and Family Social Work* 13 (2008), 91–100.

147 Stein, *Resilience and Young People Leaving Care*.

148 Centrepoint, *A Place To Call Home: Care leavers' experience of finding suitable accommodation* (London: Centrepoint, 2006).

149 Ibid

150 Dixon et al, *Young People Leaving Care*.

151 Wade and Dixon, 'Making a home, finding a job'.

152 Dixon et al, *Young People Leaving Care*.

153 Sinclair et al, *Foster Children*; Stein, *What Works for Young People Leaving Care?*; and Stein, *Living out of Care*.

154 Dixon et al, *Young People Leaving Care*.

155 Cameron et al, *Using Health, Education, Housing and Other Services*.

156 J Wade, 'The ties that bind: support from birth families and substitute families for young people leaving care', *British Journal of Social Work* 38, no 1 (2008), 39–54.

157 Ibid; see also P Marsh and M Peel, *Leaving Care in Partnership* (London: The Stationery Office, 1999).

158 Cameron et al, *Using Health, Education, Housing and Other Services*.

159 DCSF, 'Children looked after in England (including adoption and care leavers) year ending 31 March 2009', statistical first release, www.dcsf.gov.uk/rsgateway/DB/SFR/s000878/SFR25-2009Version2.pdf (accessed 31 May 2010).

160 'Scoring the informant-rated strengths and difficulties questionnaire', www.sdqinfo.com/ScoreSheets/e1.pdf (accessed 31 May 2010).

161 DCSF, *Care Matters*.

162 Ibid.

163 Ofsted, *Parents on Council Care: A report on parents' views by the Children's Rights director for England* (Manchester: Ofsted, 2008), www.ofsted.gov.uk/Ofsted-home/Publications-and-research/Browse-all-by/Care/Children-s-rights/Parents-on-council-care (accessed 31 May 2010).

164 Narey, *Beyond Care Matters*.

165 CSCI, *Supporting Parents, Safeguarding Children* (London: Commission for Social Care Inspection, 2008).

166 Narey, *Beyond Care Matters*.

167 Biehal et al, *Characteristics, Outcomes and Meanings of Three Types of Permanent Placement*; Selwyn et al, 'Paved with good intentions'.

168 Selwyn et al, 'Paved with good intentions'.

169 DfES and DCA, *Review of the Child Care Proceedings System in England and Wales* (London: Dept for Education and Skills and Dept for Constitutional Affairs, 2006), www.familieslink.co.uk/download/june07/Review of child care.pdf (accessed 31 May 2010).

170 Children Act Advisory Committee, *Annual Report 1991/92*, 2; LCD, *Scoping Study on Delay in Children Act Cases* (London: Lord Chancellor's Department, 2002).

171 Cafcass care demands quarterly figures January 2010.

172 A social work professional provided by Cafcass to represent a child independently, subject to care or adoption proceedings.

173 C Pemberton, 'Children's guardians say safeguarding is at risk', *Community Care*, 22 Jan 2010, www.communitycare.co.uk/Articles/2010/01/22/113624/Damning-Nagalro-survey-blasts-Cafcass39-management.htm (accessed 31 May 2010).

174 DfES and DCA, *Review of the Child Care Proceedings System in England and Wales*.

175 Originally used by NEF to explain aversion to using residential care – see NEF, *A False Economy*.

176 Biehal et al, *Characteristics, Outcomes and Meanings of Three Types of Permanent Placement*.

177 DfES and DCA, *Review of the Child Care Proceedings System in England and Wales*.

178 O Stevenson, 'Emotional abuse and neglect – time for re-appraisal', *Child and Family Social Work* 1, no 1, (1996), 13–18.

179 M Narey, 'Our duty of care', *Guardian*, 12 Mar 2009, www.guardian.co.uk/commentisfree/2009/mar/12/social-workers-child-protection.

180 Evidence to Children and Schools Select Committee, March 2009, Q28.

181 Cited in D Barrett, 'Take more children into care, says Barnardo's chief Martin Narey', *Telegraph*, 24 Jan 2009,

www.telegraph.co.uk/news/uknews/baby-p/4334287/Take-more-children-into-care-says-Barnardos-chief-Martin-Narey.html (accessed 31 May 2010).

182 Forrester et al, *What is the Impact of Care on Children's Welfare?*

183 J Masson, *Care Profiling Study* (London: Ministry of Justice, 2008).

184 J Dickens, 'Child neglect and the law: catapults, thresholds and delay', *Child Abuse Review* 16(2007), 77–92.

185 J Masson et al, *Protecting Powers* (Chichester: Wiley, 2007).

186 See, for example, O Stevenson, *Neglected Children and Their Families* (Oxford: Blackwell, 2007).

187 DCSF, *Care Matters.*

188 See www.parliament.uk/deposits/depositedpapers/2008/DEP2008-1751.xls (accessed 4 Jun 2010).

189 Rainer, *What Makes The Difference?: Submission to parliamentary inquiry on looked-after children* (London: Rainer, 2008).

190 Ward, 'Patterns of instability'.

191 Ibid.

192 E Farmer, W Sturgess and T O'Neill, *Reunification of Looked After Children With Their Parents: Patterns, interventions and outcomes* (Bristol: School for Policy Studies, University of Bristol, 2008).

193 N Biehal, *Reuniting Looked After Children With Their Families* (York: Joseph Rowntree Foundation, 2006); and Sinclair et al, *Foster Children.*

194 J Beecham and I Sinclair, *Costs and Outcomes in Children's Social Care: Messages from research* (London: Dept for Education and Skills, 2007).

195 Farmer, Sturgess and O'Neill, *Reunification of Looked After Children With Their Parents*.

196 E Farmer and E Lutman, *Case Management and Outcomes for Neglected Children Returned to Their Parents: A five year follow-up study* (London: Dept for Children, Schools and Families, 2010).

197 Ibid.

198 Selwyn et al, 'Paved with good intentions'.

199 Evidence to Children and Schools Select Committee March 2009, Q609.

200 Ward, 'Patterns of instability'.

201 See 'More adopted children returned to care', 10 Jul 2009, www.channel4.com/news/articles/uk/more+adopted+children+return+to+care/3259957 (accessed 31 May 2010).

202 See 'DCSF: Children looked after in England (including adoption and care leavers) year ending 31 March 2008', www.dcsf.gov.uk/rsgateway/DB/SFR/s000810/index.shtml (accessed 31 May 2010).

203 See C Pemberton, 'Parents reluctant to seek help from child mental health services post-adoption', *Community Care*, 15 Feb 2010, www.communitycare.co.uk/Articles/2010/02/15/113808/supporting-families-post-adoption.htm (accessed 31 May 2010).

204 The Children Act 1989 Guidance and Regulations, vol 2, 'Care planning, placement and case review' (2010).

205 DCSF and DoH, *Statutory Guidance on Promoting the Health and Wellbeing of Looked After Children* (London: Dept for Children, Schools and Families and Dept of Health, 2009), www.dh.gov.uk/prod_consum_dh/groups/dh_digitalassets/documents/digitalasset/dh_108592.pdf (accessed 31 May 2010).

206 Ibid.

207 Biehal et al, *Characteristics, Outcomes and Meanings of Three Types of Permanent Placement*.

208 Meltzer et al, *The Mental Health of Young People Looked After by Local Authorities in England*.

209 Sempik, Ward and Darker, 'Emotional and behavioural difficulties of children and young people at entry to care'.

210 Meltzer et al, *The Mental Health of Young People Looked After by Local Authorities in England*.

211 Sempik, Ward and Darker, 'Emotional and behavioural difficulties of children and young people at entry to care'.

212 Though this may change following 2009 guidance.

213 Ofsted, 'An evaluation of the provision of mental health services for looked after young people over the age of 16 accommodated in residential settings' (2010), www.ofsted.gov.uk/Ofsted-home/Publications-and-research/Browse-all-by/Documents-by-type/Thematic-reports/An-evaluation-of-the-provision-of-mental-health-services-for-looked-after-young-people-over-the-age-of-16-accommodated-in-residential-settings (accessed 1 Jun 2010).

214 Ibid.

215 Fostering Network, 'Huge pressure on fostering drives call for more foster carers', 17 May 2010, www.fostering.net/media/2010/huge-pressure-fostering-drives-call-more-foster-carers (accessed 1 Jun 2010).

216 Deloitte, *Determining the Optimum Supply of Children's Residential Care*.

217 Ibid.

218 Children, Schools and Families Committee, House of Commons, *Looked-after Children*, 53; and Rubin et al, 'The impact of placement stability on behavioral well-being for children in foster care'.

219 Children, Schools and Families Committee, House of Commons, *Looked-after Children*.

220 See for example Children, Schools and Families Committee, House of Commons, *Looked-after Children*.

221 NEF, *A False Economy*.

222 Ward, Holmes and Soper, *Costs and Consequences of Placing Children in Care*.

223 Deloitte, *Determining the Optimum Supply of Children's Residential Care*.

224 Ibid.

225 See DCSF, 'Education and skills in your area – England', www.dcsf.gov.uk/inyourarea/statics/las_nat_064_9.shtml (accessed 1 Jun 2010).

226 DCSF, *NEET Statistics Quarterly Brief*, Feb 2010.

227 See www.dcsf.gov.uk/rsgateway/DB/SFR/s000878/index.shtml (accessed 4 Jun 2010).

228 DfES, *Care Matters: Time for change*.

229 ONS, *Social Trends*, www.statistics.gov.uk/statbase/Product.asp?vlnk=13675 (accessed 4 Jun 2010).

230 Wade, 'The ties that bind'.

231 See, for example, Children's Rights Director, *Young People's Views on Leaving Care* (London: Office of The Children's Rights Director, 2006).

232 ESRC, *Tracking Care Leavers as They Move to Independence*.

233 Stein, 'Research review'.

234 Dixon et al, *Young People Leaving Care*.

235 Wade, 'The ties that bind'.

236 Barnardo's evidence to the Children, Schools and Families Committee, 2009.

237 See TCLF, *Setting Up: A place to call home* (Bala: The Care Leavers' Foundation, 2009), www.thecareleaversfoundation.org/documents/APlacetoCallHome-ASurveyonLeavingCareGrants.pdf (accessed 1 Jun 2010), a survey into setting up home grants for care leavers.

238 S Jackson, S Ajayi and M Quigley, *By Degrees: The first year, from care to university* (London: Frank Buttle Trust, 2003).

239 Ofsted, 'Thematic report – support for care leavers' (Jul 2009), www.ofsted.gov.uk/Ofsted-home/Publications-and-research/Browse-all-by/Documents-by-type/Thematic-reports/Support-for-care-leavers (accessed 1 Jun 2010).

240 Rainer, *Home Alone: Housing and support for young people leaving care* (London: Rainer, 2006). Rainer is now Catch22.

241 Ibid.

242 Children, Schools and Families Committee, House of Commons, *Looked-after Children*.

243 ANV, *No Place Like Home: Housing for care leavers report* (Manchester: A National voice, 2006).

244 Jackson, Ajayi and Quigley, *By Degrees*.

245 ESRC, *Tracking Care Leavers as They Move to Independence*.

246 Centrepoint, *A Place To Call Home*.

247 Dixon et al, *Young People Leaving Care*.

248 Cameron et al, *Using Health, Education, Housing and Other Services*.

249 Dixon et al, *Young People Leaving Care*.

250 See Stein, *Resilience and Young People Leaving Care*.

251 Biehal et al, *Characteristics, Outcomes and Meanings of Three Types of Permanent Placement*; and Rubin et al, 'The impact of placement stability on behavioral well-being for children in foster care'.

252 Sempik, Ward and Darker, 'Emotional and behavioural difficulties of children and young people at entry to care'; and Dixon et al, *Young People Leaving Care*.

253 For more information see www.ccfcs.org.uk/research-and-development/ (accessed 1 Jun 2010).

254 Ward, Holmes and Soper, *Costs and Consequences of Placing Children in Care*.

255 H Ward and L Holmes, 'Calculating the costs of local authority care for children with contrasting needs', *Child and Family Social Work* 13, no 1 (2008), 80–90.

256 Staff consulted by Ward et al in their study included 104 social workers, 23 family placement workers, 13 team managers, and two independent reviewing officers.

257 The Review of Children's Cases (Amendment) (England) Regulations 2004, www.opsi.gov.uk/si/si2004/20041419.htm (accessed 26 Apr 2010), outline the statutory requirement that the following process is followed at the start of each new care episode: first review within four weeks; second review within three months after previous review; third review within six months of previous review; thereafter every 6 months.

258 L Curtis, *Unit Costs of Health and Social Care 2009* (Canterbury, Personal Social Services Research Unit, University of Kent, 2009), www.pssru.ac.uk/uc/uc.htm (accessed 1 Jun 2010).

259 Ward and Holmes, 'Calculating the costs of local authority care for children with contrasting needs'.

260 See A Goodman, A Leicester and H Reed, 'A graduate tax for the UK?', www.ifs.org.uk/budgets/gb2002/chap8.pdf (accessed 1 Jun 2010) and DIUS, *Statistical First Release*, table 4, www.dcsf.gov.uk/rsgateway/DB/SFR/s000798/DIUSSFR05-2008.pdf (accessed 1 Jun 2010).

261 Taken from the 2008 Destination of Leavers from Higher Education, latest figure available on salary of those six months after graduating with their first degree.

262 According to the Annual Survey of Hours and Earnings, the 2009 median annual salary full time between ages 18 and 21 is £13,717.

263 Goodman, Leicester and Reed, 'A graduate tax for the UK?'.

264 Annual Survey of Hours and Earnings, 2009, www.statistics.gov.uk/cci/nugget.asp?id=285 (accessed 1 Jun 2010).

265 Ibid.

266 P McCrone et al, *Paying the Price: The cost of mental health care in England to 2026* (London: King's Fund, 2008).

267 'Teenage pregnancies among children in care: research', *Community Care*, 23 Jan 2008, www.communitycare.co.uk/Articles/2008/01/23/107036/teenage-pregnancies-among-children-in-care-research.htm (accessed 1 Jun 2010).

268 SCIE, *Preventing Teenage Pregnancy In Looked After Children*, SCIE research briefing 9 (London: Social Care Institute for Excellence, Aug 2005).

269 Of course only 7 per cent of care leavers go on to get a degree.

270 Children's Rights Director, *Planning, Placement and Review*.

271 J Barnes et al, *Nurse–Family Partnership Programme: Second year pilot sites implementation in England* (London: Dept for Children, Schools and Families, 2009).

272 Smith and Allen, *Early Intervention*.

273 Barnes et al, *Nurse–Family Partnership Programme*.

274 Smith and Allen, *Early Intervention*.

275 See www.ccfcs.org.uk/ (accessed 1 Jun 2010).

276 Care Planning Regulations 2010.

277 L Katz, 'Concurrent planning: benefits and pitfalls', *Child Welfare*, 78, no 1 (1999), 71–87.

278 Ibid.

279 Monck, Reynolds and Wigfall, *The Role of Concurrent Planning*.

280 Ibid.

281 Ibid. See figure 5.3, p100.

282 J Kenrick, 'Concurrent planning: a retrospective study of the continuities and discontinuities of care, and their impact on the development of infants and young children placed for adoption by the Coram Concurrent Planning Project', *Adoption & Fostering* 33, no 4 (2009).

283 Ibid.

284 See A D'Andrade and JD Berrick, 'When policy meets practice: the untested effects of permanency reforms in child welfare', *Journal of Sociology and Social Welfare* 33, no 1 (2006), 31–52; and

V Wigfall, E Monck, J Reynolds, 'Putting programme into practice: the introduction of concurrent planning into mainstream adoption and fostering services', *British Journal of Social Work* 36, no 1 (2006), 41–55.

285 M Ahmed, 'Nottingham Council pays damages to mother of baby K', *Community Care*, 18 Feb 2008, www.communitycare.co.uk/Articles/2008/02/18/107314/nottingh am-baby-case-council-agrees-to-pay-babys-mother-damages.htm (accessed 1 Jun 2010).

286 'Manchester Adoption Society is to close', www.manchesteradoption.com/ (accessed 1 Jun 2010).

287 Narey, *Beyond Care Matters*.

288 Ibid.

289 Forrester et al, *What is the Impact of Care on Children's Welfare?*

290 Family Rights Group, Audit of FGC Services, unpublished data, October 2009, quoted in report on the impact of the Public Law Outline on Family Group Conference Services in England and Wales by Family Rights Group in association with University of Birmingham, November 2009, www.frg.org.uk/ policy_papers.html (accessed 1 Jun 2010).

291 DfES, *Care Matters: Time for change*.

292 Public Law Outline, www.justice.gov.uk/guidance/ careproceedings.htm, quoted in report on the impact of the Public Law Outline on Family Group Conference Services in England and Wales by Family Rights Group in association with University of Birmingham.

293 New Care Planning Guidelines, March 2010.

294 D Howe, *Patterns of Adoption* (London: Blackwell Science, 1997).

295 Narey, *Beyond Care Matters*.

296 DCSF, *Children Looked After in England, Year Ending March 31st 2009* (London: Dept for Children, Schools and Families, 2009).

297 J Selwyn et al, 'Adoption and the inter-agency fee', www.dass.stir.ac.uk/adoption-research/exec/summary7.pdf (accessed 1 Jun 2010).

298 Harrow Council, Overview and Scrutiny Committee, agenda item, Apr 2009, http://harrow.gov.uk/www2/Published/ C00000276/M00004157/AI00049890/$AdoptionService_ v1.docA.ps.pdf (accessed 1 Jun 2010); and Ofsted, 'Harrow Council Adoption Service: inspection report for local authority adoption agency', Sep 2008; and Cardiff Council, Children and Young People Scrutiny Committee, agenda item, Jan 2008, www.google.co.uk/url?sa=t&source=web&ct=res&cd=3&ved=0CB AQFjAC&url=http%3A%2F%2Fwww.cardiff.gov.uk%2Fobjview.a sp%3Fobject_id%3D10543&rct=j&q=permanency+planning+trac king+committee&ei=sv7gS4ffHImM0gT6h- CcCA&usg=AFQjCNFIvgNvyJ-KXEL9Xwcy7LhRv4vE6A (accessed 1 Jun 2010).

299 The Care Planning Regulations published in March 2010 reassert the importance of planning for permanence: 'Permanence provides an underpinning framework for all social work with children and families from family support through to adoption. One of the key functions of the care plan is to ensure that each child has a plan for permanence by the time of the second review, as set out in the statutory guidance to the 2002 Act. Achieving permanence for a child will be a key consideration from the day the child becomes looked after.'

300 DCSF, *Statutory Guidance for Independent Reviewing Officers and Local Authorities on their Functions in Relation to Case Management and Review for Looked After Children* (London: Dept for Children, Schools and Families, 2010).

301 Selwyn et al, 'Paved with good intentions'.

302 Case study interviews with Essex County Council.

303 E Bengtsson et al, 'Introducing social pedagogy into residential child care in England: an evaluation of a project commissioned by the Social Education Trust (SET) in September 2006 and managed by the National Centre for Excellence in Residential Child Care (NCERCC)', 2008, www.ncb.org.uk/ncercc/ncercc practice documents/introducing_sp_into_rcc_in_england_feb08.pdf (accessed 1 Jun 2010).

304 Case study interviews Whistler Walk Residential Unit.

305 The Children Act 1989 Guidance and Regulations, vol 2, 'Care planning, placement and case review' (2010).

306 CAMHS, *Children and Young People in Mind: The final report of the National CAMHS Review* (London: Children and Adolescent Mental Health Service, 2008).

307 CWDC Training, Support and Development Standards for Foster Carers, standard 3.3a.

308 For example, Biehal et al, *Characteristics, Outcomes and Meanings of Three Types of Permanent Placement*; and Sempik, Ward and Darker, 'Emotional and behavioural difficulties of children and young people at entry to care'.

309 Ofsted, 'An evaluation of the provision of mental health services for looked after young people over the age of 16 accommodated in residential settings'.

310 Fostering Network, 'Learning, development and support for foster carers', www.fostering.net/together-for-change/support (accessed 2 Jun 2010).

311 DCSF, *Multidimensional Treatment Foster Care in England (MTFCE)*.

312 Children, Schools and Families Committee, House of Commons, *Looked-after Children*.

313 The Children Act 1989 Guidance and Regulations, vol 2, 'Care planning, placement and case review' (2010).

314 The Department of Health, Social Services and Public Safety is the Northern Irish equivalent of the English Department of Health and is responsible for children in care.

315 In Northern Ireland trusts have responsibility for children in care as there are no equivalents to local authorities

316 OFMDFMNI, *Our Children and Young People: Our pledge* (Belfast: Office of the First Minister & Deputy First Minister, 2008).

317 The Care Planning, Placement and Case Review (England) Regulations 2010.

318 Ibid.

319 DCSF, *IRO Handbook: Statutory guidance for independent reviewing officers and local authorities on their functions in relation to case management and review for looked after children* (London: Dept for Children, Schools and Families, 2010), 5.13 and 5.14.

320 Office for National Statistics, cited in A Browne and P Webster, 'School leaving age goes up to 18', Times Online,12 Jan 2007, www.timesonline.co.uk/tol/life_and_style/education/article1292132.ece (accessed 1 Jun 2010).

321 Office for National Statistics, *Social Trends Survey* (2007).

322 During the passage of the Children and Young Persons Bill in 2008, campaigners including the Fostering Network, NCH, Barnardo's, the Children's Society and Voice wrote an open letter to Ed Balls, seeking an amendment which would skip this piloting stage, as they felt the evidence for increasing the leaving age to 21 was so convincing that piloting was unnecessary, and 190 MPs signed an early day motion calling for the same thing.

323 M Courtney et al, *Midwest Evaluation of the Adult Functioning of Former Foster Youth from Wisconsin: Outcomes at age 21* (Chicago: Chapin Hall at the University of Chicago, 2007), www.chapinhall.org/sites/default/files/ ChapinHallDocument_2.pdf (accessed 2 Jun 2010).

324 See chapter 9.

325 The Children Act 1989 Guidance and Regulations, vol 2, 'Care planning, placement and case review' (2010).

326 E Lamont et al, *Provision of Mental Health Services for Care Leavers: Transition to adult services* (Slough: National Foundation for Education Research, 2009).

327 CAMHS, *Children and Young People In Mind*.

328 M Stein, 'Resilience and young people leaving care', *Child Care in Practice* 14 no 1, 2008, 35–44; and Stein, 'Young people leaving care'.

329 DCSF, *IRO Handbook*.

330 T Newman and S Blackburn, *Transitions in the Lives of Children and Young People: Resilience factors* (Edinburgh: Scottish Executive, 2002), www.scotland.gov.uk/Publications/2002/10/15591/11950 (accessed 2 Jun 2010).

331 See Dixon et al, *Young People Leaving Care*. Care leavers with mental health or emotional and behavioural difficulties were more likely to be living in supported accommodation, as were those whose last placement had been in a residential home.

332 19-year-old care leavers, by form of accommodation. See DCSF, 'Children looked after in England (including adoption and care leavers) year ending 31 March 2009', statistical first release.

333 DCSF, *Sufficiency: Statutory guidance on securing sufficient accommodation for looked after children* (London: Dept for Children, Schools and Families, 2010).

334 Children (Leaving Care) Act 2000, regulation and guidance, 14.

335 Children, Schools and Families Committee, House of Commons, *Looked-after Children*.

336 M Courtney et al (2009) *Midwest Evaluation of the Adult Functioning of Former Foster Youth: Outcomes at age 23 and 24* (Chicago: Chapin Hall at the University of Chicago, 2009), www.chapinhall.org/research/report/midwest-evaluation-adult-functioning-former-foster-youth (accessed 4 Jun 2010).

337 Biehal et al, *Characteristics, Outcomes and Meanings of Three Types of Permanent Placement*.

338 Sempik, Ward and Darker, 'Emotional and behavioural difficulties of children and young people at entry to care'.

339 Biehal et al, *Characteristics, Outcomes and Meanings of Three Types of Permanent Placement*.

340 DCSF, *Children Looked After in England (Including Adoption and Care Leavers) Year Ending 31 March 2009*.

341 DfES, *Statistics of Education: Children looked after by Local Authorities Year Ending 31 March 2005*, vol 1, 'National tables'(London: Dept for Education and Skills, 2006).

342 Sinclair et al, *The Pursuit of Permanence*, 32.

343 DfES, *Statistics of Education: Children looked after by Local Authorities Year Ending 31 March 2005*, vol 1, National Tables.

344 DCSF, *Children Looked After in England (Including Adoption and Care Leavers) Year Ending 31 March 2009*.

345 Biehal et al, *Characteristics, Outcomes and Meanings of Three Types of Permanent Placement*.

346 Rubin et al, 'The impact of placement stability on behavioral well-being for children in foster care'.

347 DfES, *Statistics of Education: Children looked after by Local Authorities Year Ending 31 March 2005*, vol 1, National Tables.

348 DCSF, *Children Looked After in England (Including Adoption and Care Leavers) Year Ending 31 March 2009*.

349 Biehal et al, *Characteristics, Outcomes and Meanings of Three Types of Permanent Placement*.

350 DCSF, *Children Looked After in England (Including Adoption and Care Leavers) Year Ending 31 March 2009*.

351 Ibid.

352 I Sinclair, *Fostering Now: Messages from research* (London: Jessica Kingsley Publishers, 2005).

353 Sinclair et al, *The Pursuit of Permanence*, 199.

354 Sempik, Ward and Darker, 'Emotional and behavioural difficulties of children and young people at entry to care'.

355 Sinclair et al, *The Pursuit of Permanence*, 221.

356 DfES, *Statistics of Education: Children looked after by Local Authorities Year Ending 31 March 2005*, vol 1, National Tables.

357 Sinclair et al, *The Pursuit of Permanence*, 221.

358 Farmer and Lutman, *Case Management and Outcomes for Neglected Children Returned to Their Parents*.

359 DfES, *Statistics of Education: Children looked after by Local Authorities Year Ending 31 March 2005*, vol 1, 'National tables'.

360 Sinclair et al, *The Pursuit of Permanence*, 221.

361 Dixon et al, *Young People Leaving Care*.

362 Ibid.

363 Ibid.

364 Rubin et al, 'The impact of placement stability on behavioral well-being for children in foster care'.

365 Meltzer et al, *The Mental Health of Young People Looked After by Local Authorities in England*.

366 Biehal et al, *Characteristics, Outcomes and Meanings of Three Types of Permanent Placement*.

367 DfES, *Statistics of Education: Children looked after by Local Authorities Year Ending 31 March 2005*, vol 1, 'National tables'.

368 DCSF, *Children Looked After in England (Including Adoption and Care Leavers) Year Ending 31 March 2009*.

369 Ibid.

370 Ward, Holmes and Soper, *Costs and Consequences of Placing Children in Care*.

371 DCSF, *NEET Statistics*, www.dcsf.gov.uk/rsgateway/DB/STR/d000913/index.shtml (accessed 2 Jun 2010).

372 DCSF, *Youth Cohort Study and Longitudinal Study of Young People* (London: Dept for Children, Schools and Families, 2008).

373 See www.dcsf.gov.uk/trends/index.cfm?fuseaction=
home.showChart&cid=1&iid=3&chid=13
(accessed 2 Jun 2010).

374 P Gregg, 'The impact of youth unemployment on adult
unemployment in the NCDS', *Economic Journal* 111 (2001),
F626–53.

375 McCrone et al, *Paying the Price*.

376 A Buchanan, 'Are leavers significantly dissatisfied and
depressed in later life?', *Adoption and Fostering* 23, 35–40.

377 A Chevalier and L Feinstein, 'Sheepskin or Prozac: the causal
effect of education on mental health', mimeo (2005).

378 See www.dcsf.gov.uk/trends/index.cfm?fuseaction=
home.showChart&cid=1&iid=3&chid=15
(accessed 2 Jun 2010).

379 Annual Survey of Hours and Earnings, 2009 levels,
www.statistics.gov.uk/StatBase/Product.asp?vlnk=15313
(accessed 1 Jun 2010).

380 Ibid.

381 Using the Coventry benefits calculator.

References

'DCSF: Children looked after in England (including adoption and care leavers) year ending 31 March 2008', www.dcsf.gov.uk/rsgateway/DB/SFR/s000810/index.shtml (accessed 31 May 2010).

'More adopted children returned to care', 10 Jul 2009, www.channel4.com/news/articles/uk/more+adopted+children+return+to+care/3259957 (accessed 31 May 2010).

'Teenage pregnancies among children in care: research', *Community Care*, 23 Jan 2008, www.communitycare.co.uk/Articles/2008/01/23/107036/teenage-pregnancies-among-children-in-care-research.htm (accessed 1 Jun 2010).

Adcock, M, White, R and Rowlands, O, *The Administrative Parent: A study of the parental rights and duties* (London: British Association for Adoption and Fostering, 1982).

Ahmed, M, 'Nottingham Council pays damages to mother of baby K', *Community Care*, 18 Feb 2008, www.communitycare.co.uk/Articles/2008/02/18/107314/nottingham-baby-case-council-agrees-to-pay-babys-mother-damages.htm (accessed 1 Jun 2010).

ANV, *No Place Like Home: Housing for care leavers report* (Manchester: A National voice, 2006)

Barnes, J et al, *Nurse–Family Partnership Programme: Second year pilot sites implementation in England* (London: Dept for Children, Schools and Families, 2009).

Baumrind, D, 'The influence of parenting style on adolescent competence and substance use', *Journal of Early Adolescence* 11, no 1 (1991), 56–95.

Beecham, J and Sinclair, I, *Costs and Outcomes in Children's Social Care: Messages from research* (London: Dept for Education and Skills, 2007).

Bengtsson, E et al, 'Introducing social pedagogy into residential child care in England: an evaluation of a project commissioned by the Social Education Trust (SET) in September 2006 and managed by the National Centre for Excellence in Residential Child Care (NCERCC)', 2008, www.ncb.org.uk/ncercc/ncercc practice documents/introducing_sp_into_rcc_in_england_feb08.pdf (accessed 1 Jun 2010).

Biehal, N 'Foster care for adolescents' in Schofield and Simmonds (eds) The Child Placement Handbook, 171, 2009

Biehal, N, *Reuniting Looked After Children With Their Families* (York: Joseph Rowntree Foundation, 2006).

Biehal, N et al, *Characteristics, Outcomes and Meanings of Three Types of Permanent Placement: Adoption by strangers, adoption by carers and long-term foster care* (York: University of York, 2009).

Brodie, I et al, *Improving Educational Outcomes for Looked-after Children and Young People* (London: C4EO, 2009).

Buchanan, A, 'Are leavers significantly dissatisfied and depressed in later life?', Adoption and Fostering 23, 35–40, 1999

Cameron, C et al, *Using Health, Education, Housing and Other Services: A study of care leavers and young people in difficulty* (London: Thomas Coram Research Unit, Institute of Education, 2007).

CAMHS, *Children and Young People in Mind: The final report of the National CAMHS Review* (London: Children and Adolescent Mental Health Service, 2008).

Cashmore, J, 'Promoting the participation of children and young people in care', *Child Abuse & Neglect* 26, no 8 (2002), 837–47

Centrepoint, *A Place To Call Home: Care leavers' experience of finding suitable accommodation* (London: Centrepoint, 2006).

Chase, E, Simon, A and Jackson, S (eds), *In Care and After: A positive perspective* (London: Routledge, 2006).

Chevalier, A and Feinstein, L, 'Sheepskin or Prozac: the causal effect of education on mental health', mimeo (2005).

Children Act Advisory Committee, *Annual Report 1991/92*.

Children, Schools and Families Committee, House of Commons, *Looked-after Children*, Third Report of Session 2008–09, HC 111-1 (London: HM Parliament, 2009).

Children's Rights Director, *Planning, Placement and Review: A report of a children's consultation to the DCSF by the Children's Rights Director for England* (London: Children's Rights, 2009).

Children's Rights Director, *Young People's Views on Leaving Care* (London: Office of The Children's Rights Director, 2006).

Coleman, J and Hendry, L, *The Nature of Adolescence* (London: Routledge, 1999).

Courtney, M et al, *Midwest Evaluation of the Adult Functioning of Former Foster Youth from Wisconsin: Outcomes at age 21* (Chicago: Chapin Hall at the University of Chicago, 2007), www.chapinhall.org/sites/default/files/ChapinHallDocument_2.pdf (accessed 2 Jun 2010).

CSCI, *Supporting Parents, Safeguarding Children* (London: Commission for Social Care Inspection, 2008).

Curtis, L, *Unit Costs of Health and Social Care 2009* (Canterbury, Personal Social Services Research Unit, University of Kent, 2009), www.pssru.ac.uk/uc/uc.htm (accessed 1 Jun 2010).

D'Andrade, A and Berrick, JD, 'When policy meets practice: the untested effects of permanency reforms in child welfare', *Journal of Sociology and Social Welfare* 33, no 1 (2006), 31–52.

DCSF, *Care Matters: Ministerial stocktake report* (London: Dept for Children, Schools and Families, 2009), http://publications.dcsf.gov.uk/eOrderingDownload/ Care_Matters_Stocktake.pdf (accessed 31 May 2010).

DCSF, *Children Looked After in England (Including Adoption and Care Leavers) Year Ending 31 March 2009*, www.dcsf.gov.uk/rsgateway/DB/SFR/s000878/index.shtml (accessed 30 May 2010). The figures are based on data from the SSDA903 return collected from all local authorities.

DCSF, *IRO Handbook: Statutory guidance for independent reviewing officers and local authorities on their functions in relation to case management and review for looked after children* (London: Dept for Children, Schools and Families, 2010), 5.13 and 5.14.

DCSF, *Multidimensional Treatment Foster Care in England (MTFCE): Annual project report* (London: Dept for Children, Families and Schools, 2008).

DCSF, *Outcome Indicators for Children Looked After: Twelve Months to 30 September 2009, England 21 April 2010*, http://data.gov.uk/ dataset/outcome_indicators_for_children_looked_after_twelv e_months_to_30_september (accessed 30 May 2010).

DCSF, *Statutory Guidance for Independent Reviewing Officers and Local Authorities on their Functions in Relation to Case Management and Review for Looked After Children* (London: Dept for Children, Schools and Families, 2010).

DCSF, *Sufficiency: Statutory guidance on securing sufficient accommodation for looked after children* (London: Dept for Children, Schools and Families, 2010).

DCSF, *The Pursuit of Permanence: A study of the English care system, research brief*, November 2007, www.dcsf.gov.uk/research/programmeofresearch/projectinformation.cfm?projectid=15321&resultspage=1 (accessed 30 May 2010).

DCSF, *Youth Cohort Study and Longitudinal Study of Young People* (London: Dept for Children, Schools and Families, 2008).

DCSF and DoH, *Statutory Guidance on Promoting the Health and Wellbeing of Looked After Children* (London: Dept for Children, Schools and Families and Dept of Health, 2009), www.dh.gov.uk/prod_consum_dh/groups/dh_digitalassets/documents/digitalasset/dh_108592.pdf (accessed 31 May 2010).

Deloitte, *Determining the Optimum Supply of Children's Residential Care* (London: Dept for Children, Schools and Families, 2007).

DfES, *Care Matters: Time for change*, Cm 7137 (London: Dept for Education and Skills, 2006).

DfES, *Care Matters: Transforming the lives of children and young people in care*, Cm 6932 (London: Dept for Education and Skills, 2006).

DfES, *Statistics of Education: Children looked after by Local Authorities Year Ending 31 March 2005*, vol 1, 'National tables' (London: Dept for Education and Skills, 2006).

DfES and DCA, *Review of the Child Care Proceedings System in England and Wales* (London: Dept for Education and Skills and Dept for Constitutional Affairs, 2006), www.familieslink.co.uk/download/june07/Review of child care.pdf (accessed 31 May 2010).

Dickens, J, 'Child neglect and the law: catapults, thresholds and delay', *Child Abuse Review* 16 (2007), 77–92.

Dixon, J et al, *Young People Leaving Care: A study of costs and outcomes*, report to the Department for Education & Skills (York: University of York, 2006).

DoH, *Personal Social Services Expenditure and Unit Costs England: 2005–06* (London: Information Centre, Dept of Health, 2007), quoted in M Narey, *Beyond Care Matters: Future of the Care Population Working Group Report* (London: HM Government, 2007).

ESRC, *Tracking Care Leavers as They Move to Independence* (Swindon: Economic and Social Research Council, 2003).

Farmer, E and Lutman, E, *Case Management and Outcomes for Neglected Children Returned to Their Parents: A five year follow-up study* (London: Dept for Children, Schools and Families, 2010).

Farmer, E, Sturgess, W and O'Neill, T, *Reunification of Looked After Children With Their Parents: Patterns, interventions and outcomes* (Bristol: School for Policy Studies, University of Bristol, 2008).

Feinstein, L, Bynner, J and Duckworth, K, *Leisure Contexts in Adolescence and their Effects on Adult Outcomes* (London: Centre for Research on the Wider Benefits of Learning Institute of Education, 2005).

Forrester, D et al, *What is the Impact of Care on Children's Welfare? A focussed review of the literature*, prepared for the Welsh Assembly Government 2007.

Fostering Network, 'Huge pressure on fostering drives call for more foster carers', 17 May 2010, www.fostering.net/media/2010/huge-pressure-fostering-drives-call-more-foster-carers (accessed 1 Jun 2010).

Fostering Network, 'Learning, development and support for foster carers', www.fostering.net/together-for-change/support (accessed 2 Jun 2010).

Gammell, C, 'Baby P: social workers admit string of failures', *Daily Telegraph*, 25 May 2010, www.telegraph.co.uk/news/uknews/baby-p/7760374/Baby-P-social-workers-admit-string-of-failures.html (accessed 29 May 2010).

Gentleman, A, 'Children in care: how Britain is failing its most vulnerable', *Guardian*, 20 Apr 2009, www.guardian.co.uk/society/2009/apr/20/care-system-failures (accessed 29 May 2010).

Goldstein, J, Freud, A and Solnit, A, *Beyond the Best Interests of the Child* (New York: Free Press, 1979).

Goodman, A, Leicester, A and Reed, H, 'A graduate tax for the UK?', www.ifs.org.uk/budgets/gb2002/chap8.pdf (accessed 1 Jun 2010).

Gregg, P, 'The impact of youth unemployment on adult unemployment in the NCDS', *Economic Journal* 111 (2001), F626–53.

Gwyther, R et al, *Understanding Children's Well-being: A national survey of young people's well-being* (London: The Children's Society, 2010).

Hart, A, 'Resources for transitions from care' in *Leaving Care – Where?*, conference report (London: National Association of Young People in Care, 1984).

Howe, D, *Patterns of Adoption* (London: Blackwell Science, 1997).

Hunt, L, 'Children and Young Persons Bill close to becoming law', *Community Care*, 10 Oct 2008, www.communitycare.co.uk/Articles/2008/10/10/109660/children-and-young-persons-bill-last-ditch-amendments-fail.html (accessed 30 May 2010).

Jackson, S, 'Care past and present' in Chase, E, Simon, A and Jackson, S (eds), *In Care and After: A positive perspective* (London: Routledge, 2006).

Jackson, S, Ajayi, S and Quigley, M, *By Degrees: The first year, from care to university* (London: Frank Buttle Trust, 2003).

Katz, L, 'Concurrent planning: benefits and pitfalls', *Child Welfare*, 78, no 1 (1999), 71–87.

Kenrick, J, 'Concurrent planning: a retrospective study of the continuities and discontinuities of care, and their impact on the development of infants and young children placed for adoption by the Coram Concurrent Planning Project', *Adoption & Fostering* 33, no 4 (2009).

Lamont, E et al, *Provision of Mental Health Services for Care Leavers: Transition to adult services* (Slough: National Foundation for Education Research, 2009).

LCD, *Scoping Study on Delay in Children Act Cases* (London: Lord Chancellor's Department, 2002).

Lexmond, J and Reeves, R, *Building Character* (London: Demos, 2009).

Margo J et al, *Freedom's Orphans: Raising youth in a changing world* (London: ippr, 2006).

Margo, J and Sodha, S, *Get Happy: Children and young people's emotional wellbeing* (London: NCH, 2007).

Marsh, P and Peel, M, *Leaving Care in Partnership* (London: The Stationery Office, 1999).

Masson, J, *Care Profiling Study* (London: Ministry of Justice, 2008).

Masson, J et al, *Protecting Powers* (Chichester: Wiley, 2007).

McCarthy, G, 'The developmental histories of children who experience high levels of placement instability in the care system', *Adoption and Fostering* 28, no 4 (2004), 60–5

McCrone, P et al, *Paying the Price: The cost of mental health care in England to 2026* (London: King's Fund, 2008).

Meltzer, H et al, *The Mental Health of Young People Looked After by Local Authorities in England* (Office for National Statistics: The Stationery Office, 2003).

Monck, E, Reynolds, J and Wigfall, V, *The Role of Concurrent Planning: Making permanent placements for young children* (London: British Association for Adopting and Fostering, 2003).

Narey, M, *Beyond Care Matters: Future of the Care Population Working Group Report* (London: HM Government, 2007).

Narey, M, 'Our duty of care', *Guardian*, 12 Mar 2009, www.guardian.co.uk/commentisfree/2009/mar/12/social-workers-child-protection.

NEF, *A False Economy: How failing to invest in the care system for children will cost us all* (London: New Economics Foundation, 2008).

Newman, T and Blackburn, S, *Transitions in the Lives of Children and Young People: Resilience factors* (Edinburgh: Scottish Executive, 2002), www.scotland.gov.uk/Publications/2002/10/15591/11950 (accessed 2 Jun 2010).

NICE, 'The physical and emotional health and wellbeing of looked-after children and young people, draft guidance', 2010, www.nice.org.uk/guidance/index.jsp?action=download&o=47451 (accessed 4 Jun 2010).

OFMDFMNI, *Our Children and Young People: Our pledge* (Belfast: Office of the First Minister & Deputy First Minister, 2008).

Ofsted, 'An evaluation of the provision of mental health services for looked after young people over the age of 16 accommodated in residential settings' (2010), www.ofsted.gov.uk/Ofsted-home/Publications-and-research/Browse-all-by/Documents-by-type/Thematic-reports/An-evaluation-of-the-provision-of-mental-health-services-for-looked-after-young-people-over-the-age-of-16-accommodated-in-residential-settings (accessed 1 Jun 2010).

Ofsted, *Children's Care Monitor* (Manchester: Ofsted, 2009).

Ofsted, *Parents on Council Care: A report on parents' views by the Children's Rights director for England* (Manchester: Ofsted, 2008), www.ofsted.gov.uk/Ofsted-home/Publications-and-research/Browse-all-by/Care/Children-s-rights/Parents-on-council-care (accessed 31 May 2010).

Ofsted, 'Thematic report – support for care leavers' (Jul 2009), www.ofsted.gov.uk/Ofsted-home/Publications-and-research/Browse-all-by/Documents-by-type/Thematic-reports/Support-for-care-leavers (accessed 1 Jun 2010).

ONS, *Statistics of Education: Children looked after by local authorities year ending 31 March 2005* (London: Office of National Statistics, 2006), 45.

Pemberton, C, 'Children's guardians say safeguarding is at risk', *Community Care*, 22 Jan 2010, www.communitycare.co.uk/Articles/2010/01/22/113624/Damning-Nagalro-survey-blasts-Cafcass39-management.htm (accessed 31 May 2010).

Pemberton, C, 'Parents reluctant to seek help from child mental health services post-adoption', *Community Care*, 15 Feb 2010, www.communitycare.co.uk/Articles/2010/02/15/113808/supporti ng-families-post-adoption.htm (accessed 31 May 2010).

Petrie, P et al, *Working with Children in Care: European perspectives* (Maidenhead: Open University Press, 2006).

Pritchard, C and Williams, R, 'Does social work make a difference?: a controlled study of former "looked-after-children" and "excluded-from-school" adolescents now men aged 16–24 subsequent offences, being victims of crime and suicide', *Journal of Social Work* 9 (2009), 285.

Rainer, *Home Alone: Housing and support for young people leaving care* (London: Rainer, 2006). Rainer is now Catch22.

Rainer, *What Makes The Difference?: Submission to parliamentary inquiry on looked-after children* (London: Rainer, 2008).

Robson, R et al, *Couldn't Care Less: A policy report from the children in care working group* (London: Centre For Social Justice, 2008).

Rowe, J and Lambert, L, *Children Who Wait* (London: Association of British Adoption Agencies, 1973)

Rowlands, J and Statham, J, 'Numbers of children looked after in England: a historical analysis', *Child and Family Social Work* 14 (2009), 79–89.

Rubin, DM et al, 'The impact of placement stability on behavioral well-being for children in foster care', *Pediatrics* 119 (2007), 336–44.

Rushton, A, 'Outcomes of adoption from public care: research and practice issues', *Advances in Psychiatric Treatment* 13 (2007), 305–11.

Rushton, A and Dance, C, 'The adoption of children from public care: a prospective study of outcome in adolescence', *Journal of the American Academy of Child and Adolescent Psychiatry* 45, no 7 (2006), 877–83.

Rutter, M, 'Resilience concepts and findings: implications for family therapy', *Journal of Family Therapy*, 21 (1999), 119–44.

Rutter, M, Giller, H and Hagell, A, Antisocial Behaviour by Young People (Cambridge: Cambridge University Press, 1998), as cited in M Stein, 'Young people leaving care' in G. Schofield and J. Simmonds (eds.) The Child Placement Handbook: Research, policy and practice, British Association for Adoption & Fostering

Sargeant, H, *Handle with Care: An investigation into the care system* (London: Centre for Policy Studies, 2006).

Schofield, G and Beek, M, 'Risk and resilience in long-term foster care', *British Journal of Social Work* 35 (2005) 1283–301.

SCIE, *Preventing Teenage Pregnancy In Looked After Children*, SCIE research briefing 9 (London: Social Care Institute for Excellence, Aug 2005).

Selwyn, J, Frazer, L and Quinton, D, 'Paved with good intentions: the pathway to adoption and the costs of delay', *British Journal of Social Work* 36 (2006) 561–76.

Selwyn, J et al, 'Adoption and the inter-agency fee', www.dass.stir.ac.uk/adoption-research/exec/summary7.pdf (accessed 1 Jun 2010).

Sempik, J, Ward, H and Darker, I, 'Emotional and behavioural difficulties of children and young people at entry to care', *Clinical Child Psychology and Psychiatry* 13, no 2, (2008), 221–33.

Simon, A 'Early access and use of housing: care leavers and other young people in difficulty', *Child and Family Social Work* 13 (2008), 91–100.

Simon, A and Owen, C, 'Outcomes for children in care what do we know?' in Chase, Simon and Jackson (eds), In *Care and After* (2006).

Sinclair, I, *Fostering Now: Messages from research* (London: Jessica Kingsley Publishers, 2005).

Sinclair, I et al, *Foster Children: Where they go and how they get on* (London: Jessica Kingsley, 2005).

Sinclair, I et al, *The Pursuit of Permanence: A study of the English care system* (London: Jessica Kingsley, 2007).

Smith, ID and Allen, G, *Early Intervention: Good parents, great kids, better citizens* (London: Centre for Social Justice and the Smith Institute, 2008).

Stein, M, *Living out of Care* (Ilford: Barnardo's, 1990).

Stein, M, 'Research review: young people leaving care', *Child and Family Social Work* 11, no 3 (2006), 273–9.

Stein, M, *Resilience and Young People Leaving Care: Overcoming the odds* (York: Joseph Rowntree Foundation, 2005).

Stein, M, 'Resilience and young people leaving care', *Child Care in Practice* 14 no 1, 2008, 35–44.

Stein, M, *What Works for Young People Leaving Care?* (Barkingside: Barnardo's, 2004).

Stein, M, 'Wrong turn: the consensus that children in care are failing, and that the system is to blame, is plain wrong', *Guardian*, 6 December 2006, www.guardian.co.uk/society/

2006/dec/06/childrensservices.guardiansocietysupplement1 (accessed 30 May 2010).

Stein, M, 'Young people leaving care' in G Schofield and J Simmonds (eds), *The Child Placement Handbook* (London: British Association for Adoption and Fostering, 2009).

Stevenson, O, 'Emotional abuse and neglect – time for re-appraisal', *Child and Family Social Work* 1, no 1, (1996), 13–18.

Stevenson, O, *Neglected Children and Their Families* (Oxford: Blackwell, 2007).

TCLF, *Setting Up: A place to call home* (Bala: The Care Leavers' Foundation, 2009), www.thecareleaversfoundation.org/documents/APlacetoCallHo me-ASurveyonLeavingCareGrants.pdf (accessed 1 Jun 2010), a survey into setting up home grants for care leavers.

Wade, J, 'The ties that bind: support from birth families and substitute families for young people leaving care', *British Journal of Social Work* 38, no 1 (2008), 39–54.

Wade, J and Dixon, J, 'Making a home, finding a job: investigating early housing and employment outcomes for young people leaving care', *Child and Family Social Work* 11, no 3 (2006), 199–208.

Ward, H, 'Evidence concerning the outcomes of care', unpublished submission to the Laming Inquiry.

Ward, H, 'Patterns of instability: moves within the English care system: their reasons, contexts and consequences', *Child and Youth Services Review* 31 (2009), 1113–18.

Ward, H and Holmes, L, 'Calculating the costs of local authority care for children with contrasting needs', *Child and Family Social Work* 13, no 1 (2008), 80–90.

Ward, W, Holmes, L and Soper, J, *Costs and Consequences of Placing Children in Care* London: Jessica Kingsley Publishers, 2008).

Wigfall, V, Monck, E and Reynolds, J, 'Putting programme into practice: the introduction of concurrent planning into mainstream adoption and fostering services', *British Journal of Social Work* 36, no 1 (2006), 41–55.

Demos – Licence to Publish

The work (as defined below) is provided under the terms of this licence ('licence'). The work is protected by copyright and/or other applicable law. Any use of the work other than as authorised under this licence is prohibited. By exercising any rights to the work provided here, you accept and agree to be bound by the terms of this licence. Demos grants you the rights contained here in consideration of your acceptance of such terms and conditions.

1 Definitions

A **'Collective Work'** means a work, such as a periodical issue, anthology or encyclopedia, in which the Work in its entirety in unmodified form, along with a number of other contributions, constituting separate and independent works in themselves, are assembled into a collective whole. A work that constitutes a Collective Work will not be considered a Derivative Work (as defined below) for the purposes of this Licence.

B **'Derivative Work'** means a work based upon the Work or upon the Work and other pre-existing works, such as a musical arrangement, dramatisation, fictionalisation, motion picture version, sound recording, art reproduction, abridgment, condensation, or any other form in which the Work may be recast, transformed, or adapted, except that a work that constitutes a Collective Work or a translation from English into another language will not be considered a Derivative Work for the purpose of this Licence.

C **'Licensor'** means the individual or entity that offers the Work under the terms of this Licence.

D **'Original Author'** means the individual or entity who created the Work.

E **'Work'** means the copyrightable work of authorship offered under the terms of this Licence.

F **'You'** means an individual or entity exercising rights under this Licence who has not previously violated the terms of this Licence with respect to the Work, or who has received express permission from Demos to exercise rights under this Licence despite a previous violation.

2 Fair Use Rights

Nothing in this licence is intended to reduce, limit, or restrict any rights arising from fair use, first sale or other limitations on the exclusive rights of the copyright owner under copyright law or other applicable laws.

3 Licence Grant

Subject to the terms and conditions of this Licence, Licensor hereby grants You a worldwide, royalty-free, non-exclusive, perpetual (for the duration of the applicable copyright) licence to exercise the rights in the Work as stated below:

A to reproduce the Work, to incorporate the Work into one or more Collective Works, and to reproduce the Work as incorporated in the Collective Works;

B to distribute copies or phonorecords of, display publicly, perform publicly, and perform publicly by means of a digital audio transmission the Work including as incorporated in Collective Works; The above rights may be exercised in all media and formats whether now known or hereafter devised. The above rights include the right to make such modifications as are technically necessary to exercise the rights in other media and formats. All rights not expressly granted by Licensor are hereby reserved.

4 Restrictions

The licence granted in Section 3 above is expressly made subject to and limited by the following restrictions:

A You may distribute, publicly display, publicly perform, or publicly digitally perform the Work only under the terms of this Licence, and You must include a copy of, or the Uniform Resource Identifier for, this Licence with every copy or phonorecord of the Work You distribute, publicly display, publicly perform, or publicly digitally perform. You may not offer or impose any terms on the Work that alter or restrict the terms of this Licence or the recipients' exercise of the rights granted hereunder.You may not sublicence the Work. You must keep intact all notices that refer to this Licence and to the disclaimer of warranties. You may not distribute, publicly display, publicly perform, or publicly digitally perform the Work with any technological measures that control access or use of the Work in a manner inconsistent with the terms of this Licence Agreement. The above applies to the Work as incorporated in a Collective Work, but this does not require the Collective Work apart from the Work itself to be made subject to the terms of this Licence. If You create a Collective Work, upon notice from any Licensor You must, to the extent practicable, remove from the Collective Work any reference to such Licensor or the Original Author, as requested.

B You may not exercise any of the rights granted to You in Section 3 above in any manner that is primarily intended for or directed toward commercial advantage or private monetary compensation. The exchange of the Work for other copyrighted works by means of digital filesharing or otherwise shall not be considered to be intended for or directed toward commercial advantage or private monetary compensation, provided there is no payment of any monetary compensation in connection with the exchange of copyrighted works.

C   If you distribute, publicly display, publicly perform, or publicly digitally perform the Work or any Collective Works, You must keep intact all copyright notices for the Work and give the Original Author credit reasonable to the medium or means You are utilising by conveying the name (or pseudonym if applicable) of the Original Author if supplied; the title of the Work if supplied. Such credit may be implemented in any reasonable manner; provided, however, that in the case of a Collective Work, at a minimum such credit will appear where any other comparable authorship credit appears and in a manner at least as prominent as such other comparable authorship credit.

5   Representations, Warranties and Disclaimer

A   By offering the Work for public release under this Licence, Licensor represents and warrants that, to the best of Licensor's knowledge after reasonable inquiry:

  i   Licensor has secured all rights in the Work necessary to grant the licence rights hereunder and to permit the lawful exercise of the rights granted hereunder without You having any obligation to pay any royalties, compulsory licence fees, residuals or any other payments;

  ii   The Work does not infringe the copyright, trademark, publicity rights, common law rights or any other right of any third party or constitute defamation, invasion of privacy or other tortious injury to any third party.

B   except as expressly stated in this licence or otherwise agreed in writing or required by applicable law, the work is licenced on an 'as is' basis, without warranties of any kind, either express or implied including, without limitation, any warranties regarding the contents or accuracy of the work.

6   Limitation on Liability

Except to the extent required by applicable law, and except for damages arising from liability to a third party resulting from breach of the warranties in section 5, in no event will Licensor be liable to you on any legal theory for any special, incidental, consequential, punitive or exemplary damages arising out of this licence or the use of the work, even if Licensor has been advised of the possibility of such damages.

7   Termination

A   This Licence and the rights granted hereunder will terminate automatically upon any breach by You of the terms of this Licence. Individuals or entities who have received Collective Works from You under this Licence, however, will not have their licences terminated provided such individuals or entities remain in full compliance with those licences. Sections 1, 2, 5, 6, 7, and 8 will survive any termination of this Licence.

B   Subject to the above terms and conditions, the licence granted here is perpetual (for the duration of the applicable copyright in the Work). Notwithstanding the above, Licensor reserves the right to release the Work under different licence terms or to stop distributing the Work at any time; provided, however that any such election will not serve to withdraw this Licence (or any other licence that has been, or is required to be, granted under the terms of this Licence), and this Licence will continue in full force and effect unless terminated as stated above.

8   Miscellaneous

A   Each time You distribute or publicly digitally perform the Work or a Collective Work, Demos offers to the recipient a licence to the Work on the same terms and conditions as the licence granted to You under this Licence.

B   If any provision of this Licence is invalid or unenforceable under applicable law, it shall not affect the validity or enforceability of the remainder of the terms of this Licence, and without further action by the parties to this agreement, such provision shall be reformed to the minimum extent necessary to make such provision valid and enforceable.

C   No term or provision of this Licence shall be deemed waived and no breach consented to unless such waiver or consent shall be in writing and signed by the party to be charged with such waiver or consent.

D   This Licence constitutes the entire agreement between the parties with respect to the Work licensed here. There are no understandings, agreements or representations with respect to the Work not specified here. Licensor shall not be bound by any additional provisions that may appear in any communication from You. This Licence may not be modified without the mutual written agreement of Demos and You.